The Persian Gulf

Its Past and Present

The
Persian Gulf

Its Past and Present

Svat Soucek

MAZDA PUBLISHERS, Inc. ◆ Costa Mesa, California ◆ 2008

Major funding for the publication of this volume
was provided by a grant from
The A. K. Jabbari Trust,

and by a grant from
The Iranica Institute, Irvine California

Mazda Publishers, Inc.
Academic Publishers since 1980
P.O. Box 2603, Costa Mesa, California 92628 U.S.A.
www.mazdapub.com
A. K. Jabbari, publisher
Copyright © 2008 by Svat Soucek
Maps copyrights © 2008 by Mazda Publishers, Inc.
Library of Congress Cataloging-in-Publication Data

Soucek, Svatopluk.
The Persian Gulf: Its Past and Present/ Svat Soucek.
p.cm.
Includes maps, bibliographical references and index.

ISBN 13: 978-1-56859-120-9
ISBN: 1-56859-120-9
(alk. hard cover)

1. Persian Gulf. I. Title.
DS326.S68 2004
953.6—dc22
2004048890

CONTENTS

The Persian Gulf: the Concept, the Name, the Purpose

At first sight, the concept poses no problem. Like several other branches of the oceans, the Persian Gulf has a distinct geographical identity enhanced by the narrow strait that both joins it to the Gulf of Oman—and thereby to the Indian Ocean—and contributes to its distinctiveness: the Strait of Hormuz performs a function similar to that of Bab al-Mandab between the Red Sea and the Arabian Sea and the Indian Ocean, of the Strait of Gibraltar between the Mediterranean Sea and the Atlantic Ocean, and of Øresund between the Baltic Sea and the North Sea and the Atlantic Ocean. Historically, however, the destinies of the Persian Gulf have been intimately linked with those of the Gulf of Oman, and the story of one would be incomplete without that of the other.

As for the name, the Persian Gulf is the prevalent appellation today, and has been so since classical antiquity. That other names have also existed in the past should not be surprising. It does not negate the overwhelming predominance of the principal name whose earliest known use appeared in Greek as *Persikos Kolpos*, and from there spread across Europe through its Latin translation *Sinus Persicus*. Its equally universal use in Arabic, most often as *Bahr Fars* or *al-Bahr al-Farsi*[1] (the Sea of Persia, the Persian Sea), or *al-Khalij al-Farsi* (the Persian Gulf) may also have Greek roots, although a possible alternative is direct Persian influence during the domination of the Gulf by the Sasanian Empire of Iran before the rise of Islam and the conquest of the area by Arabs.

---

[1] Or Farisi; both forms were used, but for the sake of consistency we shall use the form Farsi.

This historical scenario has recently been perturbed by a tidal wave of nationalism. In the 1960s the Arab Gulf—*al-Khalij al-Arabi*—appeared in the Egyptian press and spread throughout the Arab world,[2] where it has now completely replaced the traditional name. One would in vain search for "al-Khalij al-Farsi" in any newspaper, journal, or book published today anywhere from Morocco to Iraq. Nevertheless, while the switch to "Arab Gulf" is virtually absolute in the Arab world, in the West—and the rest of the world—the traditional name still predominates, and is likely to retain this position. So far, this common usage has been reflected in the official nomenclature used by governments and international organizations. Thus "Persian Gulf", established by the U.S. Department of State as the Gulf's official appellation in 1917, is still valid today; in 1994 and again in 1999 the United Nations Secretariat issued directives that "Persian Gulf" is the name the organization must use; the standard subject heading according to the American Library Association is "Persian Gulf"; and while people in all walks of life immediately understand whenever the Persian Gulf is mentioned, most would ask what was meant by the "Arab" Gulf. Some professional groups have up to a point bowed to this revisionism, however, and have recourse to one of the following solutions: an outright adoption of the neologism, compromise by coining the term Arabo-Persian Gulf, avoidance of the problem by simply calling it the Gulf, or personal choice of a different name. As an example of the first solution which at the same illustrates the incongruousness of the innovation, we can cite the admirable book by the archaeologist D.T. Potts, *The Arabian Gulf in Antiquity* (Oxford: Clarendon Press, 1990, 2 vols.). In the title and the text, the author uses the neologism; in virtually all the citations and quotations, however, he has no choice but to use the term Persian Gulf.

---

[2] The first public figure to announce the new name apparently was General Abd al-Karim Qasim after the coup which in 1958 brought down the monarchy and established the Republic of Iraq, and there apparently were even earlier proponents in the 1950s. The principal propagator of the "Arab Gulf" was, however, Colonel Gamal Abd al-Nasir (Nasser), president of Egypt, who in the 1960s assumed the role of leadership in the Arab world and adopted an attitude of hostility toward Iran, then an ally of the United States.

This rather unnecessary problem elicits the question of why the modern Arabs have abandoned a time-honored name that their ancestors always used without any qualms, and replaced it with a new one which the latter would have found puzzling or might have taken to mean the Red Sea. Changing the name of a territory is understandable, for it can have the purpose of defending or acquiring it, or again of determining the identity or political allegiance of its inhabitants; but the oceans and their extensions are by definition international, and neither Iran nor Arabia will ever own this branch of the Indian Ocean beyond the universally recognized limits of territorial waters.[3] Perhaps the question of the Gulf's continental shelf, some of which harbors rich oil deposits, looms as a possible argument bolstered by the name. But the motivation may be pure and simple nationalism seeking to enhance the status of its vanguard's identity and influence.

The standard name, Persian Gulf, owes its origins to illustrious pre-Islamic dynasties ruling Iran and Iraq, starting with the Achaemenid conquest of Babylon in 539 BC. By then, however, Mesopotamia already had a glorious past of three millennia behind it, and the Gulf occupied an important niche in the material civilization of Sumerians, Babylonians, and Assyrians. In Sumerian and early Babylonian times the name applied to it was the generic Lower Sea, as distinct from the Upper Sea, that is, the Mediterranean. Both names appear in a Sumerian text of Lugal Zagesi, King of Uruk (2340-2334 BC), stating that "from the Lower Sea, by the Tigris and Euphrates, as far as the Upper Sea, [the god Enlil] provided him with clear routes."[4] An inscription of King Sargon of Akkad (2334-2279 BC) states that Enlil gave him the Upper and the Lower Sea (*Tamtu Elenitu* and *Tamtu Shaplitu* in Akkadian). The name "Bitter River" (*Nar Marratu*)

---

[3] "Territorial waters" are usually recognized up to a distance of 3 nautical miles (1 nautical mile = 1,852 meters); many countries, however, have extended this to 12 nautical miles, and some even to 24 miles. Such extensions would amount to over 22 or 44 kilometers, which could play a role if applied especially to insular possessions in the Persian Gulf.

[4] D. D. Luckenbill, *Ancient Records of Assyria and Babylon*, Chicago 1927, 2: 123, 246; E. Sollberger, *Inscriptions royales sumériennes et akkadiennes*, Paris 1971, s.v. the rulers.

is applied to the Persian Gulf in a cuneiform account of the Assyrian king Sennacherib's (704-681 BC) naval expedition down the Euphrates-Tigris and the Gulf against the Elamites.[5]

The Greeks began to acquire an idea of the Persian Gulf at the time of the intensification of their contacts with the Achaemenid Empire of Iran, which they called *Persis*, thus naming it after this dynasty's core province, Pars,[6] and the Gulf as *Persikos Kolpos*. The earliest author known to have used the name was Hekataios of Miletus, who wrote his *Periegesis* ("Circumambulation of the Earth") around 494 BC, the year in which he was one of the ambassadors of the Ionian cities to the Persian satrap at Sardes. Its use became standard with most classical historians and geographers; at the same time, they also paid attention to the Red Sea, which they called the Arabian Gulf. Strabo (63 BC-25 AD), in addition to his own observations, used a variety of sources; for the passages relevant to our subject, his most frequent references are to the no longer extant writings of the Alexandrian scientist and librarian Eratosthenes (276-194 BC). The following examples taken from Book 16 of Strabo's *Geographia* [7] illustrate his usage of both names, Persian Gulf and Arabian Gulf.

> 1: 8. The country of the Babylonians is surrounded on the east by the Susians and Elymaeans and Paratacenians, and on the south by the Persian Gulf and the Chaldaeans as far as the Mesenian Arabians...
> 3: 1. The northern side of Arabia Felix is formed by the above-mentioned desert, the eastern by the Persian Gulf, the western by the Arabian Gulf, and the southern by the great sea that lies outside both gulfs and is called Erythra.

---

[5] Georges Roux, *La Mésopotamie: Essai d'histoire politique, économique et culturelle*, Paris, 1985, p. 281. This excellent book at the same time illustrates the current dilemma faced by the academic community. The author writes: "En 694, Sennacherib décida de s'emparer des cités élamites "de l'autre coté du fleuve Amer (le golfe Arabo-Persique)..."

[6] The consonants p and f are virtual twins in the physiology of human speech, and passage from one to the other in either direction is a frequent phenomenon. *Fars* is thus an Arabised form of *Pars*.

[7] *The Geography of Strabo...* Ed. & tr. Horace Leonard Jones. London: Heinemann, 1954, vol. 7.

3: 2. The Persian Gulf is also called the Persian Sea, and Eratosthenes describes it as follows: its mouth, he says is so narrow that from Harmozi, the promontory of Carmania, one can see the promontory at Macae in Arabia...

3: 6. Such are the statements of Eratosthenes concerning the Persian Sea, which, as I was saying, forms the eastern side of Arabia Felix.

3: 7. Nearchos goes on to say that there is an island at the beginning of the Persian Gulf where quantities of valuable pearls are to be found.

4: 1. Arabia commences on the side of Babylonia with Mesene. In front of Mesene, on one side, lies the desert of the Arabians, and on another side lie the marshes opposite the Chaldaeans, which are formed by diversions of water from the Euphrates, and on another side lies the Persian Sea.

4: 2. But I return to Eratosthenes, who next sets forth his opinions concerning Arabia. He says about the northerly, or desert, part of Arabia, which lies between Arabia Felix and Coele-Syria and Judaea, extending as far as the recess of the Arabian Gulf, that from the City of Heroes, which forms a recess of the Arabian Gulf near the Nile...

Another example is a famous text on navigation from the Red Sea to India known as *Periplus of the Erythraean Sea* compiled in the first century AD.[8] It shows that the name *Persikos Kolpos* had become standard by then:

> #34: "After coasting due north along the next stretch of the shore [of Oman], in the vicinity by now of the entrance to the Persian Gulf, you meet numerous islands..."; #35: "In the vicinity of the furthest tip of the Isles of Kalaios... a little further on is the mouth of the Persian Gulf, where there is much diving for pearl oysters... beyond, the Persian Gulf, a vast expanse, spreads up to places deep within it. At its very head is a legally limited port of trade called Apologos, lying near Charax Spasinou and the Euphrates River."

The usage of the two terms, *Persikos Kolpos* and *Arabios Kolpos* with these connotations was generalized by the Alexandrian astronomer and geographer Ptolemy (active in the first half

---

[8] *The Periplus Maris Erythraei*; text with introduction, translation, and commentary by Lionel Casson. Princeton, 1989.

of the second century AD) through his work *Geographike Hy-phegesis*. In Book 5, chapter 16, entitled *Arabias Petraias thesis* (The situation of "Stony" Arabia), the Red Sea is without exception called *Arabios Kolpos*, while in chapters 18 and 19, entitled *Arabias Eremou thesis* (The situation of "Desert" Arabia) and *Babylonias thesis* (The situation of Babylonia), the Persian Gulf is called *Persikos Kolpos*. Ptolemy's *Geography* had fundamental influence first on Islamic and later on European scholarship, especially during the renaissance and early modern periods. In Europe, Ptolemy's work spread through its Latin translation, and the two gulfs—or the gulf and the sea—thus became known as *Sinus Persicus* and *Sinus Arabicus*.

With the blossoming of the Islamic civilization in Abbasid Iraq (8th-10th centuries), "Persian Gulf" became the prevalent name for the Gulf both in Arabic and Persian. The term Muslim authors used invariably had the attribute "Persian" (Farsi/Farisi) or "Persia" (Fars). Arabs had a word for gulf, *khalij*, but in this case they more often used the word *bahr*, sea: thus *Bahr Fars* or *al-Bahr al-Farsi* (or *Farisi*). To give three examples from among many, first a passage from the *Muruj al-Dhahab*, a work by the Arab traveler and scholar Masudi (d. 956). Having described the "gulf" which extends from the "al-Bahr al-Habashi"—the western part of the Indian Ocean—all the way to Qulzum (the Red Sea), Masudi continues:[9]

> 1:238 Another gulf branches off from this sea, it is the <u>Sea of Fars</u>, and it ends at Ubullah, the Khashabat, and Abbadan, of the province of Basra... 1: 241 This sea is the <u>Persian Gulf</u>, [also] known as the <u>Persian Sea</u>; it is bordered, as we have described, by Bahrain, Fars, Basra, Oman, and Kirman, all the way to the Cape of the Skull; between the <u>Persian Gulf</u> and the <u>Gulf of Qulzum</u> are Aylah, Hijaz, and Yemen; the overland distance between the two gulfs is one thousand five hundred miles, [across] a protrusion of land into the sea, which surrounds it on most sides... [i.e., the Arabian peninsula]

Another famous work of Islamic literature, the *Kitab Surat al-Ard* (The Geography of the World) by a younger contemporary

---

[9] The quotation is based on vol. 1 of the standard edition and French translation: Maçoudi, *Les Prairies d'Or*; texte et traduction par C. Barbier de Meynard et Pavet de Courteille, Paris, 1861-77, 9 vols.

of Masudi, the Arab traveler and geographer Ibn Hawqal, intro-
duces the subject in the following manner:[10]

> "I have classified the lands of Islam region by region... and I
> began by describing the Arab lands... and after the Arab
> lands, having drawn all the mountains, deserts, roads and riv-
> ers there which flow into the <u>Persian Gulf</u>, I have proceeded to
> the <u>Persian Gulf</u>, because it borders a great part of their lands,
> and I have depicted its attachment to them..."

Moreover, the first of the several maps accompanying this
text has the title *Surat Bahr Fars* (= Map of the *Sea of Persia*).
Like the bulk of Islamic cartography of the classical period, it is
extremely stylized, and only the title and the legends along the
coasts reveal what the map represents; at the same time, the map
also confirms an additional use of the term *Bahr Fars* at this period, for it means here not only the Persian Gulf but also the
northern part of the Indian Ocean, in a manner reminiscent of the
Erythraean Sea of the classical period.

Finally a passage from another book on world geography, the
Ahsan al-Taqasim, by the renowned Arab geographer Idrisi (12th
century AD) may be worth quoting:

> "<u>The Persian Gulf</u>: its right-hand coast belongs to the Arabs,
> its left-hand coast belongs to the Persians... As for Ahsa: it is
> a city near [lit. on] <u>the Persian Gulf</u>, facing Uwal [i.e. Bah-
> rain]... As for the city of Qatif, it is on the [coast of] <u>the Per-
> sian Gulf</u>."

From among the occasional exceptions in Islamic literature,
naming the Gulf for Basra is the most common and lasting one.
Its earliest appearance occurred in the 9th century. Thus Abu Ja-
far Muhammad al-Khwarazmi (d. 847), when discussing the
Bahr Kabir or Indian Ocean, states that it has six extensions, one
of which is the *Bahr al-Basra*.[11] In a similar vein but even more

---

[10] The quotation is from the standard edition: *Opus Geographicum*, ed.
Leiden: Brill, 1967 (*Biblotheca Geographorum Arabicorum*, vol. 2).,
pp. 42 ff.
[11] Muhammad ibn Musa al-Khwarazmi, *Kitab surat al-ard*, ed. Hans
von Mžik, Leipzig 1926, p. 74.

exceptionally, the name of Iraq is used in the cosmography *Hudud al-alam*, written in Persian in the 10th century by an unknown author: *Khalij-e Iraq*[12]:

> "Discourse on the disposition of the Seas and Gulfs. ...Another large sea is the one called the Great Sea (Bahr al-Azam, i.e. the Indian Ocean)...This sea has five gulfs:...The third gulf starts from the frontiers of Fars and stretches in a northwestern direction until the distance between it and the Gulf of Ayla [=the Red Sea] amounts to 16 stages on swift camels; it is called the Gulf of Iraq. All the Arab lands lie between these two gulfs, i.e. the Gulf of Ayla and the Gulf of Iraq. The fourth gulf is that of Pars which starts from the limit of Pars, where it has a small breadth [i.e. the Strait of Hormuz], and extends to the frontiers of Sind..."

The *Hudud al-Alam* thus does use the name Persian Gulf, but it applies it to what is more commonly known as the Gulf of Oman. For the Red Sea, on the other hand, it uses the name Arabian Gulf:

> "Another gulf (which) adjoins [the Great Sea] takes a northern direction up to the confines of Egypt, growing narrow till its breadth becomes one mile; it is called the Arabian Gulf or the Gulf of Ayla or Qulzum..."[13]

Until the end of the middle ages, the Persian Gulf was essentially a preserve of the Arabs and Persians. A new era began in the 16th century with the intrusion of two alien groups: Europeans and Ottoman Turks. One of the effects of this intrusion was the appearance of a few modifications and alternative names for the Persian Gulf, but two aspects stand out: we *never* encounter the name Arab or Arabian[14] Gulf as applied to the Persian Gulf; and as time wore on, the alternatives receded and the traditional

---

[12] *Hudud al-Alam: "The Regions of the World", a Persian Geography, 372 A.H.-982 A.D.*, tr. & explained by V. Minorsky, 2nd ed., London 1970, p. 137.

[13] *Ibid.*, p. 52.

[14] The variants of *Arab* and *Arabian* exist only in English; Arabic and Persian use `Arabi as the only form. See below my remark on the English usage of *Arabian* in this context.

name Persian Gulf, which had never really ceased to occupy the center stage, regained its time-honored place.

Once the Portuguese had established themselves at Hormuz by 1515, they began to write about the events and the people and places they were encountering, and to depict cartographically this world which was new to them. They had a choice in naming the Persian Gulf between the classical or scholarly European tradition, the Islamic tradition (in so far as it was accessible to them), and the features that struck them most vividly upon their arrival. *Sinus Persicus* appeared in numerous Latin editions, both manuscript and printed, of the aforementioned *Geography* of Ptolemy which were proliferating in renaissance Europe. It is thus the name most commonly encountered in Portuguese writings and those of other 16th century authors and cartographers, increasingly also in such variations as *Mare Persicum* and eventually also in vernacular translations and related literature. We thus see *Sino Persico* used by Fernão Lopes de Castanheda (1500-59) in his *Historia do descubrimento e conquista da India pelos Portugueses*.[15] João de Barros (1496-1570) in his *Decadas* mentions the two straits leading to the Red Sea and the Persian Gulf as *"dois estreitos do Mar Roxo, e Persio,"* and describes Bahrain as *"Ilha Baharem, que esta no seio do Mar da Persia pegada na costa da Arabia."*

This tradition is also prevalent in the writings of 16th century English authors and travelers. One of them was Ralph Fitch, who in 1583 journeyed through Iraq and the Persian Gulf to India, and wrote in his account:

"Basora standeth neere the Gulfe of Persia, and is a Towne of great trade of Spices and Drugs which come from Ormus…I went from Basora to Ormus downe the Gulfe of Persia, in a certaine ship made of bordes, and sowed together with Cayro, which is threed made of the huske of Cocoes…"[16]

A new twist came with the entry of Ottoman Turks on the scene. Piri Reis, a mariner and cartographer, while describing the

---

[15] *Historia do descubrimento e conquista da India pelos Portugueses*, 3rd ed., Coimbra 1924-33, vol. 2, p. 365.

[16] Samuel Purchas, *Hakluytus Posthumus or Purchas His Pilgrimes*, Glasgow: James MacLehose, 1905, vol. 10, p. 167.

Persian Gulf in the versified introduction to his *Kitabi Bahriye*, writes:[17]

> Now that you have learned about the Indian Ocean,
> Hear also about the <u>Persian Sea</u>.
> While it is called the <u>Persian Sea,</u>
> They also call it the <u>Sea of Hormuz</u>.
> This sea is a gulf from the Indian Ocean,
> And there are nine islands there.

Piri Reis wrote this book in 1526, thus before he or other Ottoman Turks came to the Persian Gulf. As he himself states on several occasions, he drew both on Islamic and European sources. During the next three decades the Turks conquered Iraq and eastern Arabia, thus establishing their presence in the Persian Gulf area. Another remarkable mariner and author, Seydi Ali Reis, sailed in July 1554 from Basra with Suez as his destination, but after entering the Gulf of Oman his fleet was deflected by storms and the Portuguese toward India, whence he and his companions returned overland to Turkey. In his account of these adventures Seydi Ali calls the Gulf *Derya-yi Hormuz,* the Sea of Hormuz (*derya,* a Persian loanword naturalized in Turkish, is a synonym of the Arabic *bahr*). The traditional name appears, however, in the *Cihannuma,* a book of cosmography compiled by the great Ottoman polyhistor Kâtip Çelebi (also known as Hajji Khalifa, 1609-1657).[18] Like Piri Reis, Kâtip Çelebi too used a variety of Islamic and European sources; among the latter was what he called "*Atlas Major'un* muhtasari olan *Atlas Minor'u*"(Atlas Minor, an abridgement of [Blaeu's] Atlas Major")[19]. Here is a passage from the Cihannuma:

---

[17] Piri Reis, *Kitab-ı Bahriye*, Ankara: Türk Tarih Kurumu, 1935, pp. 61-62.

[18] Kâtip Çelebi died before printing in Turkish was permitted in Ottoman Turkey. His manuscript was published for the first time at the renowned Müteferrika Press in 1732.

[19] *Atlas Major* was a sumptuous six-volume atlas made by the Dutch cartographer Joan Blaeu (1599-1673); a copy had been presented by the Dutch ambassador to the Ottoman Sultan. The *Atlas Minor* used by Katib Celebi, however, apparently was a Mercator-Hondius work published in 1621, which the Turkish scholar mistook for an abridgement of Blaeu's Atlas.

The Sea of Persia: they call it Sinus Persicus, which
means the Persian Gulf; they attribute it to the Land of
Persia, which occupies its eastern coast; and they also say
Mare Persicum.

In the 17th century, we begin to find other names, sometimes
side by side in a text or on a map. The most frequent attributes
are Hormuz, Qatif, and Basra, combined with either Gulf or Sea.
We thus see here a convergence of essentially bookish, scholarly
traditions with alternatives deriving from current experience and
evolution. *Basra Körfezi*, the Gulf of Basra (*körfez*, a loanword
from Greek, is more common than *haliç*, a loanword from Arabic, barring such exceptions as Haliç used for the Golden Horn
in Istanbul), became increasingly frequent in Turkish; this may
be a result of the psychological impact which Basra, the Turks'
major port and outlet into the Gulf, and Hormuz, occupied by
their formidable rivals the Portuguese at the other end, had on
them.

In some texts, and even more on maps, two or three names for
the Gulf appear at the same time. Thus on a map by Giacomo
Gastaldi (fl. Venice, 1539-66) dated 1561, we find the Gulf labeled as "Mare Elcatif", "Golfo di Persia", and "Golfo de Ormus". However, a close inspection reveals that the cartographer
had a purpose. Mare Elcatif is meant to designate the upper portion of the Gulf between Qatif and Basra; Golfo di Persia, the
lower portion between Qatif and Hormuz; and Golfo de Ormus
stands here for the Gulf of Oman. This nomenclature still existed
a century later, for we find it in the above-mentioned *Atlas
Maior*, although with a further nuance: *Mare Elcatif olim Sinus
Persicus* ("The Sea of Qatif, formerly the Persian Gulf"), while
Ormus also appears in the interior where the country of Oman is
located, clearly a confusion of Hormuz and Oman caused by the
similarity of the two words. The association of the Gulf with
Qatif, relatively brief, is somewhat surprising. Qatif was a port
and oasis on the coast facing Bahrain and functioned, together
with Uqair, as an entrepot for trade with the Arabian interior, but
it never gained the prominence of Basra or Hormuz, for example.

In the 18th century, the name Persian Gulf reasserted itself as
the prevalent appellation for this body of water in all languages
except Turkish, where *Basra Körfezi* became standard. The latter
name did appear in Arabic as well, but seldom, and then only in

Iraq. A good illustration is a classic of modern Arab historiography, the *Tarikh al-Iraq Baina Ihtilalain* (History of Iraq Between Two Occupations) by the Iraqi scholar Abbas Azzawi. In its eight volumes we see *Khalij Fars* routinely used from volume 1, published in Baghdad in 1935 to the final volume published there in 1956, with the exception of *Khalij al-Basra* used once in volume 6 (1954). The most significant fact, however, is that prior to the 1950s, we *never* encounter *al-Khalij al-Arabi* either in this book or anywhere else as applied to the Persian Gulf, and for good reason: as we have already remarked, people would have wondered what the name meant or might have thought that it meant the Red Sea. The aforementioned application of *Khalij al-Arabi* to the Red Sea, common in the past, has been pushed out, together with the less common *Bahr Qulzum* (The Sea of Qulzum, thus named after the port — the classical Clysma — at the northwestern end of the Red Sea) by *Bahr Ahmar* (Red Sea), although not completely; we find it thus used in another classic of modern scholarship, the Arab-American historian Philip Hitti's *History of the Arabs* (many editions, including a translation into Arabic). The fact remains that until its creation in the 1960s, the term *Arab Gulf* as applied to the Persian Gulf did not exist. The sheer weight of its exclusive acceptance in the Arab world since then has forced its way into the English language as well, but, as we have stated, marginally and with a nuance. The *Arabios Kolpos* of the Greeks and *Sinus Arabicus* of the Romans and renaissance Europeans, applied to the Red Sea, is usually translated not as *Arab Gulf* but as *Arabian Gulf*. On the other hand, we should concede that using the neologism for the Persian Gulf may appear justified to scholars, businessmen, journalists and other professionals active within the framework of the Arab world, motivated as they must be by a gamut of reasons ranging from matters of tact and courtesy to the rigors of their vocation.[20]

---

[20] Until recently, the question of the name of the Persian Gulf was only incidentally touched upon in scholarly or other literature, chiefly because its emotional or propagandistic impact had not yet fully matured. It is discussed in this dispassionate manner by C. Edmund Bosworth in his excellent introductory chapter "The Nomenclature of the Persian Gulf" to the book *The Persian Gulf States: a General Survey*, ed. Alvin J. Cottrell, Baltimore and London, The Johns Hopkins University

The purpose: The history of the subject, and reasons for adding one more book.

The interest and importance of the Persian Gulf as a subject of study is self-evident, but less easy is the definition and justification of an attempt to write its history. How does one write the history of a body of water? If natural history were meant, the task would be clear: physical structure and animal population provide ample matter for study, thought and description, from the extension, depth and salinity of the water to the dolphins, oysters, seagulls, and mangroves that inhabit it or grow along its shores. The discussion would give their due to the islands and coastlines, where the Gulf's natural history ends, with the exception of paying some attention to the major rivers as its extensions of sorts. But our book is an attempt to present the human history of the Persian Gulf, which is the reverse of its natural history: it begins at the coastline and proceeds a certain distance inland. This unavoidable fact thus presents a problem and a challenge. If the project really intends to focus on the Persian Gulf, how much of the "inland history" is relevant, once one has give due space to man's seafaring, trading, fishing, pearling, piracy, and naval warfare? And how does one go about teasing out this inland history's components relevant to the Gulf — or vice versa, what aspects of the Gulf are relevant to the history of the riparian countries, or even of the whole world? Compiling a historical geography of the coastlands and ports would be a plausible approach, whether in a consecutive topographical fashion or in dictionary form, but too restrictive if a broader tableau is the author's goal.

Press, 1980, pp. xvii-xxxiii. Nevertheless, since its rise as an issue in the 1960s, the name has received increasing attention also among Persian scholars and journalists. Besides the *Atlas of Geographical Maps and Historical Documents on the Persian Gulf* edited by A. Sahab, Tehran, Sahab Geographic and Drafting Institute, 1971, one can cite as examples the article *"Hamishah Khalij-e Fars budeh ast"* ("It has always been the Persian Gulf") in the 25 December 2004 issue of the literary weekly *Kitab-e Haftah*; it includes an interview with Dr. Piruz Mujtahedzadeh, author of numerous publications dealing with the Persian Gulf. A recent book specifically devoted to this question is *Nam-e Khalij-e Fars, bar payah-e asnad-e tarikhi va naqshah-ha-ye jughrafiyayi* (The Name of the Persian Gulf, on the basis of historical documents and maps) by Iraj Afshar Sistani (Tehran, 1381/2002).

There is thus no easy answer to these questions, especially if an author makes the downright presumptuous attempt to write a brief account of the Persian Gulf from the dawn of history to the present. We have made this attempt in the belief that despite — and partly because of — many excellent studies dealing with special or specific aspects of the Persian Gulf published in recent decades, no accessible overview has come out since the publication of Arnold Wilson's basic *The Persian Gulf: an Historical Sketch from the Earliest Times to the Beginning of the Twentieth Century* (Oxford: The Clarendon Press, 1928). In 1928 the Persian Gulf, although important to the Persians, Arabs, and British, was still a backwater on the global scene; since then it has moved to the center of world events. It is this vertiginous rise of the Gulf's importance that has prompted us to supplement, though hardly displace, Sir Arnold's book.

Recent Literature on the Persian Gulf

To the best of our knowledge, only one book in English, besides Arnold Wilson's, covers the Persian Gulf in the totality of its history and current situation: the above-mentioned *The Persian Gulf States: A General Survey*, edited by Alvin J. Cottrell (Baltimore: The Johns Hopkins University Press, 1980). Written by a consortium of distinguished scholars, this large volume provides an excellent coverage of the subject. There is an abundance of specialized treatments of various aspects of the Persian Gulf. To give examples which also illustrate the wide range of the subject's aspects: the already cited *The Arabian Gulf in Antiquity*, by Daniel Potts; *Bahrain, Oman, Qatar and the United Arab Emirates: Challenges of Security,* by Anthony H. Cordesman (Westview Press, 1997); *The Ottoman Gulf and the Creation of Kuwayt, Saudi Arabia and Qatar, 1871-1914*, by Frederick Anscombe (New York: Columbia University Press, 1997); *The Making of the Modern Gulf States: Kuwait, Bahrain, Qatar, the United Arab Emirates and Oman*, by Rosemarie Said Zahlan (2nd ed., Ithaca Press, 1998); or *Security in the Persian Gulf: Origins, Obstacles, and the Search for Consensus*, by Lawrence Potter and Gary Sick (Palgrave Macmillan, 2002). Literature in Persian and Arabic is even more voluminous, from Iraj Afshar Sistani's works such as his *Jughrafiya-ye Tarikhi-ye Darya-ye* Pars (*His-*

torical geography of the Persian Gulf; Tehran, 1997) to contributions to international symposia held in Tehran on the subject of the Persian Gulf (*Hamayish-e Bain al-Milali-e Khalij-e Fars*); the eleventh symposium was published by the Ministry of Foreign Affairs in 1380/2001. To name just one of many Arabic books on the subject, there is the *al-Khalij al-Arabi* by Qadri Qalaji (Beirut, 1992). Coverage in periodical literature is abundant, and impossible for a single person to keep track of if the whole span of history and current events is the goal. Furthermore, the Internet offers access to an immense variety of sources, including Persian and Arabic news media, journals and newspapers. The author of this book is indebted in various degrees and ways to a selection of these sources, from Sir Arnold's classic and Anthony Cordesman's studies to articles and reports on the Internet.

Spelling and Transliteration

Arabic and Persian are both written in the Arabic alphabet. At first sight this should facilitate the task of transliterating them into English, but in fact it is one of the most daunting challenges to anyone trying to write a book involving both languages. First of all, a naturally "correct" system of transliteration does not exist, and each one is a matter of accepted convention. This approach works if the adopted system serves a specific community that is familiar with the convention. A good illustration is the *Encyclopedia of Islam*, in which one system is used throughout for Arabic as well as Persian and is perfectly clear to the community of its readers. Once we leave the sheltered enclosure of scholarship, however, we are faced with an often bewildering assortment of spellings and inconsistencies. *Abu Dhabi* is the most commonly used spelling for this emirate in newspapers and journals, but it appears as *Abu Zaby* on the maps of the National Geographic Society. The problem is even more complicated with Persian names and words. The system used by the *Encyclopaedia of Islam* is the same as for Arabic, disregarding the phonetic differences of modern standard Persian pronunciation. We thus find the spelling Masdjid-i Sulayman (the *d*, unnecessary in English, is used by this encyclopedia to harmonize it with the French edition), whereas the actual pronunciation is Masjed-e

Soleiman; significantly, even the National Geographic Society makes allowance for this difference. In our book, we are adopting what we think is a practical though admittedly inconsistent approach. For Arabic words, we follow the *Encyclopaedia of Islam*, but without the diacritics which we deem unnecessary and even confusing in a book intended for a wider audience. For Arabic names, we do so whenever reasonable, but follow general usage when it is clearly prevalent (thus Abu Dhabi and not Abu Zaby; Bahrain instead of Bahrayn). For Persian words and names, we use a transliteration that is closer to the actual pronunciation, or the generally accepted forms. For Turkish words and names, we use the modern Turkish alphabet which is Roman, with the necessary diacritics.

The author wishes to express his warmest thanks for the assistance he has received, in the preparation of this book, from several friends and colleagues. Especially helpful have been Michael Cook, Kambiz Eslami, and Mark Farrell of Princeton University, and Gamil Youssef of the Asian and Middle East Division, The New York Public Library.

LIST OF MAPS

Introduction

1. The Persian Gulf: The Natural Setting

The Persian Gulf and the Gulf of Oman lie in the core of the Middle East, with Iran, Afghanistan, Central Asia and Pakistan to the east and northeast; Iraq, Syria and Turkey to the northwest; and the Arabian Peninsula to the west and southwest. The Gulf of Oman merges with the Arabian Sea at the level of Ras al-Hadd or Cape of the Extremity, the easternmost point on the Arabian Peninsula. The Arabian Sea in turn is part of the Indian Ocean, of which the two gulfs under discussion can thus be considered to be branches or extensions. In political terms, the states with coastlines along one or both gulfs are Iran, Iraq, Kuwait, Saudi Arabia, Bahrain, Qatar, United Arab Emirates, and Oman.[21]

---

[21] Besides the *Encyclopaedia of Islam* (henceforth cited as *EIs*) (S.F. Beckingham, "Bahr Faris," vol. 1, pp. 927-29) and the *Encyclopaedia Iranica* (henceforth cited as *EIr*), most major encyclopedias offer adequate surveys of the relevant aspects of the subject: physical geography, natural history, human history and the present-day economic and political situation; for example *Encyclopaedia Britannica*, 1970 ed., vol. 17, pp. 649-52; *al-Mawsuah al-Arabiyah*, Damascus, vol. 8 (2003), "al-Khalij al-Arabi". An invaluable reference tool is J.G. Lorimer's *Gazetteer of the Persian Gulf, Oman and Central Arabia*, in this case vols. 7-9: *Geographical & Statistical* (henceforth cited as Lorimer, *Gazetteer*). First printed at Calcutta in 1908, it has been reprinted (Gerrards Cross, Buckinghamshire, 1986). *Iraq and the Persian Gulf*, published by the British Admiralty, London 1944, includes thorough geographical descriptions. Also useful are the official manuals of sailing directions, mostly government publications such as *Sailing Directions for the Persian Gulf*, Washington, DC, The United States Hydrographic Office, and its British counterpart, *The Persian Gulf Pilot*, both repeatedly updated.

The two gulfs communicate through the Strait of Hormuz, which is formed by the northward thrust of the Hajar mountain range of northeastern Arabia (in political terms, of the Sultanate of Oman and the United Arab Emirates), ending in Cape Musandam (Ras Musandam). The strait, between 60 and 100 km wide, is a result of this protrusion and a corresponding break in the otherwise fairly straight coast of Iran, which here makes a wide arc inward, forming a large bay at the head of which we find the small island of Hormuz.

The Strait of Hormuz is thus both a link and a dividing, though not separating, point of the two gulfs. This fact somewhat complicates the approach we have chosen to our subject. In certain situations, we shall have to specify which of the two gulfs we mean; at other moments, "Gulf" or even "Persian Gulf" will mean both. Here we shall start with the Persian Gulf in the narrower sense—the body of water extending from the head of the gulf at the Iranian-Iraqi border to the Strait of Hormuz.

The Gulf extends in a generally northwest-southeast direction from the estuary of the Shatt al-Arab, at the Iranian-Iraqi border, until it makes a sharp turn northeastward as it narrows on its approach to the Strait of Hormuz. The Shatt al-Arab[22] or "the Arabs' River" is formed by the confluence of the Tigris and Euphrates near the Iraqi town of Qurnah, whence its water flows southeastward towards the Gulf. It is 179 kilometers long, and for the last 70 kilometers of its course, from the point where it passes by the Iranian town of Khurramshahr,[23] it also forms the border between Iran and Iraq.

---

[22] Amatzia Baram, "Shatt al-Arab," *EIs* 9: 368-69; M. Kasheff, "Arvand-Rūd", *EIr* 2: 679-81; Lorimer, *Gazetteer*, 7: 94-115 (Arab, Shatt-al-). "Shatt" is an Arabic word meaning bank, shore, coast. Here it means the final joint course of the Tigris and Euphrates rivers. It is a historical name that goes back to the Middle Ages. In the 20th century, however, the official name used in Iran has been the impeccably Persian Arvand Rūd, instead of the Arabic Shatt al-Arab that moreover might suggest Arab nature or possession of it.

[23] "Khurramshahr" is a Persian name formed by combining two words and meaning "The Joyous City". Here, too, national sensibilities have played a role, for the place used to be known by a completely different Arabic name, Muhammarah. See Lorimer, *Gazetteer*, 8: 1262-65 (Muhammarah Town); Roger M. Savory, "Khurramshahr," *EIs* 3: 65-66.

Geologically, the Persian Gulf is part of a shallow that extends from northern Iraq to the Strait of Hormuz. This trough is hemmed in on the north by the Taurus Mountains of southeastern Turkey, on the east by the Zagros Mountains of Iran, on the west and south by the continental block of the Arabian Peninsula, and on the southeast by the Hajar Mountains of Oman. It thus forms a long and somewhat irregular rectangle, whose bottom side on the southeast is shaped by the Ras al-Musandam peninsula that restricts, though without obstructing, its communication with the Gulf of Oman and the Indian Ocean. The Gulf itself measures a little over 800 kilometers in length from the mouth of the Shatt al-Arab to Ras al-Musandam, and varies between 80 and 300 kilometers in width.

One of the salient features of this trough is its relative uniformity over a distance of some 1,600 kilometers from northern Iraq to the Strait of Hormuz. The vast extended low landscape of southern Iraq continues as a long shallow gulf that is lined by an equally low landscape on the Arabian side, and the narrow coastal strip between the Zagros chain and the sea on the Iranian side. The shallowness of the Persian Gulf is striking: some 150 meters at most along the Persian coast, 50 meters or less along the Arabian coast.[24] The shoals along almost the whole length of the latter and parts of the former make a fertile ground for the proliferation of pearl oysters, in particular the Great Pearl Bank between Sharjah and Qatar, but also in the vicinity of Bahrain and Kuwait. Pearling as an industry in the Persian Gulf has virtually vanished, the main reason being the introduction of cultured pearls by Japan in the 1920s. By an almost uncanny coincidence of geological, geographical, and historical circumstances, the same offshore areas have been exploited, since the 1950s, as one of the richest sources of oil in the world. Pearl oysters were of course not the only product of the waters of the twin gulfs: they abound in fish and marine mammals, and in this respect the mostly inhospitable coastland has offered man compensation, besides pearling and before oil. Tuna, swordfish, sea

---

[24] Comparison with the Red Sea can help us grasp this special aspect. The median depth of the Red Sea is 491 meters, with a maximum of 3,000 meters. While the Persian Gulf is part of a trough or depression, the Red Sea is part of the great continental rift that extends from Syria all the way to East Africa.

bass, mackerel, and sardines are among the principal varieties caught in the Gulf.

The extremely hot and humid summers and scarcity of rain around the Persian Gulf have had a debilitating effect on vegetation and agriculture, but several features have mitigated this drawback. One is the presence of a considerable underground aquifer in the Arabian plateau with a west-east incline, which has created a number of natural springs and provided for man-made wells in eastern Arabia and the Bahrain archipelago; fresh water even gushes forth from the sea bottom in the vicinity of the latter. This has enabled man to create a number of sometimes vast oasis complexes, renowned especially for their date palm groves.

The other feature that has enabled man to settle here and practice agriculture is the rivers descending from the Taurus and Zagros Mountains. The Euphrates and the Tigris have played the principal role in this respect. Both originate in the mountains of eastern Turkey not far from each other (42 kilometers), but when they emerge from the Taurus range into northeastern Syria and northwestern Iraq, they first form wide arcs west and east, flowing at one point as far as 300 km from each other before gradually drawing closer until at the level of Baghdad they are separated by a mere 60 kilometers; then they again diverge to a distance of 200 kilometers before drawing closer once more and finally uniting at Qurnah. The two rivers could be viewed as a double spinal cord of the area, both graphically and culturally. It was thanks to them that man emerged from prehistory to develop irrigated agriculture, settle in urban communities, and towards the end of the fourth millennium before our era, to create the earliest civilization with written records; he then proceeded to shape this civilization through an ever rising level of sophistication and variety of forms.

The crucial role played by the Euphrates and Tigris should not make us forget several other rivers that have also made their contribution to human settlement and civilization. One especially could be compared with them in terms of the effect it had on the birth of civilization and its early development: the Karun, which originates in the central Zagros Mountains and eventually enters the Iranian side of the lowlands at the head of the Gulf, into which it flows through two arms, one of them by entering the Shatt al-Arab near the above-mentioned Khurramshahr.

The land thus marked by the Euphrates and Tigris can be viewed as an extension of the Persian Gulf, just as the Gulf continues the trough through which the two rivers flow. Mesopotamia or "[country] between[two] rivers", as it was named by the Greeks, is the landward half of this complex. Like many other geographical terms, its meaning does not include any precise boundaries. To most observers and commentators, rather than specifically designating territory *between* the two rivers, it refers to the general area through which they pass on their course, after they emerge from the Taurus Mountains, all the way to the Persian Gulf. It can be used as an approximate synonym for Iraq, with the possible addition of adjacent territories in Iran and Syria.

The Islands of the Persian Gulf

A number of islands line both the northern, Iranian coast of the Gulf, and the southern, Arab one. Several have played considerable economic, political, or cultural roles at various points in history, and some still do so today. They are, on the Persian side, Kharak, Kish, Qishm, and Hormuz, and they all belong to the Republic of Iran; on the Arab side, Warbah, Bubiyan, Failakah, and the Bahrain archipelago. Warbah, Bubiyan, and Failakah belong to Kuwait; Bahrain is an independent state. One might also add the special case of the tiny trio of the Greater Tunb, Lesser Tunb and Abu Musa; lying between the two coasts near the Strait of Hormuz, they are Iranian possessions but claimed by the United Arab Emirates. Finally a number of other islands, small but important historically, politically and economically, are strewn over the southern segment of the Gulf along the coast of the United Arab Emirates. They will be discussed in the course of our narrative.

The Gulf of Oman

If we bracket, in the longitudinal sense, the Persian Gulf proper by the estuary of the Shatt al-Arab and the Strait of Hormuz, we can use the eastern bracket that is Hormuz as the western end of the Gulf of Oman; the decision as to where it ends in the east as it merges with the Arabian Sea is somewhat arbitrary, but here

both geography and politics come to our aid. The already mentioned Ras al-Hadd can serve as a distinct landmark on the south,
while the small bay of Gavater, some 320 kilometers northeast of
this cape, delimits it on the north. Gavater is also the name of a
small port on the western shore of this bay, which is on its northern shore marked by the Iranian-Pakistani border. The Gulf of
Oman is about 550 kilometers long, if we adopt this delimitation;
we reduce it to some 310 kilometers if we start on the west, with
the Dimaghah-e Kuh or Ras al-Kuh, a cape on the Persian coast,
and the already familiar cape Ras al-Musandam on the Omani
coast. The final part of the Strait's arc assumes a roughly north-
south trend, and the Dimaghah-e Kuh marks its end; from there
on, the Iranian coast proceeds in an easterly direction towards
the Pakistani border. This southernmost and easternmost coast of
Iran delimits the Gulf of Oman on the north. Its immediate hinterland, traversed by ranges of low mountains running parallel
with the coast, has been known as Makran since pre-Islamic
times. Today it is politically divided into the Persian provinces
of Hormuzgan and Baluchistan, and the Pakistani province of
Baluchistan. On the Iranian side, the principal ports on the Mak-
rani coast are, proceeding from west to east, Jask, Chahbahar and
Gavater; on the Pakistani side, Gwadar and Pasni.

2. The Persian Gulf: The Human Dimension

Before embarking on a narrative of the Gulf's past, it may be
helpful to briefly sketch the basic ethno-linguistic, cultural and
religious identity of the people who today live along its coasts.

Our task is facilitated by a pronounced uniformity, although
we shall have to deal with often considerable complexity behind
this façade. Two languages are spoken around the Gulf: Persian
in Iran, Arabic everywhere else. Persian is an Indo-European
tongue, thus related to most idioms spoken on the European
continent and to English. Arabic is a Semitic language, whose
only major living relations are Hebrew and Amharic. Persian and
Arabic use the same system of writing, the Arabic alphabet. As
the principal language used by a government, taught in schools,
and found in newspapers and the greater part of what is pub-

lished or written, Persian is restricted to only one country, Iran.[25] Arabic, on the other hand, is the official language of a great number of countries from Mauritania to Iraq. An educated Iraqi, Egyptian, or Moroccan feels at home in any of these countries when it comes to reading newspapers, listening to the radio or conversing with his peers. Besides their national identities, they thus feel united by a common linguistic identity as Arabs. The languages spoken in informal conversation and by those who have received no education do display dialectal differences to such a degree that one could consider them separate languages, but that does not negate the determining factor of official linguistic unity.

On the religious level, the façade is even more uniform: Islam is the religion of the overwhelming majority of the inhabitants. This is thus an even more unifying trait, especially in the case of relations with the outside world of unbelievers, traditionally regarded as a hostile world. At the same time, however, the paradoxically divisive force inherent within most religions has also been in play here. Sunni or Orthodox Islam claims official approval in the Arab countries, while Shia or Schismatic Islam governs Iran. This division caused a series of bloody wars between the Ottoman sultans, Iraq's overlords, and the shahs of Iran from the 16th to the 18th century; it has also contributed to tensions in Iraq itself, where the southern segment of the country is predominantly Shia, and where Saddam Husayn's wrath descended upon this group as one of the consequences of the Gulf War in the early 1990s. The other schismatic movement of Islam, the Kharijites, is mostly extinct today except in a few places, the Sultanate of Oman being one of them. A special form of this denomination, that of the Ibadites, has survived there since its introduction in the 8th century. An elected Imam ruled part of Oman as recently as 1955.

---

[25] Persian, however, is one of the two official languages of Afghanistan, where it is called Dari; and Tajik, the language of the Republic of Tajikistan, is a mutually intelligible close relative of Persian (or, according to some, Tajik *is* Persian, only a notch closer to the sterling purity of the language spoken and written a millennium ago by the greatest national poet of Iran, Firdawsi).

3. The Persian Gulf: The Historical Dimension

An admittedly somewhat artificial but nonetheless practical tool of the historian is periodization. In a discussion of the Persian Gulf, its use seems justified.

The Persian Gulf before it became Persian, ca 3100 BC—539 BC. The first known writing system, dated to about 3100 before our era, was created in Sumer, a group of city-states in an area encompassed today by the Iraqi cities of Samawa, Nasiriya and Basra. This was the earliest recorded culture, and signified the inception of the Mesopotamian civilization that would pass through several stages, languages and empires. This civilization was dominant in the Gulf area until its conquest and absorption by the Achaemenid empire of Iran in 539. The fall of Babylon to Cyrus II (Cyrus the Great) symbolized the dawn of a new era during which Persian dominance extended over much of the Middle East, including the Persian Gulf area. This period is discussed in chapters 1-2.

The Persian Gulf under Persian rule, 539 BC—637 AD. Domination of Mesopotamia and the Persian Gulf by a succession of Iranian empires, intermittently interrupted by Hellenistic, Roman, and Byzantine rivals, continued until the rise of victorious Islam. In 539 BC, the city of Babylon was conquered by the Achaemenid king Cyrus the Great; in 637 AD, the Arab Muslims defeated the Persians at the Battle of Qadisiyah and conquered the Sasanian capital Ctesiphon. This period is discussed in chapters 3-4.

The Islamic Persian Gulf, 637—1507. This is the period when the Persian Gulf and Mesopotamia were under exclusive Muslim domination, with Arabs and Persians playing the leading roles. This period is discussed in chapters 5-9.

The Persian Gulf since the implantation of European, and most recently American, presence. This period can be divided into two phases, 1507-1971, and 1971-present. The Portuguese made a dramatic irruption into the Persian Gulf by seizing Hormuz in 1507, a step which symbolized the dawn of European dominance there as over most of the world's seas and oceans. This dominance came close to converting the Persian Gulf, on the level of naval strategy, into a British lake between 1820 and 1971. On 30 November 1971, Great Britain abrogated her protectorate over what for over a century had been the Trucial Coast principalities, but now became fully independent United Arab Emirates. Oil and strategy have since then quickened the pace of the Persian Gulf's history towards a dramatic present in which the United States plays the leading role. This period is discussed in chapters 10-14.

Part I

HISTORICAL NARRATIVE

Period 1. The Persian Gulf Before it Became Persian

Period 2. The Persian Gulf Under Persian Rule,
539 BC – 637 AD

Period 3. The Islamic Persian Gulf,
637-1507

Period 4. Persian Gulf Under Western Domination

Chapter 1

Sumerians and Elamites[26]

Towards the end of the 4th millennium before our era, two peoples at the head of the Gulf, one between the lower Euphrates and Tigris and along the former river's western bank (thus in present-day Iraq), the other to the east of the lower Tigris (thus in present-day Iran), emerged from the mists of prehistory, practiced irrigated agriculture, and began to record certain business or administrative transactions. They were the Sumerians and Elamites, and spoke now extinct languages whose origins have so far defied an incontrovertible identification.[27] Sumerian does display, though, certain agglutinative features which to some scholars suggest a possible link with the Altaic family of Central Asia (Turkish and Mongolian are its principal representatives), and thus an Inner Asian origin of its speakers, but this link is tentative at best. The Elamites, in contrast, are believed to have arrived from the southeast, speaking a language

---

[26] Literature on the subject is vast, and most of the references cited in the book include often extensive bibliographies. Among the best general overviews the following four books stand out: *Cambridge Ancient History* (henceforth cited as *CAH*), vols. 1, part 2 – vol. 2, parts 1-2, Cambridge, 1971-73; Martinus Adriaan Beek, *Atlas of Mesopotamia: a survey of the history and civilisation of Mesopotamia from the Stone Age to the fall of Babylon*, London 1962 (a translation of his *Atlas van het Tweestromenland*); Michael Roaf, *Cultural Atlas of Mesopotamia and the Ancient Near East*. New York: Facts on File, 1990; and Georges Roux, *Ancient Iraq*. 3rd ed. Penguin Books 1993 (a translation of his *La Mésopotamie: essai d'histoire politique, économique et culturelle*. Paris: Seuil, 1985).
[27] W.F. Albright and T.O. Lambdin, "The Evidence of Language," *CAH* 1: 2: 122-155.

that had sprung up among the Dravidian populations of the Indian subcontinent (Malayalam is a modern example of this linguistic family).

Among several Sumerian urban centers, two deserve special mention. Erech or Uruk, whose ruins lie some 15 kilometers north of the town of Khidr on the left bank of the Euphrates, is memorable especially for its religious precinct of Eanna: this is where archaeologists have found clay tablets inscribed with ideographic characters. Dated to 3,100 BC, they are mankind's earliest known written records.[28] The other center is Ur, whose ruins lie farther down the river toward Basra, in a cluster of archaeological sites. The Kingdom of Ur rose in the course of the 3rd millennium to become an important political and commercial center with trading partners in the Gulf and even beyond it: Dilmun, now identified as modern Bahrain; Magan, probably Oman; and Melukha, believed to have been the Indus Valley.[29] This trade consisted chiefly in luxury items for the state and the wealthy elites. While some merchants from as far away as Melukha came to Ur and even resided there, others used Dilmun as the main entrepot. Pearls were acquired from the Gulf itself, while carnelian, lapis lazuli, ivory, and gold were brought all the way from Melukha; among exported or re-exported items were textiles, olive oil, barley, and silver. There also seems to have been trade with southern Arabia and Africa, for which Magan played the role of intermediary or entrepot partner. In all cases, the Persian Gulf was this traffic's main avenue.

---

[28] C.J. Gadd, "The Cities of Babylonia," *CAH* 1: 2: 93-96.

[29] Daniel T. Potts, *The Arabian Gulf in Antiquity*, Oxford 1990, vol. 1, p. 142 and passim (see index for Dilmun, Magan, Meluhha).

Chapter 2

Akkadians, Babylonians and Assyians

While Sumer blossomed along the lowermost courses of the Euphrates, a neighboring people to the northwest along the Euphrates and the Tigris arose in the course of the 3rd millennium to create their own civilization. These were Semites, whose tribes had for some time been moving into Mesopotamia from northern Arabia. Both they and the language they spoke and wrote are known by several appellations which more or less correctly reflect certain variables: Akkadians, Babylonians, Assyrians. Linguists call their language Akkadian and classify it as eastern Semitic[30] – the only one of this category and distinct from western Semitic, which includes Aramaic, Phoenician, and Hebrew; and southern Semitic, of which Arabic is the principal living representative. In other words, the immediate neighbors of the Sumerians and Elamites spoke a language totally different from theirs, or, put in different terms, the three groups – Sumerian, Elamite, and Semitic – formed a cluster of unrelated linguistic and racial identities. Yet astonishingly, despite the inevitable wars, conquests and razings of cities, the three developed an essentially common civilization using the same cuneiform writing system and borrowing one another's pantheon. Moreover, the Babylonian civilization was for a long time bilingual, with Akkadian only gradually restricting Sumerian to the role of a dead though still venerated and studied literary and religious vehicle.

---

[30] C.J. Gadd. "The State of Babylonia under the Dynasty of Agade...," *CAH* 1: 2: 417-63, esp. pp. 450-51.

By 2350 BC, in one of these Semites' royal cities, Kish,[31] a resolute and able upstart named Sargon had pushed aside the ruling monarch and launched his own rule and dynasty, that of the Akkadian Sargonids (2350-2230). He then founded his own capital, named Agade, whose site archaeologists have so far failed to locate with certainty but which was probably somewhere to the northwest of Kish. More memorable were his conquest of the Sumerian city of Uruk and subsequent creation of the first recorded multinational empire, whose borders may have stretched from the Persian Gulf to the Mediterranean coast in Syria and Lebanon. Agade itself probably lay on the Euphrates or on one of its navigable canals, for one of Sargon's inscriptions states that its quay was frequented by ships from Dilmun, Magan, and Melukha. If this is true, then the first imperial capital in Mesopotamia also functioned as a Persian Gulf port.

Ships thus carried merchants and merchandise to and from Mesopotamia, and the successive empires that replaced the Sargonids were eager customers and suppliers of the trade coming via the Persian Gulf. The Akkadian Sargonids lasted only a little over a century, and their capital, Agade, disappeared with them. It was they who inaugurated the reign of the Semites in Mesopotamia, however, and their rule was an expression of the energy and creativity that had been gathering momentum. Under them the Akkadian language, written in cuneiform script, came of age not only as an administrative and business language, but also as a literary one.

The Akkadian empire of the Early Sargonids fell victim to the invasion of the Guti, barbarians of unknown origin who irrupted into Mesopotamia from the Zagros Mountains and installed their rule for the next hundred years. Southernmost Mesopotamia – in other words, Sumer – was less affected and eventually reached one of the high points of its civilization with the Third dynasty of Ur (2130-2021). By the end of the 3rd millennium, however, there arose another Akkadian kingdom whose capital, Babylon, would in due course become one of the most venerated and famous cities of antiquity. Its ruins lie some 10 km east of the present course of the Euphrates near the modern town of Hilla. Babylon passed through many vicissitudes during its long his-

---

[31] The ruins of Kish lie some 20 kilometers northeast of the Iraqi city of Hilla.

tory, but two phases deserve special attention. The first, often referred to as "Old Babylonian," lasted from about 2000 to about 1590;[32] the second, "New Babylonian," appeared a millennium later, from about 1130 to 539, albeit with long interruptions and domination by Assyria.

The Semites who transformed Babylon into a famous religious center and imperial capital were the Amurru or Amorites. They spoke a dialect that pertained to the Western Semitic family, in contrast to Akkadian which was Eastern Semitic. They soon ceased using it, however, and became what we might call "Akkadianized" or "Babylonized". What is more, it was under them that the classical Old Babylonian civilization came to full bloom. Akkadian, impressed in cuneiform script on clay tablets or engraved as inscriptions on steles and monuments, besides retaining its role as a vehicle for royal edicts and correspondence, now also became a literary language. Of the former category the most celebrated monument is the Law Code of Hammurabi, engraved on a diorite stele by order of King Hammurabi (1792-1750), the 6th king of the First Dynasty of Babylon (1894-1595).

We have mentioned the Guti, who had invaded Mesopotamia and put an end to the First Akkadian Dynasty ca 2280. Similar invasions also marked the following millennium, and had similar effects. Some of the invaders would then impose their rule; but even if it was a prolonged one, they would not succeed in implanting their own languages or civilizations; more often they would respect what they found or even endeavor to adopt it for themselves. This was the case of the Kassites, another people of unknown origin and language, who like the Guti had arrived from the Zagros Mountains in Iran. Kassite rule succeeded that of the Babylonians in 1595 and lasted until 1150. Their appearance earlier in the 2nd millennium coincided with that of the Hittites, who had invaded northwestern Mesopotamia from Anatolia, where they had created an impressive civilization of their own, partly inspired by that of Mesopotamia. The Hittites spoke an Indo-European tongue but adopted the Akkadian cuneiform script to write it. It was their king Mursili I who with a sudden raid on Babylon brought down the First Babylonian Dynasty; but

---

[32] C.J. Gadd, "Babylonia c. 2120-1800 B.C.," *CAH* 1: 2: 595-643; esp. p. 637.

he immediately withdrew, and the void was quickly filled by the Kassites, as we have seen.

Meanwhile the same Eastern Semites who had populated the northern part of Babylonia and created the first empires, Akkad and Babylon, had begun to assert themselves farther north along the two rivers, but especially along the upper Tigris. Toward the end of the 2nd millennium they founded a mighty empire that became known by the name of their principal deity and the city which was named after it, Assur or Ashur. The land which they inhabited could still be considered part of Mesopotamia, since it straddled the Tigris and thus what lay to the west of the river was also between it and the Euphrates. Here, however, the Euphrates flows at its farthest from the Tigris, and the concept of Mesopotamia is as elastic in this area as when applied to the lowermost course of the two rivers as they approach the Persian Gulf though a unified bed. Comparison as well as contrast is also worthwhile for another reason. The wide crescent-like swath of territory on both sides of the upper Tigris, from the foothills of the Zagros on the east all the way to the west where the upper Euphrates flows through the Syrian desert, has good soil and is blessed with enough rainfall to make "dry" farming possible. It indeed seems that this region witnessed the earliest human settlement and cultivation of grain, and over the ages it gained fame as the "Fertile Crescent".[33] Once the farmers and settlers in Assyria acquired some of the sophisticated tools of civilization such as writing from their Babylonian neighbors to the south, they began their ascent toward building a city-state, which in due course would grow into a powerful empire and create an impressive civilization. Assyria as a kingdom and empire made its appearance in the 14th century BC, when King Ashur-uballit ascended the throne, and lasted until 612 when it collapsed under the joint blows of the Medes and Babylonians. Tiglath-pileser I (1116-1076) conquered Babylon, but showed respect for the sacred city and its god by allowing a local king to govern it. Subsequent centuries witnessed recurrent military campaigns, initially defensive but eventually turning into grandiose and ruthless conquests. Among the Assyrians' adversaries were the Arameans, Semitic tribes that towards the end of the 2nd millen-

---

[33] And Jazirah ("Island" or "Peninsula") in Arabic.

nium, having emerged along the fringes of Mesopotamia from the deserts of northern Arabia, spread over a wide swath of territory between Syria on the northwest and the Persian Gulf on the southeast. In both areas – that of the northwest with Damascus and Bit-Adini, now an archaelogical site on the Euphrates, and that on the southeast in a region more or less coterminous with the former Sumer in lowermost Iraq, the Arameans would found local kingdoms whose significance went beyond the confines of the territories under their control; still more important was their penetration, chiefly as merchants, of much of Mesopotamia and lands as far west as the Mediterranean.

The Assyrian rise from kingdom to empire gained momentum with kings Ashurnasirpal (844-859) and Shalmaneser III (859-824). Shalmaneser conquered lands that would become the core of the empire: Babylon itself and those of the two Aramean kingdoms on the Euphrates and by the Persian Gulf. The Arameans in the latter area, which was also called "Sealand" in Babylonian, had meanwhile begun to assert themselves to the point where one of their names, Chaldean, started to supersede the term Babylonian and the still older Sumerian in that quarter, so that the region came to be known as Chaldea; centuries later, this name, whether applied to the region, people, or the language they spoke, came to replace that of Babylonia. The name of the famous city itself, however, always remained Babylon.

The Assyrian apogee came under the dynasty of the Sargonids (722-627). Its founder, Sargon II (722-705),[34] in 710 defeated the Chaldean Merodach-baladan who had made himself king of Babylon; he then pushed on farther south and east all the way to Elam. These conquests allowed him to add to his titles that of "King of Sumer and Akkad", but significantly, out of respect for Babylon he called himself there a mere "Governor of Babylon". The reign of his successor Sennacherib (704-681) included a famous naval expedition to the Persian Gulf. It was triggered by a revolt in Babylonia, where in 703 BC Merodach-baladan had again seized power. Sennacherib suppressed it in 700 and installed there one of his sons as king; six years later, wishing to chastise the state of Elam situated east of the Shatt al-

---

[34] Not to be confused with the aforementioned Sargon I of the Early Sargonids.

Arab, he had two fleets built by shipwrights from the Mediterranean port of Tyre in the Euphrates harbor of Til Barsip and the Tigris harbor of Nineveh. Manned by Phoenician mariners, the two squadrons sailed down the rivers. At a place where Baghdad would later be located, the Tigris squadron was hauled overland to the Euphrates, where it joined its counterpart. The combined fleet then sailed all the way down to the Persian Gulf, where it exited into the open sea (Nar Marratu, or "Bitter River", in Akkadian, a name derived from the difference between maritime and fluvial water) and, turning east and entering the Karun, attacked Elam from this unexpected quarter.[35] Til Barsip no longer exists, but the site, some 50 km south of the Syrian-Turkish border, lies near the river harbor of Birecik, 20 km north of this border. In the Ottoman period Birecik functioned both as the empire's vital base for river traffic on the Euphrates and as an arsenal, gathering materials such as wood that would then be shipped to the shipyard of Basra. A certain analogy can be found on the Tigris. Nineveh was destroyed in 612 BC by a coalition of Medes and Assyrians, but modern Mosul in the site's vicinity still functions as a river port.

The last prominent Sargonid, Ashurbanipal (669-631), is remembered as a ruthless conqueror, but he also was a cultivated monarch who founded a great library in Nineveh. It was under Ashurbanipal that Assyrian material and artistic culture reached its peak. Commerce flourished, and Assyrian trading colonies followed a network of trade routes, especially in Anatolia. The Assyrian empire now included not only Palestine but also Egypt, where Ashurbanipal defeated the Kushite monarch and seized Thebes. At the other pole of the empire, in Babylon, the "Sealand," and Elam, rebellions and attacks had been partly caused by Ashurbanipal's involvement with Egypt. Once back from that campaign, the king launched a four-year war, during which he defeated his opponents and sacked the capital of Elam, Susa. Worthy of notice is the increasing presence of Arabs, nomadic tribes that had followed the Aramaean example by emerging from the desert, eager to get a share of Mesopotamian wealth. They lent their services to Shamash-shuma-ukin, the elder brother of Ashurbanipal, who had been assigned by their father

---

[35] D.D. Luckenbill, *Ancient records of Assyria and Babylonia.* University of Chicago Press, 1927. 2 vols. vol. 2, sections 318-21.

Esarhaddon not the imperial succession at Ashur but the local (though still respectable) throne of Babylon. Shamash-shuma-ukin eventually rebelled against his younger suzerain, and in the ensuing war (which he lost) he used Arab auxiliaries mounted on camels. A depiction of these nomads fleeing from Assyrian troops is included on a wall relief in Ashurbanipal's palace at Nineveh. The presence of camels is significant: it was the Arameans and especially the Arabs who domesticated this animal and then spread its use throughout the Middle East.

After Ashurbanipal the Sargonid dynasty soon collapsed and with it the existence of Assyria as an independent and at times imperial state. The main cause of its end may well have been the internal disintegration of a dynasty whose brilliant reign had run its course, but it was speeded up by a special alliance the magnitude of whose consequences few could have predicted at the time. In neighboring Iran, the Medes, a people closely related to the Persians, had forged an extensive kingdom centered on the city of Hamadan. Meanwhile Nabopolassar, a Chaldean employed by the Assyrians as an official in southern Babylonia, declared himself King of Sealand during the confusion following Ashurbanipal's death, and made an alliance with Cyaxares, king of Media. The two then attacked Assyria and in 612 took its capital Nineveh. Nabopolassar became king of Babylonia, inaugurating the rule of the so-called Chaldean or Neo-Babylonian dynasty.

Nabopolassar was succeeded by his son Nebuchadnezzar II (605-562). The first phase of his reign was spent on building a Babylonian empire as extensive as that of the Assyrian Sargonids had been, minus Egypt. This empire enabled him to amass great wealth from the home provinces as well as from international trade whose network spanned the Near East from the Persian Gulf to Iran and the Mediterranean. The outstanding symbol of his might, prosperity and genius was the city of Babylon itself, which may have grown to become the largest city in the Near East. A double wall surrounded the city, with a moat between the inner and outer walls. The Euphrates flowed through the city, and the wall was strengthened by bulwarks of bricks at the river's points of entry and exit. Within Babylon was the sacred precinct of the god Marduk, with a temple and a *ziggurat*, the temple tower ("the Tower of Babel") of a type characteristic of Mesopotamia. A straight-walled street linked the temple pre-cinct to the western gate; the walls were lined with glazed bricks showing the symbols of Babylon's main deities: the dragon of Marduk, the lion of Ishtar, the bull of Adad. Marduk himself was elevated above all other gods – the Sumerian Enlil and Assyrian Ashur had hitherto been accorded similar status – but he also received a new name, Bel or Bal – the Biblical Baal (this was a Chaldean word, a symptom of the ever-rising importance of the Aramaic linguistic family, of which Chaldean was a part, in Mesopotamia). In other words, *henotheism* made its appearance, a parallel or forerunner of monotheism. Meanwhile the spoken language was shifting from Babylonian to Aramaic, although for some time to come, the former continued to be used as a vehicle for the written word. Even after the extinction of Assyrian and Babylonian supremacy brought about by the Iranians, Babylo-nian survived for some time, although only as a ceremonial lan-guage; its ultimate exit and the victory of Aramaic may have been accelerated by practical aspects – the phonetical alphabet borrowed by Aramaic from Phoenician had a definite advantage over the unwieldy Akkadian cuneiform, originally developed from ideograms.

While the Arameans and Arabs were emerging during the reigns of Sargonid Assyrians in the approaches to Mesopotamia, a third Semitic group, the Hebrews, were moving into Palestine. This was their second arrival during their wanderings; the first one, led by Abraham possibly from the area of Ur, is believed to have occurred at the time of the Old Babylonian empire.[36] The local kingdoms they now established in the Promised Land be-came frequent targets of Assyrian and Babylonian expansion. Jerusalem was the most notable kingdom, and Nebuchadnezzar conquered it twice: in 597 BC, after which, having imposed a heavy tribute on the king, he withdrew; and in 587, when he punished the city for its rebellion by deporting a large segment of the population, some of it to Babylon itself. The years of

---

[36] It should be noted that doubts have been expressed of late as to the historicity of Abraham's origins in Ur, or even of Abraham himself. Scholars have so far disproved neither, however, nor have they offered convincing alternative explanations of *Genesis* xi, 31: "And Terah took Abram his son...; and they went forth ...from Ur of the Chaldees, to go into the land of Canaan..."

"Babylonian captivity" that followed became proverbial in the entire Judeo-Christian civilization, and with them King Nebuchadnezzar and the Tower of Babel.

The Mesopotamian empires were landward-oriented, not maritime. Seaborne trade, though lively, must have been private, and thus left little record in official documents or narrative literature.[37] There were merchant ships and perhaps even fleets, but no major naval undertakings.[38] This pattern, characteristic of the Persian Gulf, and in fact of the Indian Ocean as well, would apply to all subsequent periods until the arrival of the Europeans in the 16th century.

---

[37] A bill of lading recorded on a tablet found in Ur and dating from ca 1900 BC lists gold, ivory, pearls, precious stones, copper ore, and hardwoods among the contents of a ship's hold, but it only indirectly reflects commercial sailings to Dilmun, Magan, or Melukha.

[38] There are two known notable exceptions. The first, admittedly somewhat hypothetical, goes back to Sargon of Akkad, who, according to literary sources, sent a naval expedition to Dilmun (modern Bahrain); the second is the documented campaign mounted by the Assyrian king Sennacherib via the Euphrates and the Persian Gulf to attack Elam.

Chapter 3

The Achaemenids

The Persian king who in 539 conquered Babylon was Cyrus II (ruled 559-530), honored in historiography as "Cyrus the Great". The home of the Achaemenid dynasty which rose to prominence with him was a region in southwestern Iran known today as Fars, or "land of the Persians", a branch of the Iranian tribes.[39] The Iranians had populated much of Central Asia and Iran in the course of the second millennium BC. Setting out from his home province, Cyrus first conquered all of Persia and then Anatolia, Mesopotamia, and Egypt, creating the greatest multinational state the world had yet seen, the Persian Empire. Its destinies would be intimately intertwined with those of the Greeks, who had meanwhile spread from their homeland in Greece to populate the Aegean islands and the maritime fringes of western Anatolia. Cyrus had imposed his rule on the rest of the Iranians and thereby extended the name of his own group, the Persians, to what we might call the entire nation; and the Greeks followed suit by applying the name Persia to their gigantic neighbor. This name then remained dominant in the West until 1935, when Reza Shah Pahlavi, the founder of the last dynasty to rule Persia, ordered that the name of the country be changed to Iran, and the West again followed suit.

The ceremonial capital of the Persian Empire was a city which the Greeks called Persepolis, or City of the Persians. Its ruins, known as Istakhr in Islamic literature, lie near modern Shiraz in southern Iran. For administrative purposes the realm

---

[39] J.M Cook, "The Rise of the Achaemenids and Establishment of their Empire," *Cambridge History of Iran* (henceforth cited as *CHIr*), 2: 200-291.

was divided into satrapies. One of them, the 9th, was Mesopotamia, which the Persians called Babirush, Babylonia. The 8th satrapy included ancient Elam, whose metropolis, Susa, became the Persian Empire's political and administrative capital. A royal road led from Susa southeastward to Persepolis and northwestward to Sardis in western Anatolia, but a lateral branch struck out due west across central Mesopotamia to connect it with Babylon. Both the choice of Susa and the respect shown to Babylon were symptomatic of pre-Islamic Persia's Mesopotamian focus and inspiration. The language that the Persians spoke was totally unrelated to Sumerian, Elamite, or the Semitic idioms (Akkadian, Aramaic, Arabic) dominant in Mesopotamia. Nonetheless, the Persians not only adopted the cuneiform script, but also much of the Mesopotamians' administrative practice and manner of keeping records. Aramaic was now the language of trade and bureaucracy, but official inscriptions were often bilingual or even trilingual – in Persian, Elamite, and Akkadian.[40] At its peak the Persian Empire was huge indeed. It comprised a wide swath of territory from the Bosporus in the west to the Indus in the east and Egypt in the south. The indispensable art of writing and record-keeping may have been borrowed, but the genius of organizing such an essentially harmonious polity was entirely Persian, just as in most other respects the Iranian civilization was original and creative.

Most important for our story, however, is the fact that Persia was the first major state directly bordering the Persian Gulf over at least one-half of its coastline. The former "Sealand" at the head of the gulf with its main rivers, the Euphrates/Tigris and the Karun, accessible to smaller sea-going ships, continued to serve as the terminus of maritime trade that had the potential of further expansion, given the wealth and means of the principal customer or partner, the Persian Empire. No such development, however,

---

[40] It is worth noting that Sumerian had by then dropped out of the picture, whereas Elamite stubbornly resisted extinction much longer. The explanation may be the completion of the "Babylonization" of the land of Sumer by the time the Persians had entered the scene. The land of Sumer merged or overlapped Akkadian-speaking territory of Babylonia, whereas Elam was separated from it by distance and the Tigris; Elamite seems to have been spoken as late as the first centuries of Islam.

occurred. First of all, the state itself showed no interest in launching a maritime expansion into the Persian Gulf or the Indian Ocean, whether for purposes of conquest or trade. No navy was created on that side of the empire, in contrast to the Mediterranean, where chiefly Phoenician fleets performed this function on behalf of the Persian king. One special exception that only confirmed this rule was the expedition led by Scylax of Caryanda, a Greek mariner in Persian service. King Darius I (522-486) ordered a small fleet under this commander to sail down the Indus and proceed from there to the Red Sea with Suez as the final destination.[41] Darius had indeed paid greater attention to that maritime route, and even ordered that a canal linking the head of the Red Sea with the Nile, previously dug by one of the pharaohs, be revived. This canal made seaborne communication, whether commercial or military, possible between the Mediterranean and the Red Sea, and was the precursor of a system that in several forms and despite interruptions has lasted to our own day. Darius, however, may have missed an opportunity while pursuing an imperial dream. He could have turned Persia into a great naval and commercial power if he had based it on the Gulf; concentrating on the Red Sea made this hardly possible. His main goal may have been strategy of the moment: acquiring a firmer grasp on the recalcitrant Greeks in the Aegean and on the unstable Egyptians. This does not mean that the Persian Gulf ceased to be what it had been since the dawn of history, an avenue of seaborne commercial traffic and source of such littoral treasures or commodities as pearls and dates. It does suggest, however, that the Red Sea would become a lasting parallel or competitor for long-distance seaborne trade, with primacy alternating between the two. Also, as in the case of the Sumerians and Babylonians, we can suspect increasing participation of Persian ships, traders and mariners, but again, without sufficient written evidence on their part.

---

[41] Herodotus, *History*, Book 4, chapter 44.

Chapter 4

The Seleucids, Parthians and Sasanians

The Achaemenid Empire lasted until 331 BC, when Alexander the Great defeated Darius III at the Battle of Gaugamela. This event inaugurated the Hellenistic era, which was represented in Mesopotamia, Iran and the Persian Gulf by one dynasty, that of the Seleucids (305-125). For our purposes, the noteworthy phase of this era is Alexander's own time. He organized a fleet on the Indus at the end of his conquests in the East, and sent it under the command of his captain Nearchos to the Gulf. The voyage was recorded in a journal now lost, but its substance seems to have been preserved in the *Indika*, a work by the historian Arrian (Arrianus Flavius, 96-180).[42] The fleet set out from the delta of the Indus and, hugging the coast of present-day Pakistan and Iran, sailed all the way to Teredon near the head of the Persian Gulf. Lowermost Mesopotamia had changed since Sumerian times. The silt brought by four rivers (Euphrates, Tigris, Karkhah, Karun) had pushed the head of the Gulf southward closer to its present coastline; the first two converged near modern Qurnah and proceeded to the Gulf by a joint estuary, the Shatt al-Arab, while the Karkhah no longer reached the sea but flowed into the Shatt. New harbors and cities were making their appearance, and older ones had to be reached through the Shatt. One of the latter was Teredon. Its location has not been identified with certainty, but it had then

---

[42] A good summary of Arrian's account is in Wilson, *The Persian Gulf*, pp. 36-43, based on a translation by William Vincent, *The Voyage of Nearchus from the Indus to the Euphrates.* This translation is included in vol. 1 of Vincent's *Commerce and navigation of the ancients in the Indian Ocean*, 2 vols., London 1807.

the reputation of being 'the emporium of the sea-borne trade in frankincense and all the other fragrant productions of Arabia', and may have lain to the west of the combined estuary of the Euphrates and Tigris. Nearchos, having arrived at Teredon, had at that point received news that Alexander was approaching Susa; he made his fleet turn back and, passing the Shatt estuary, enter the third major river at the head of the Gulf, the Karun, then called the Euleaus or Pasitigris. Like the other two rivers, the Karun was accessible to seagoing craft a considerable distance upstream, and the fleet proceeded all the way to the bridge serving the royal highway from Persepolis to Susa near the modern city of Ahvaz. There, on 24 February 325, it linked up with Alexander's troops, which had just arrived from their epic anabasis.

The progress of the fleet from the Indus to the Euphrates/Tigris may in some respects have mirrored the by then already age-old sailings of merchant vessels between India and the Gulf, mostly hugging the northern, thus Persian coast despite the innumerable hazards of shoals and rocks. One can surmise, though, that merchants strove to cover the distance in fewer than the 146 days needed by the Greek fleet. In most cases, ships probably had to call at several points to replenish water and victuals, and on occasion to hire local pilots; the success of Nearchos's fleet in doing both may be indicative of the frequency of maritime traffic between the Persian Gulf and India.

Although many of the geographical features mentioned in Arrian's account have had their names changed over the centuries, most have been identified, and with frequent comments by the Greek author they provide valuable historical information. As the fleet approached the entrance to the Strait of Hormuz, it anchored 'off a barren coast (the coast of Makran), whence they descried a headland projecting far out into the sea...about a day's sail distant. Persons acquainted with those regions asserted that this cape belonged to Arabia, and was called Maketa (Ras Musandam), whence cinnamon and other products were exported to the Assyrians.'

The fleet then entered the strait and anchored at the mouth of the Anamis, in a country called Harmozeia, 'a hospitable region rich in every production except only the olive'. The Anamis was the river Minab, and the town near its estuary, today also called

Minab, was the original Hormuz. The fleet anchored there, while Nearchos proceeded inland in order to meet Alexander and his troops, who were reported to have reached a point a mere five days' journey away. Meanwhile the ships were repaired and provisioned, the crews enjoyed some respite on land, and on Nearchos's return the fleet resumed the voyage. It passed by Organa, an unassuming, desolate, rocky island whose days of glory as New Hormuz were hidden in the distant future. The ships anchored at the next island, 'of considerable size and inhabited, called Oarakta, which produced vines, palm trees, and corn'. This was Qishm, which would later become the main provider of food and water for New Hormuz. While describing the features observed during the voyage along the coast of Persis, the modern Fars, the narrative mentions 'another inhabited island where there is a fishery for pearls as there is in the Indian Sea', probably Kish.

The voyage of the Greek fleet under Nearchos can thus also be construed as an exploration of the Persian side of the Gulf, but Alexander did not neglect the other side either. His genius also encompassed maritime exploration down the Persian Gulf along the coasts of Arabia. Three expeditions sent by him in the reverse direction, from the head of the Gulf along the coast of Arabia, are mentioned by Strabo and Arrian. One led by Archias reached Tylos, thus Bahrain, and observed the pearl fisheries there; another, led by Androsthenes of Thasos, sailed some distance past it; a third one, under Hieron of Soli, reached the promontory of Maketa, thus Ras Musandam. All this may have been preparatory reconnaissance with a view to a planned sailing, again led by Nearchos, around the Arabian Peninsula. The fleet was ready in 323 BC when Alexander suddenly died in Babylon, probably of plague.

Much of what Alexander, Nearchos and the others were endeavoring to explore must have been common knowledge among the mariners of the Persian Gulf and Indian Ocean for perhaps as long as two millennia. The novelty of the Alexandrine projects lay in their incorporation in a great conqueror's vision, which, had he lived, might have laid the foundations of an empire that would have been not only land based but also seaborne. Alexander was an exception, however. True overseas expansion undertaken by a state had to wait until the age of discoveries which ushered in the modern era.

Alexander's empire was parceled out on his death among his generals. Mesopotamia with the territories east to the Indus fell to Seleucus I Nicator (305-281).[43] Seleucus founded a new capital for his kingdom, Seleucia-on-the-Tigris. Babylon [-on-the-Euphrates, we might add] had not yet turned into an archaeological site; in fact, it still was an important urban and religious center, but the Greek general who had been newly made king clearly wished to make a fresh start. Seleucia lay on the west bank of the Tigris some 60 kilometers north of Babylon, or, put in different terms, some 35 kilometers to the southeast of where Baghdad would be founded a millennium later. Like several of its predecessors and successors as capitals, the city lay in the central part of Mesopotamia where the Euphrates and Tigris draw closest to one another. In this instance, they were even linked by a "royal canal", thus prefiguring the "Isa canal" which in Islamic times would connect the Tigris with the Euphrates at the level of Baghdad.

The shift of the political center of gravity from Babylon to Seleucia may also have had another effect. First of all, the power elite was Greek-speaking, and the government functioned in that language, at least in the early stage of the dynasty's rule. The population was mixed; some of it may have been Persian, but the most common language was Aramaic, probably spoken also by the growing Jewish community; meanwhile Akkadian had entered its death throes as the religious language of declining Babylon.

With the Hellenistic and then Classical eras we begin to obtain a richer array of written sources about the trade passing through the Persian Gulf. One of the authors is Megasthenes, who wrote at the time of Seleucus Nicator. His work about India has been preserved in quotations by Arrian and Strabo, and mentions among other features Taprobane, later known as Ceylon and today as Sri Lanka. This large island was a pivot of maritime trade between the Persian Gulf, the southern Indian Ocean, and the Far East, as a mart for Oriental goods destined

---

[43] E. Bickerman, "The Seleucid Period," *CHIr*, 3:1: 3-20; Daniel T. Potts, *The Arabian Gulf in Antiquity*, vol. 2, pp. 2-22.

for Western markets, and as both a source and consumer of pearls and precious metals.

In the Persian Gulf itself, a place named Gerrha comes into prominence in the Seleucid period as an emporium and entrepot for both caravan and seaborne trade.[44] Situated on the Arabian shore facing Dilmun – thus Bahrain – in a region later known as al-Ahsa, it may have been a predecessor of the port city of Qatif. Its people were the already familiar Chaldeans, thus of the same Aramaic-speaking stock that populated lowermost Mesopotamia to the point of imprinting their own identity on this formerly Sumerian and Babylonian area. Gerrha was the terminus of caravans bringing spices from Hadramaut in southern Arabia and Aelana (the modern Elat), the port of Petra, on the Gulf of Aqaba. Some of these goods would then be shipped to the ports of Mesopotamia such as Teredon, Charax, and Seleucia itself. The Seleucid king Antiochus III (223-187), tempted by Gerrha's riches, undertook in 205 a campaign to conquer it, but was bought off by a tribute of silver, frankincense and myrrh. As the Greek historian Polybius tells us, "The Gerrhaeans begged the king not to destroy what had been given to them by the gods: eternal peace and freedom".

A reference to a special feature in the Persian Gulf area of an entirely different but prophetic kind can be found in the work of the Alexandrine geographer Eratosthenes (276-194), quoted by Strabo: "Asphaltus is found in great abundance in Babylonia. The liquid asphaltus, which is called naphtha, is found in Susiana…It is of a singular nature. When it is brought near the fire, the fire catches it; and if a body smeared over with it is brought near the fire, it burns with a flame which it is impossible to extinguish, except with a large quantity of water." The presence of petroleum had indeed been known since Babylonian times, and the substance received some attention and application. Its overwhelming role had to wait, however, until the 20th century.

Despite the benefits the Seleucids drew from trade coming via the Persian Gulf, they themselves displayed little initiative to participate by investing the resources of the state in shipping ventures or a navy for protection and conquest. The shippers,

---

[44] Christopher Brunner, "The Quadrant of the West," *CHIr* 3:2: 752-63; Daniel T. Potts, *The Arabian Gulf in Antiquity*, vol. 2, pp. 85-97.

merchants, mariners, and their specific activities remained chronically hidden in the haze of anonymity until Muslim authors of the Abbasid period lifted the veil to reveal a fascinating and dynamic breed of Persian and Arab seafarers. We can only surmise that they came from among the Chaldean, Arab, and Persian populations living in the coastlands of the Gulf and the Arabian peninsula. This state of affairs would continue under the next dynasty to rule Persia and Mesopotamia, the Arsacids or Parthians.[45]

The name is derived from Arsaces, a leader of the Parni, an Iranian tribe which in his time – the 3rd century BC – lived in what is today the Central Asian republic of Turkmenistan. From his capital at Dara, Arsaces expanded the territory under his control to include Parthia and Bactria, the northeastern provinces of the Seleucid empire. His successors further expanded their empire, until Mithridates I (171-139) seized Seleucia and Babylon in 141, annexing the greater part of Seleucid Mesopotamia. The Parthian empire, as it came to be known after the province in northeastern Iran from whence the Arsacids had fanned out on their conquests, stretched from the Euphrates to the Indus. Although not as large as that of the Achaemenids, it was still an impressive state and represented a renaissance of Iranian supremacy over a large segment of the Middle East. Significantly, though, like their Achaemenid predecessors and Sasanian successors, the Parthians, once they had secured control of Iran, placed their political center not in Iranian territory but in Mesopotamia. They built their capital, Ctesiphon, on the eastern bank of the Tigris a short distance to the northeast of Seleucia, which was on the river's western bank. The proximity of the earlier capital as well as of several other towns gave rise to an alternative name for the new city, Mahoze – "Cities", in Aramaic, which after the Islamic conquest would be Arabized as Mada'in.

The centuries of Parthian rule, conventionally stated as 238 BC – 224 AD, coincided with the decline of Hellenism and the rise of Rome. By the 1st century of our era, Rome, having absorbed Greece and Anatolia, became Persia's immediate neighbor, and Mesopotamia came to be the usual battleground of the two rival empires. Intermittent warfare did not put a stop to the

---

[45] A.D.H. Bivar, "The Political History of Iran under the Arsacids," *CHIr* 3: 1: 21-99.

long-distance trade that passed between east and west, however. Commercial exchange grew in intensity with the growth of powerful and wealthy empires in China, India, Iran, and Rome; and as usual, it had two main axes, a terrestrial and a maritime one. For the latter, we have seen, the Persian Gulf had been the principal or final avenue communicating with the affluent customers of ancient Mesopotamia. The Red Sea began to play a similar role, serving Egypt, western Arabia and the countries bordering the eastern Mediterranean. The vigor of this seaborne trade, in which the Gulf route probably had long held a slight advantage, now seems to have shifted to the Red Sea, and for several reasons. One was the quite sudden entry on the scene of wealthy Rome as an avid customer for exotic spices and products, which made transit via Suez and Egypt more practical. The other was the fact that Parthian Iran could obtain such wares by means of overland routes. Moreover, some of these routes continued to end at Antioch and to afford the merchants there a share in the Roman extension.

The last pre-Islamic dynasty to rule Iran and intermittently Mesopotamia was that of the Sasanians (224-651).[46] It surpassed its predecessors in most respects. At its peak, the Sasanian Empire rivaled that of the Achaemenids in size, for it extended from the Bosporus to the Indus, and in the south it included Egypt and the Yemen. Several spectacular victories over Rome overshadowed all earlier military exploits of the Persians. And, especially relevant for our purposes, the Sasanians can be said to have conquered the Persian Gulf by occupying and integrating its Arabian side from Bahrain to Oman.

Like the Achaemenids, the Sasanians were Persians *par excellence* – the home province from which they had issued was Fars, and while the Achaemenids had begun building their empire by first overcoming that of their Iranian kinsmen the Medes, the Sasanians started with the Parthians. Once they had conquered Mesopotamia, they too moved their political capital from Istakhr to Ctesiphon, echoing the Achaemenid move from Persepolis to Susa. The language they spoke and wrote, which scholars call Pahlavi, was a descendant of Old Persian, but Aramaic,

---

[46] Richard N. Frye, "The Political History of Iran under the Sasanians, *CHIr* 3:2: 116-80; Wilhelm Eilers, "Iran and Mesopotamia," *ibid.*, 3:2: 481-504.

the *lingua franca* of trade, business and administration since Achaemenid times, was now the principal everyday idiom of Mesopotamia; it also became the liturgical language of the growing Manichaean and Christian communities. The religion that accompanied Sasanian rule, Mazdaism, was also descended from the Zoroastrian religion of ancient Iran.

Some of the Semitic tribes moving from the interior of the Arabian peninsula into the fringes of Mesopotamia, however, kept their ethnolinguistic identity even when they settled and founded flourishing kingdoms. These were the Arabs, and one of their kingdoms, that of the Lakhmids of Hira (early 4th century – 602), was a contemporary and usually a vassal of the Sasanians.[47] Hira was a city situated near the Euphrates a short distance to the southeast of present-day Najaf. Originally pagan, the kings of Hira later converted to Christianity. The civilization that blossomed in their kingdom during the final centuries before the rise of Islam had as one of its effects the appearance of a mature Arabic language able to handle not just practical but also cultural and religious themes.

Hira was the neighbor to the west and southwest of the Persian provinces of Asorestan (Babylonia), Mesene (Maysan), and Khuzistan (roughly coterminous with ancient Elam); west of the Shatt, it may have controlled some of the lowermost Mesene and Characene, vassal principalities of the Sasanians partly coterminous with ancient Sumer but with the added area created by silt brought by the rivers to the Persian Gulf. Arab authority, and up to a point the Arabic language, thus gained ascendancy over the local Chaldean principalities. Caravan and maritime trade flourished, and much of it passed through Hira or its territories.

The Sasanians, as we have said, were the first Persian dynasty to become actively involved in seaborne trade and connections with the Arabian Peninsula and beyond. The founder of the Sasanian empire, Ardashir I (224-241), sent expeditions to occupy Bahrain and Oman, both areas gradually populated by Arab tribal groups moving in this direction from the south and southwest of the Arabian Peninsula. For the time being, the Persian hold here was weak or intermittent, and eventually the Arabs of

---

[47] C.E. Bosworth, "Iran and the Arabs before Islam," *CHIr*, 3:2: 593-612.

Bahrain[48] were strong enough to reverse the tide and land on the coast of Fars, raiding the province to some distance in the interior. According to the 10th century Persian historian Tabari writing in Arabic,[49]

> "...A large number of them set out by sea from the regions of Abd al-Qays, Bahrain and Kazimah, and landed at Rashahr and on the shores of Ardashir Khurrah and the coastland of Fars..."

Henceforward the Arab presence in the coastal areas of Fars and Kirman would never cease and at times would impose its own rule and identity well into the latter part of the 19th century – just as the Persian presence on the Arab side would do.

The Arab expedition across the Gulf to Fars provoked a vigorous Persian reaction. King Shapur II (310-379), once he came of age in 325, mounted a retaliatory expedition. Again quoting Tabari,[50]

> "Then he crossed the sea with his troops and arrived at Khatt and explored the land of Bahrain killing the populace...Then he proceeded to Wajhah and arrived in Hajar whose inhabitants were the Arabs of the tribes of Tamim, Bakr bin Wa'il and `Abd al-Qays, and he spread the killing among them and spilled their blood..."

According to the historian Hamza al-Isfahani, Shapur's campaign made such a strong impression on the Arabs of the region that he became engraved in their memory under the nickname they gave him, *Dhu l-Aktaf* or "He who [perforated their] shoulders", meaning that he had the prisoners tied together by perforating their shoulders.[51]

---

[48] In early Arabic terminology, Bahrain had a wider connotation than it has now; it designated also or primarily the Arabian coastland between Qatar and Qatif.

[49] Tabari, *Annals*, ed. de Goeje, 1:1: 836.

[50] *Ibid.*, 1: 1: 838-9.

[51] Most modern Persian historians dismiss the "perforated shoulders" account as an exaggeration or a fabrication.

Shapur's overseas expedition to Bahrain and Yamama, an oasis crossroads deeper in the interior, was part of his efforts to secure the empire's frontiers on the west and southwest against nomadic Arab tribes; this policy included the deportation of some of the Arabs to Khuzistan and Kirman, and erecting a wall and digging a trench, the Khandaq Sabur, in lower Iraq. The motivation of these measures may not have been purely defensive, however. It had elements of what in modern times would be called colonial expansion – securing trade routes to the empire's advantage, and gaining a foothold at strategic points for this purpose or for penetration of productive areas. The Sasanian settlement on an island off the tip of the Musandam peninsula, commanding the sea lane through the Strait of Hormuz and possibly dating from Shapur's time, seems to have served such a purpose. Oman, Hadramaut, and Yemen, all of which included productive farming areas and were the principal maritime front of the Arabian Peninsula, with access to the Indian Ocean and its lucrative commerce, were the objects of Sasanian interest and expansion.[52] Shapur claimed possession of Mazun, now believed to have meant Oman, in his inscription at Naqsh-e Rustam. Eventually Persian garrisons were placed at Suhar and Rustaq. Since antiquity and throughout the early Middle Ages, Suhar was the principal port of Oman and port of call for ships sailing from the Persian Gulf to the Indian Ocean. Rustaq served as the administrative base for the Persian governor; its position in the northern and thus seaward slopes of the Jabal Akhdar range made it logistically part of the fertile Batinah coastland and its ports, while roads along the passes through the mountains linked it with the interior part of the country, the Zahirah, and cities like Nizwa and Ibri. The Arabs of those quarters, mostly of the Azdi tribal group, recognized the rule of the Al Julanda clan who – not unlike the Lakhmids of Hira – in turn were the vassals of the Sasanians. The Persian presence lasted until the Muslim conquest, and the two pivots of its economic motivation, trade and agriculture, flourished. The geographical configuration of Oman lent itself especially well to a system of irrigation, long practiced in Persia, by means of underground conduits dug from mountain

---

[52] John Craven Wilkinson, "The Origins of the Omani State," in Derek Hopwood, ed., *The Arabian Peninsula: Society and Politics*, London 1972, pp. 71-73.

slopes towards lower lying areas; in Iran they were called *kariz* or *qanat*, but came to be known in Oman by the Arabic term *falaj*, pl. *aflaj* or *fuluj*. This expansion thus represented an essential integration of the Persian Gulf and the Gulf of Oman within the orbit of the Persian Empire. We could visualize it as based, on the Arab side, on three key areas: the Lakhmid Arab kingdom of Hira, the coastal region of Bahrain, and Oman.

A fourth case of Sasanian expansion into Arabia, an expedition to Yemen, had a different motivation and was relatively brief and atypical of Persian policy. In the first half of the 6th century, Himyar, the kingdom of South Arabia, had come under the rule of the Ethiopians. A revolt erupted toward 570 against Masruq ibn Abraha, the Ethiopian governor. Sayf ibn Dhi Yazan, its leader, tried to get help from the Byzantines and then from their vassals the Ghassanids; disappointed there, he appealed to the Sasanian Khusraw I Anushirvan (531-579). The king somewhat reluctantly sent an amphibious force that included 800 cavalrymen and was commanded by Vahriz. The force disembarked on the Yemeni coast and pushed all the way to the capital Sana, where Vahriz installed Sayf as king of Himyar and as a tributary to and vassal of the Sasanians. Once the Persians left, however, trouble reappeared; Sayf was killed, and the Ethiopians came back. This in turn provoked the return of the Persians, led by the able Vahriz, who expelled the African invaders and installed Sayf's son Ma`di Karib as vassal ruler in Sana. This time a Persian garrison with a governor was left in the Yemeni capital, and stayed there until the rise of Islam. The Prophet Muhammad, by then ruler of a newly established theocratic state in Medina, sent envoys to Sana demanding conversion or submission. This happened in the late 620s, when Iran's losing war with the Byzantines ruled out any help for the Persian garrison. Badham, the commander, and then his son (whose exact name seems to be unknown), not only accepted the terms and promised to convert with the entire garrison, but even helped the Muslims suppress the revolt of a local prophet, Aswad. The garrison converted to the new religion and became Arabized, although their Persian origin was long remembered, as would also be that of Persians who came as merchants and mariners to the ports of Yemen and the Red Sea.[53]

The Yemeni episode was atypical. It was by the same token characteristic of Persian reluctance to conceive of a truly maritime, commercial, overseas empire. Yemen was both a source of valuable commodities and a transit area for long-distance trade, especially between its coastal zones and emporia like Aden. With mastery of the Persian Gulf and the Gulf of Oman assured, seizing and holding the Yemeni emporia should have been both attractive and feasible. Such a policy would have required permanent attention to a navy and an at least partly state-sponsored merchant fleet, with lucrative trade as the justification of the investment. Iran, ever since its definitive formation by the Achaemenids as a large and powerful state with a long waterfront, was well suited to become a mighty oceanic empire. In Sasanian times and perhaps even earlier, Persian merchants and skippers had sailed on their trading voyages to Arabia, India, Taprobana (Ceylon, Sri Lanka) and probably as far as southern China. Had they received government backing and participation, buttressed by an adequate naval force, they might have established lasting colonies and emporia at critical points of this vast commercial orbit of the Indian Ocean. This kind of vision, however, remained alien to the empires of the Orient. I realize that the argument advanced in this paragraph contradicts my earlier statement that Shapur's and some of his successors' penetration of the Arab side of the Persian Gulf and the Arabian Sea had elements of colonial expansion. The answer is that there is a difference of degree, which then turns into one of kind. Oman and

---

[53] C.E. Bosworth, "Iran before Islam," *CHIr* v. 3 pt. 1 pp. 606-7; A. Christensen, *L'Iran sous les Sassanides,* 2nd ed., Copenhagen-Paris 1944, pp. 368-69; Th. Nöldeke, *Geschichte der Perser und Araber zur Zeit der Sassaniden, nach der arabischen Chronik des Tabari*, Leiden 1879, pp. 349-51.

Bahrain was how far the Persians were ready to go and persevere; Yemen was just too far, to say nothing of Taprobana.

Chapter 5

The Muslim Conquest of Iraq and of the Persian Gulf Area

In 602, the Sasanian emperor Khusraw II Parviz (590-628) chastised Nuʿman III for his attempts to free himself from the state of vassalage hitherto observed by his predecessors. He annexed Hira and executed the Arab king.

602 was also the year when the Byzantine Emperor Maurice was assassinated. This gave the *shahanshah* – or King of Kings, as the rulers of the Persian Empire styled themselves – the opportunity to punish the murderers and by the same token to launch an offensive against Iran's perennial rival, the Byzantine Empire. Things went well at first, for the tumult caused by the regicide in Constantinople weakened Byzantium, and the Persian armies overran virtually the entire Byzantine territory outside of Europe: Anatolia, Syria, Palestine, and Egypt were conquered, and Khusraw could see himself as the sovereign of an empire as immense as that of the great Achaemenids had been. The triumph did not last, however. The Emperor Heraclius, enthroned in 610, needed twelve years to affirm his authority and prepare for war; but when he passed to the offensive in 622 he inflicted on the Persians a series of defeats. Forced to withdraw all the way to Ctesiphon, Khusraw Parviz was deposed and assassinated in 628. Confusion followed, and when his grandson Yazdagerd III (632-651) ascended the throne, he had to face an even more formidable enemy than the Greeks.

Closer to his Mesopotamian home, in northwestern Arabia Khusraw had also eliminated the other renowned Arab kingdom, that of the Ghassanids. The Lakhmids and Ghassanids had acted as buffer states, softening the frequency and impact of collisions between the two giant empires; at the same time, while the Lakhmids had been Persia's shield against the Bedouin tribes of the northern Arabian desert, the Ghassanids performed the same function for the Byzantines. Khusraw's conquests removed the buffer and the shield. This did not by itself cause the coming confrontation with Byzantium, but it made the collision that much more devastating; and the exhausting wars that had weakened the two superpowers handed the desert nomads an unprecedented opportunity.[54]

In the same year of 622 in which Heraclius launched his campaigns of reconquest, Muhammad, the founder of Islam, left his birthplace Mecca for the city of Yathrib, later known as Medina or City [of the Prophet]. He established there a vigorous theocratic state which sent out missions to convert and armies to conquer much of Arabia. Muhammad was the head of this state, and when he died in 632 his successor, the caliph Abu Bakr, inherited a dynamic force of Bedouin warriors who, when ably led and propelled by an inspiring creed, proved almost irresistible. Sent by him and by his two successors, Umar (634-644) and Uthman (644-656), they carried out what none of the Byzantine emperors had achieved, the conquest of Iran – and that of the Persian Gulf.[55]

We have schematically defined this period in the history of the Persian Gulf as beginning in 637; that was the year when the Muslims defeated Yazdegerd's forces at the Battle of Qadisiah, a place in the vicinity of Hira. Here Bedouin warriors overcame elite Persian troops backed by a column of elephants. Things went fast from then on. In 641, Yazdegerd made his last stand at Nihavend in northwestern Iran; his defeat delivered the country to the conquering Arabs. In an uncanny replay of historical drama, the Sasanian monarch, like his Achaemenid predecessor almost a millennium earlier, fled to his collapsing empire's eastern marches, in this case to Khurasan, where in 651 he was assassinated by a local governor.

---

[54]C.E. Bosworth, "Iran and the Arabs before Islam," *CHIr*, vol. 3:1, pp. 593-612; Richard N. Frye, *The Heritage of Persia,* Cleveland and New York 1963, pp. 230-31.

[55] Abd al-Husain Zarrinkub, "The Arab conquest of Iran and its aftermath," *CHIr*, vol. 4, pp. 1-56.

In 651 Uthman, the third caliph, still resided at Medina, and until his assassination five years later, Muslim armies continued their prodigious march east and west. They had conquered Khurasan and Egypt, and were ready for further advance. These far-flung campaigns might obscure the crucial importance of the conquest of Iraq, and its subsequent role as the province from which all the Iranian east would be administered for another century. Following a favorite pattern, the commanders, rather than basing their headquarters in conquered cities, preferred their own armed camps, which often developed into new cities. Kufa thus came into being in 638, and functioned as the seat of the caliph's governor with authority over all of Iraq and Iran. It was situated to the west of the Euphrates not far from Hira, thus in a strategically and economically favorable position for interaction between the *badiya* or desert land of the Arab Bedouins and the *sawad* or agricultural lowland of Mesopotamian farmers and city-dwellers.

Another city that came into being in a similar manner was Basra.[56] Utbah b. Ghazwan, one of the Prophet's *ashab* or companions, in 637 or 638 established a military camp that would become one of the most renowned cities of early Islamic civilization. The basic source for this event, *Tarikh al-rusul wa l-muluk* by Persian historian Tabari (d. 923) writing in Arabic, presents an invaluable portrayal of how the conquering Muslims viewed and experienced this part of lower Iraq, the Tigris and the approaches to the Persian Gulf with their role as the maritime gate toward the Orient. Ubullah was the principal port at the time, and Basra functioned at first only as a settlement a certain distance inland connected with the Tigris by a canal dug for the purpose of bringing drinking water from the river. Tabari relates

---

[56] Ch. Pellat, "al-Basra", *EIs* 1: 1085-6; idem, *Le Milieu basrien et la formation de Ǧahiz*, Paris 1953; G. Le Strange, *The Lands of the Eastern Caliphate*, Cambridge University Press 1905, pp. 43-46 and passim. This classic of historical geography (henceforward cited as Le Strange, *The Lands*) has remained indispensable a full century after its first publication; the author has used the AMS Press reprint, New York, 1976.

the event by presenting several versions which he had culled from the sources. Here are some examples:[57]

The Building of al-Basra

> In this year – meaning the year 14/635-36 – Umar b. al-Khattab dispatched Utbah b. Ghazwan to al-Basra and ordered him to encamp in it with those who accompanied him and cut off the supplies of the Persians in al-Mada'in and the vicinity. This is according to the version of al-Mada'ini.
>
> Sayf [b. Umar] maintained that al-Basra was established in the spring of the year 16/637-38 and that Utbah b. Ghazwan set out for al-Basra from al-Mada'in after Sa`d had finished [the battles] of Jalula', Takrit, and al-Hisnan. [The caliph] Umar said to Utbah b. Ghazwan: "God the Exalted has conquered at the hand of your brethren al-Hirah and its vicinity. One of the chieftains of al-Hirah was killed. I do not feel safe that their Persian brethren will not help them. I therefore wish to send you to the Land of India[58] in order that you may prevent the people of that area from assisting their brethren against your brethren..."
>
> Utbah set off with three hundred and ten odd men and was joined by some Bedouins and inhabitants of the desert. He reached Basra with five hundred men...and encamped there in the month of Rabi al-Awwal or Rabi al-Akhir of the year 14/635-36. At that time Basra was called "the Land of India," and there were white, coarse stones in it.
>
> According to Sayf – Muhammad, Talhah, al-Muhallab, and Amr: When Utbah b. Ghazwan al-Mazini set out from al-Mada'in to the Opening of India[59], he halted at the shore, facing the Arabian peninsula. He stayed there for a while, then moved elsewhere. The people then complained about this until finally, after three attempts at settlement, Umar ordered him to halt in

---

[57] The quotations are based on the de Goeje edition, al-Tabari, *Ta'rikh al-rusul wa-al-muluk*, Leiden, 1879-1901, 1: 5: 2377 ff. (Dhikr Bina' al-Basra), and Yohanan Friedmann's translation and annotation, *The History of al-Tabari*, Volume XII, pp. 161 ff. (The Building of Basra).

[58] "Land of India" (*Ard al-Hind*) could serve as an epithet for the ports and their surroundings at the head of the Persian Gulf. Here Ubullah may be meant, while immediately below the site of future Basra receives this appellation.

[59] Here, Tabari calls Ubullah *Farj al-Hind*, or the Gateway (lit. Opening) to India.

the desert...They halted in a stony tract (al-Basra)(al-Basra is used for any land of which the stones are gypsum). He ordered them to dig a canal through which water could be made to flow from the Tigris, so they dug a canal for drinking water to al-Basra.

According to Umar b. Shabbah – Ali – Abu Ismail al-Hamdani and Abu Mikhnaf – Mujalid b. Said – al-Shabi: Utbah b. Ghazwan came to al-Basra with three hundred men. When he saw a field of reeds and heard the croaking of frogs, he said: "The Commander of the Faithful ordered me to halt at the most distant edge of the Arab desert and at the nearest point of the cultivated Persian land. This is the place where we must obey the orders of our imam."...At that time, five hundred Persian horsemen were in al-Ubullah defending the city. al-Ubullah was a port for ships from China and from less distant places. Utbah moved forward and halted before al-Ijjanah and stayed there for about a month. Then the garrison of al-Ubullah came out to [fight] him, and Utbah stood up against them. ...The two armies confronted each other...God routed the Persians; they took to flight and withdrew into the city. Utbah returned to his camp and stayed there for a few days. God put fear in the hearts of the people of al-Ubullah; they left the city, carried their light belongings with them, crossed [the Tigris] to the city of al-Furat, and abandoned al-Ubullah. The Muslims entered the city, capturing various goods, weapons, prisoners, and money. They divided the money between them, and every man received two dirhams. Utbah put Nafi` b. al-Harith in charge of the spoils of al-Ubullah; he set aside a fifth and divided the rest among those to whom God restored it. He wrote about it [to the Caliph, sending the letter] with Nafi` b. al-Harith.

The significant aspect of these conquests and foundations for our purposes is the role which lower Iraq and the Persian Gulf assumed in early Islamic history, and in the subsequent flowering of Islamic civilization, both material and cultural, which took place there during the first four centuries of Islam. The constituent elements of this evolution were complex, but two deserve special mention. One is continuity. The civilization, culture, and trade had their roots, as we have seen, in the remotest past of Mesopotamia and the already respectable antiquity of Persia, both of which converged in southern and central Iraq; the other is the dynamism of the young Muslim community, at the beginning chiefly Arab-dominated, then increasingly Persianized, under the two great dynasties of unified Islam, the Umayyads and the Abbasids.

The Muslim conquest of the Arabian littoral of the two gulfs – the Persian Gulf and the Gulf of Oman – had meanwhile proceeded apace and in fact preceded that of Iraq, and can be considered to have been completed by the time of the Prophet's death in 632. Most of these early campaigns in Arabia were, in contrast to that of hard-won Iraq, peaceful, mainly consisting of political treaties with local or tribal chieftains acknowledging Muhammad's spiritual and political suzerainty. A brief passage from the historian Ahmad b. Yahya al-Baladhuri (d. 892) illustrates this process:

> Bahrain[60]. It has been reported: The land of Bahrain was part of the domain of the Persians, but many of its inhabitants were Arabs of the Abd al-Qais, Bakr bin Wa'il, and Tamim [tribes]. The chieftain appointed over them by the Persians at the time of the Prophet was al-Mundhir b. Sawa, one of the Banu Abd Allah bin Zaid; this Abd Allah bin Zaid [was called] al-Asbadhi, [a name] linked to a village in Hajar called al-Asbadh, [but] it is [also] said that [he was so named] because he belonged to the Asbadhis, a people in Bahrain who worshiped the horse[61]. In the year 8 [i.e., 629 or 630] the Prophet sent Ala' b. Abd Allah ibn Imad al-Hadrami to Bahrain in order to summon its people to accept Islam or the [payment of] the poll tax, and he sent with him a letter to al-Mundhir b. Sawa as well as to Sibukht, the [Persian] marzban (governor) of Hajar, summoning them to accept Islam or the payment of

---

[60] Ahmad b. Yahya al-Baladhuri, d. 892. *Futuh al-buldan*. Ed. M.J. de Goeje, Leiden 1866, vol. 1, pp. 78-79. The passage quoted illustrates the difference between what the name meant in early Islamic times and what it means today. The earlier connotation referred primarily to the coastal area facing the island and its archipelago (while the island itself was called Uwal or Uwali – most probably Dilmun of the Sumerian and Tylos of the Hellenistic periods), and partly overlapped with what was meant by Hajar, and what is today the Sharqiyah province of Saudi Arabia; the present connotation refers exclusively to the principal island, and in political terms, to the whole archipelago – now the Kingdom of Bahrain.

[61] The name does indeed contain elements of the Iranian term for horse, *asb* or *asp*.

the poll tax. They converted, and with them all the Arabs and some of the Persians too. As for those inhabitants who were Zoroastrians or Jews or Christians, they made peace with Ala', who wrote an agreement [lit. letter] between himself and them as follows: "In the name of God the Merciful the Compassionate. This is [the stipulation] upon which Ala' ibn al-Hadrami concluded peace with the people of Bahrain: That they should be supportive of our efforts, and that they should share with us their date [crops]. Whoever does not honor this pledge, on him be the curse of God, of the angels, and of all the people."

Again in contrast to Iraq, Islam's initial triumph here was fragile. One symptom of this fragility was the religious and political hiatus that occurred once the founder of Islam was dead, and his vassals at the more extreme corners of Arabia thought the religion he had founded had died with him. What followed was a series of "wars of *Riddah*" or wars of [the suppression of] apostasy, which quickly restored the position of the new faith.

It was the conquest of Iran that eventually brought the Persian Gulf into the orbit of Islam. The campaigns, whose goal here was the province of Fars, were ultimately directed from Basra, but they started with amphibious operations across the Gulf from Bahrain and Julfar on the Arabian coast.

In 635 Ala' ibn al-Hadrami, whom the Prophet had appointed governor of Bahrain, sent `Arfaja b. Harthama al-Bariqi on a maritime expedition which took an island off the coast of Fars and raided the coastal strip there. This was an unauthorized undertaking and displeased Umar b. al-Khattab, the second caliph, who reprimanded the governor. Two years later, however, news reached Umar of a mustering of Sasanian military elements in the coastal areas (*shutut*) of Fars. He thus ordered the new governor, Uthman b. Abi al-`As, to cross to Fars in order to prevent a consolidation of Sasanian military strength there; he also instructed the two Julanda rulers of Oman, Abd and Jayfar, to join this expedition with a group of their Azd tribesmen. The troops gathered at Julfar,[62] where they embarked and crossed to the is-

---

[62] Julfar functioned as one of the principal ports on the Omani coast of the Persian Gulf in the Middle Ages; today it is an archaeological site just north of Ras al-Khaimah, by which it was replaced as a port in the course of the 18th century.

land of Bani Kavan.[63] The commander of the Persian garrison made peace without a fight, but Yazdegerd, the Sasanian king, ordered the governor of Kirman to cross to Bani Kavan and stop the invaders; the Persians embarked at Hormuz and landed on the island, but were defeated. This was an important victory for the Arabs, for it enabled them to impede the passage of Persian shipping in and out of the Gulf by controlling the Strait of Hormuz – a decisive step toward making the Persian Gulf a Muslim lake. Moreover, the resulting control of the littoral facilitated the establishment of a garrison at Tawwaj,[64] a strategically located site from which summer campaigning, sometimes in conjunction with Basran forces, was carried out.[65]

The entry of the Persian Gulf and the Gulf of Oman into the orbit of the Islamic world also meant, however, that the triple schism of Islam – the three major denominations of the new religion: Sunni or Orthodox Islam, Shii Islam, and Khariji Islam – would soon make its appearance here.

Finally it should also be pointed out that factors of logistics and economy always played a role in the location and success of most of the sites founded by the conquering Arabs: from Kerbela to Kufah, Najaf, and Basra, we can observe their role as ports – maritime as well as desert – on caravan and pilgrimage routes spanning the Islamic East from Central Asia to Mecca, and on shipping routes through the Persian Gulf linking the Indian subcontinent and Africa to Iraq and the rest of the Near East.

The incorporation of the Persian Gulf into the dynamic Islamic empire that became consolidated under the Umayyads could not but further enhance its role as the great waterway of east-west maritime trade. The greatest florescence of the Gulf, however, came with the rise of the Abbasids and lasted as long as this dynasty made Iraq the center of the Islamic world, thus

---

[63] The present-day Qishm or Qeshm. Its earlier names were also Abarkavan, Laft, and Jazirah Tawilah ("Long Island").

[64] Tawwaj no longer exists today, and its ruins have not been positively identified; according to Le Strange (*The Lands*, p. 259), it was a famous place at the time of the first Muslim conquest. Its approximate location must have been half-way between Kazarun and the coast.

[65] Martin Hinds, "The First Arab conquests in Fars," *IRAN: Journal of the British Institute of Persian Studies*, vol. 22 (1984), pp. 39-53.

during the first two and a half centuries of Abbasid rule. Only the oil boom of the 20th century would overshadow that almost legendary era of its past.

Chapter 6

Iraq and the Persian Gulf as the Center of the Islamic Empire

Like the Umayyads (661-750),[66] the Abbasids (750-1258)[67] were Arabs, and in this sense theirs too was an Arab Islamic empire. What is more, not only did they belong, like their predecessors, to the tribe of Quraysh from which the Prophet Muhammad had issued, but the ruling line's eponym, al-Abbas, was Muhammad's uncle: his father Abd al-Muttalib was the Propher's grandfather. Their legitimacy by ascent may not have been, in the eyes of the stricter Shiis, as valid as that by descent claimed by the descendants of the Prophet's daughter Fatima married to his cousin Ali, but it still could be used in their campaign against the Umayyads. In this sense, the change of dynasties in 750 has little relevance for our purposes, but the course of the Abbasids' rise to power and subsequent foundation of their empire are of capital importance. The "Abbasid revolution", although planned from the Iraqi city of Kufa, was organized in Iran's east and, setting out from there, it acquired and then retained a pronounced Persian touch. The seat of the caliphate and thus the center of the empire moved eastward with the Abbasids to Iraq, an area of overlapping or merging Arab and Persian cultures and that much closer to Iran's heartland, the province of Fars. Most important for the context of our discus-

---

[66] G.R. Hawting, "Umayyads," *EIs*, vol. 10, pp. 840-47; Clifford Edmund Bosworth, *The New Islamic Dynasties: a chronological and genealogical manual*, New York: Columbia University Press, 1996, pp. 3-5 (henceforth cited as Bosworth, *Dynasties*).

[67] B. Lewis, "Abbasids," *EIs*, vol. 1, pp. 15-23; Bosworth, *Dynasties*, pp. 6-10.

sion is the fact that the maritime dimension of the Islamic empire shifted from the Red Sea and the Mediterranean towards the Persian Gulf and the Indian Ocean.

After the first caliph, al-Saffah (750-754), had rooted out the Umayyad family (save a survivor who fled to Spain and reestablished Umayyad rule there), his brother and successor, al-Mansur (754-775), embarked on organizing the empire and choosing the site for a new capital. His choice fell on a place where the Tigris and Euphrates approach each other the closest, not far from where the monarchs of the last three pre-Islamic dynasties, the Seleucids, Arsacids, and Sasanians, had built their capitals. Baghdad thus came into being in 762, and within a century it became one of the greatest cities of the early Middle Ages.[68] Islamic tradition ascribes to the caliph words which may be apocryphal in form but are convincing in substance. According to the historian Yaqubi, Mansur said:

> ... [Baghdad] is an island between the Tigris and Euphrates. The Tigris is to the east of it, the Euphrates to the west of it, and it is the world's crossroads. Everything that comes on the Tigris from Wasit, Basra, Ahwaz, Ubulla, Fars, Oman, Yamamah, Bahrain, and the neighboring places, can go up to it and anchor at it. Likewise, whatever arrives from Mosul, Diyar Rabi`ah, Azerbaijan and Armenia, is among the [wares] brought by ships on the Tigris; and whatever comes from Diyar Mudar, Raqqah, Syria, the Frontier Marches, Egypt, and Maghrib – [wares] carried by ships on the Euphrates – alights there and is unloaded. [Baghdad] can also be a meeting-place for the people of the Jabal and Isfahan and the regions of Khurasan."[69]

Baghdad thus functioned as a real international crossroads of maritime and caravan trade, a location unmatched by any other city in the Middle East. Although it is unlikely that regular ocean-going ships ascended the Tigris all the way to it, the Abbasid capital still functioned as a seaport receiving goods transshipped to smaller ships or river craft at the ports of Ubulla and

---

[68] A.A. Duri, "Baghdad," *EIs* 1: 894-908; G. Le Strange, *The Lands*, pp. 30-33 and passim.
[69] Yaqubi, *Kitab al-buldan*, ed. M.J. de Goeje, Leiden 1892, pp. 237-38 (*Bibliotheca Geographorum Arabicorum*, vol. 7).

Siraf. This role was further enhanced by the Nahr `Isa ("Jesus's Canal"), the canal that linked the Tigris with the Euphrates at the level of Baghdad.

Basra's foundation (638) antedated that of Baghdad by over a century, but its full flowering coincided with that of the Abbasid capital. The site, the camp, and then the city had great military, economic, and cultural assets. The city's five quarters reflected the five Arab tribal groups whose members constituted Basra's elite population and supplied the troops that participated in the subsequent conquest of Persia. Its position gave Basra the role of a gateway on one of the trunk routes linking Iraq with Arabia and Syria, and – at first in tandem with Ubulla – as the principal port of Iraq on the Persian Gulf. The original Basra lay some 12 kilometers to the west of the Shatt al-Arab, but was eventually linked to it by two canals, the Nahr Ubulla and Nahr Ma`qil. The Nahr Ubulla met the Shatt at the level of Ubulla, which was located on the northern side of the juncture and on the Shatt's western bank; the Nahr Ma`qil met the Shatt a few kilometers to the north of there. The two canals, flowing towards Basra, converged as they reached the city. Ubulla was the principal Abbasid port at the head of the Persian Gulf despite, or partly because of, the proximity of Basra, for the sea-going ships used it as their terminus.[70] Goods were transferred at Ubulla onto smaller craft and ferried to al-Kalla', Basra's harbor. It was an ideal partnership, for the city also functioned as a desert port: its western quarter of Mirbad was the gateway for caravans leaving for the Arabian and Syrian west or arriving from there,[71] often as part of the giant commercial network spanning Asia from China to the Mediterranean and Europe. Goods could indeed be brought from the Far East via the Persian Gulf to Ubulla and taken from there to Basra or Baghdad by river craft and from there to further destinations. Ubulla does not exist any more, or rather its site and function became absorbed by Basra, which in the later Middle Ages gradually inched eastward toward it and eventually became the number one port on the Shatt al-`Arab. The prosperity and brilliance of the Abbasid era were gone by then, but Basra never

---

[70] J.H. Kramers, "al-Ubulla," *EIs* 10: 765-66; Le Strange, *The Lands*, pp. 44, 46.

[71] *Mirbad* is an Arabic word which means "a place where a camel kneels down", thus an apt name for a caravan terminus.

lost its basic function as the prime port at the head of the Persian Gulf.

In the second half of the 9th century, Basra was the staging area of the Zanj uprising that shook the Abbasid caliphate to its foundations.[72] It was produced by the combination of a down-trodden social class, namely black African slaves, and a charismatic figure, Ali ibn Muhammad. Born in Iran but of Arab ancestry, he represented a case of a leader who exploited social discontent for his own personal gain, and who did so through the standard claim of a religious or even divine mandate coupled with promise of bettering his followers' lot. The slaves, employed in clearing the alluvial soil for agriculture, lived in harsh conditions; Ali ibn Muhammad, who became known as Sahib al-Zanj ("Master of the Blacks") or Muhammad al-Zanji, came from a comfortable milieu where he received an excellent education. He lived for some time at Samarra, the then capital city of Abbasid caliphs, busy composing poetry as one of the Caliph's panegyrists. He eventually left Iraq and moved to Hajar,[73] where he strove to acquire a following with the purpose of rebelling against the Abbasid caliph. Dissatisfied with the insufficient response, he left and joined the Bedouin in the desert, on occasion claiming Alid descent, or to have received a mysterious message from Heaven. Ali ibn Muhammad then returned to Iraq, first to Basra, where he and his small following were dispersed by the Abbasid governor's troops. He then proceeded to Baghdad, where he resumed proselytizing for his cause. Meanwhile factional strife brought Basra close to anarchy, and Ali ibn Muhammad returned to its vicinity. This time he gained for his cause a new segment of the population, the black African slaves. In September 868 he and his group intercepted and freed a gang of fifty slaves being taken to their work place, and the scene,

---

[72] Alexandre Popovic, "al-Zandj," *EIs* 11: 445-46; idem, *The Revolt of African Slaves in Iraq in the 3rd/9th century*. Princeton: Markus Wiener, 1999; and bibliography on pp. 159-88 of this excellent book; Tabari, *Ta'rikh*, English translation *The History of al-Tabari*, vol. 36: *The Revolt of the Zanj*, translated and annotated by David Waines, Albany 1992.

[73] Hajar (today known as Hufuf) was once the capital of al-Ahsa', a province then referred to as Bahrain (while the island thus named today was called Uwal).

repeated many times over, took on a momentum that soon provided the army he needed to challenge the Caliphate. The struggle took the form of *jihad*, holy war, symbolized by his silken
standard with a Coranic inscription, and propped up by promises
to the slaves of freedom and wealth. After laborious beginnings,
the revolt spread and encompassed much of southern Iraq and
Khuzistan with a radius marked by Basra, Ahvaz, and Wasit. Ali
ibn Muhammad built for himself a new fortified capital, al-
Mukhtarah ("The Chosen [City]"), on the western bank of the
Shatt al-Arab downstream from Ubulla. The Abbasid caliphs al-
Mu`tazz and al-Muhtadi, beset by troubles elsewhere, were un-
able to mount effective campaigns against the insurgents. The
tide turned only under the caliph al-Mu'tamid (870-92). The special terrain of the Batihah and the Shatt al-Arab area, crisscrossed by canals, required the preparation of a partly amphibious force, which descended the Tigris and set about methodically
reducing the area occupied by the Zanj; even so, the operation
took four years before it was brought to a successful conclusion
with the seizure of the rebel capital and the death of Ali ibn
Muhammad in August 893.

While the Zanj uprising was going on, Hamdan Qarmat was
proselytizing for the Ismaili cause in the area of the Iraqi city of
Kufah. He sent one of his followers, Abu Sa`id al-Jannabi, to
Bahrain, where in 887 Abu Sa`id founded the first Ismaili politi-
cal formation. The Ismaili movement, then gaining strength as
the most dynamic form of Shia Islam, had its ideological center
in the Syrian town of Salamiyah, where in 899 Ubaid Allah,
upon acceding to the leadership, proclaimed himself to be the
mahdi. Hamdan Qarmat refused to recognize this claim, and a
schism ensued that signified the birth of the Qarmati form of Is-
maili-Shia Islam. While many other schismatic groups of Is-
mailism developed over time, the Qarmati State in Bahrain and
the Fatimid Caliphate first in Tunisia and then in Egypt stood out
as its most prominent political expressions. In Bahrain it developed as an original and unusual community, which endured until
1076. The above-mentioned city of Hajar was the Qarmati
State's capital; Qatif was its principal port, and Uwal, as the
main island of the Bahrain archipelago, also belonged to it; revenues from the customs levied on entrepot trade passing through
Uwal were distributed among the descendants of Abu Said al-

Jannabi. At the peak of their power the Qarmatians even seized
Mecca in 930 and carried off the Black Stone to Hajar, where
they kept it for two decades before restoring it to the venerable
sanctuary of the Kabah. The fortunes of the Qarmati state depended to a large extent on their relations with the Arab tribes of
the area. In 987 they suffered a defeat by the Muntafiq; in 1057 a
chieftain of the `Abd al-Qais defied them by reestablishing Sunni
Islam on Uwal in the name of the Abbasid caliph al-Qa'im; and
in 1067 the tribe of `Amir Rabi`ah of the `Uqail, guardians of
Uwal for the Qarmatians, suffered defeat in a naval battle at
Kaskus, an island off Qatif. An uprising followed in Qatif, and in
1070 Abd Allah ibn Ali al-Uyuni, the Arab tribal chief of the
Banu Murra b. Amir of Abd al-Qais, defeated them in battle. He
then laid siege to Hajar, which fell after a seven-year-long siege
in 1077, after which Bahrain – the province and the island – was
ruled by the Uyunids until in the 13th century another tribal Arab
family, the Usfurids, succeeded them.[74]

While Basra was the number one port of the Persian Gulf in
the heyday of the Abbasid Empire, Siraf was the leading port of
the Persian side of the Gulf.[75] Like that of Ubulla, its name is
forgotten today, but unlike Ubulla, Siraf has not survived in a
newer garb but is now an archaelogical site just west of the
small port of Taheri on the coast of the province of Fars. While
Basra/Ubulla was the port of Iraq and Arabia, Siraf served as the

---

[74] M.J. de Goeje, *Mémoire sur les Carmathes du Bahraïn et les
Fatimides*, Leiden 1886; W. Madelung, "Karmati," *EIs* 4: 660-65;
idem, "Fatimiden und Bahrainqarmaten," *Der Islam* 34 (1959), pp. 34-
88, and bibliographies in these works.

[75] C.E. Bosworth, "Siraf," *EIs 9:* 667-68; Le Strange, *The Lands*, pp.
258-59; Paul Schwarz, *Iran im Mittelalter nach den arabischen
Geographen,* Leipzig 1929 (henceforth cited as Schwarz, *Iran*) , pp. 59-
64; David Whitehouse, "Siraf: a medieval port on the Persian Gulf,"
World Archaeology 2 (1970), and reports, published in *IRAN,* on the
results of excavations carried out by a team under this scholar's leadership; Monique Kervran, "Forteresses, entrepôts et commerce: une histoire à suivre depuis les rois sassanides jusqu'aux princes d'Ormuz, "
Itinéraires d'Orient: hommages à Claude Cahen, Bures-sur-Yvette:
Groupe pour l'Étude de la Civilisation du Moyen-Orient, 1994, pp.
325-51 (*Res Orientales*, vol. 6). This excellent article focuses mainly
on Bahrain, but is also relevant for Siraf, Hormuz and the Persian Gulf
in general.

terminus of caravan routes covering the network of the Persian interior. At the same time, however, Siraf also functioned as a transshipment entrepot for goods, some of them coming all the way from China and destined for Iraq, and may indeed have received visits of ships from China. Whether these were actual Chinese ships or Persian and Arab ones so named for their long voyages is a matter of debate.

Our knowledge of Siraf's fame as an emporium is based on accounts found in the abundant Arabic geographical literature of the 9th and 10th centuries, and on recent archaeological excavations sponsored by the British Institute of Persian Studies. Thus the 10th century geographer Muqaddasi states that its trade rivaled that of Basra. The anonymous geographical compendium *Hudud al-alam,* dating from the same century, speaks of Siraf as "the merchants' haunt and the emporium of Fars." Its buildings, several storeys high and built of teak-wood (*saj*) brought from the "Zanj country," East Africa's Zanzibar area, overlooked the sea, and the merchants who lived there were renowned for their wealth. The imported goods redistributed from Siraf included aloe-wood, amber, camphor, precious gems, bamboos, ivory, ebony, paper, sandal-wood, and various kinds of perfumes, drugs, and condiments. Linen veils and napkins were manufactured in Siraf, and the place was a market for pearls. The prosperity of Siraf coincided with the Abbasid apogee, but lasted well into the 12th century, at least if we can judge from the case of the *nakhuda* or ship-owner Abu l-Qasim Ramisht (d. 1140), who ran commercial operations stretching all the way to China.

The central part of Iran's Persian Gulf coast became known in early Islamic times by three names, Sif Muzaffar, Sif Zuhayr, and Sif `Umarah.[76] *Sif* is one of the Arabic words for coast; Muzaffar, Zuhayr, and `Umarah were names of Arab tribes that had crossed the Gulf to settle in the coastal segments of the province of Fars. Siraf was on the coast of Sif Zuhayr, while Sif Muzaffar stretched to the northwest from the medieval port of Najiran past modern Bushehr to the level of the Khark island, and Sif `Umarah stretched to the southeast of Sif Zuhayr past the island of Kish toward the Strait of Hormuz. Arabs had begun crossing over and settling on the northern side of the Gulf in pre-

---

[76] Le Strange, *The Lands,* pp. 256-58.

Islamic times, and continued to do so for centuries to come. Gradually many of these people became "Persianized", but others kept their identity. Meanwhile the reverse was also taking place, although in a somewhat different form. While the Arabs tended to move in tribal groups and to give their new abodes a political identity, Persian migrations to the Arabian and African side of the sea lacked such affiliations but rather retained memories of regional origins, those from Shiraz being the most prominent. The symbiosis of the two nationalities in the Persian Gulf region and at sea was as complex and contradictory as it was undeniable. Many of the seafarers undoubtedly spoke Persian but the memoirs and sailing directions they wrote were in Arabic interlaced with Persian nautical terms; and the hero of the romanticized tales spun off from the great adventures and weaved into the Arabian Nights, Sindbad the Sailor, had a Persian name.

Chapter 7

The Persian Gulf and its Seafarers

Seafaring in the Persian Gulf was, we have seen, almost as ancient as the civilizations that arose along its northern fringe, starting with the Sumerians. From our perspective most of it occurred anonymously, for neither the mariners nor their sponsors and customers saw fit to record, except for certain business entries, any aspect of this complex and fascinating enterprise. One reason for the lack of interest or attention may have been the simple fact that this navigation was chiefly commercial. Kings and chroniclers are eager to commemorate battles and to expatiate on the exploits of war heroes, or to narrate the romantically horrifying lives and acts of buccaneers, whereas skippers and merchants and ships, once they have delivered the goods, pass into oblivion. Had there been major naval battles, we would know more; the remarkable difference between seafaring in the Mediterranean and that in the Persian Gulf and the Indian Ocean was precisely this: no battles even remotely comparable to those of Salamis or Lepanto or Aboukir ever took place to the east of Suez and of the Shatt al-Arab.

Fortunately, there are some refreshing records. The major and most famous one is the existence of a body of Arabic literature about seafaring and seafarers from the Abbasid period; another is a collection of Arabic sailing manuals compiled in the 15th and 16th centuries by several authors, the most remarkable of whom was a native of the Persian Gulf, Ibn Majid. The burst of energy propelling the Omani fleets across the Gulf to the coast of Persia and across the ocean to India and Africa in the 17th, 18th and 19th centuries, much better recorded and known, will be mentioned in due course.

The earliest known specific testimony about mariners from the Persian Gulf in the Orient since the appearance of Islam refers to its remotest quarter, China. Moreover, the sources are chiefly Chinese. The port of Canton functioned as the main commercial base of merchants, among whom a large number were from the Middle East, especially from the Persian Gulf. Three basic groups are discernible in Chinese sources: the *Posse*, meaning the Persians who had not converted to Islam;[77] the *Ta-shih*, or Muslims, both Arab and Persian; and Jews.

Muslim sources chronicle the Arab conquests advancing from Persia across Afghanistan to India, and eventually also the voyages of seaborne trade and pilgrim travel. Some of the principal authors, merchants and mariners have Persian names, and the Persian port of Siraf appears there as one of the main entrepots; nevertheless, the texts themselves are predominantly in Arabic, for that was the language central to the growth of Islamic civilization under the Abbasids. Ibn Khurradadhbih, who wrote his book *Kitab al-Masalik wa-l-Mamalik* in about 850, includes a maritime itinerary from the Persian Gulf to China. Information about the coasts of the Gulf, India and Africa is also found in the works of the already quoted Yaqubi (fl. 892), Ibn al-Faqih al-Hamadhani, Ibn Rustah (both about 903), Istakhri (ca 950), Ibn Hawqal (ca 980), and Marwazi (ca 1120).[78]

Especially noteworthy, however, are three compilations describing commercial voyages between the Persian Gulf and the Orient or elaborating on the exotic features abounding in the eastern seas. The earliest, the *Akhbar al-Sin wa-l-Hind*, is a collection of reports about the sea route from Siraf to Canton; it

---

[77] Po-sse: *Po-sse,* the pronunciation of two Chinese characters, is believed to have meant Persians who had not yet converted to Islam – thus Zoroastrians.

[78] From among the sources used in the preparation of this chapter, two stand out: George Fazlo Hourani, *Arab Seafaring in the Indian Ocean in Ancient and Early Medieval Times,* 2nd ed. revised and expanded by John Carswell, Princeton University Press 1995; and Hadi Hasan, *A History of Persian Navigation*, London 1928. The latter also exists in Persian translation: *Sarguzasht-e kashtirani-e Iraniyan: az dirbaz ta qarn-e shanzdahum-e miladi. Tarjumah-e Umid Iqtidari; tashih, tahshiyah va taliqat va payvastha [az] Ahmad Iqtidari.* [Mashhad]: Asitanah, 1371.

dates from 851 and is anonymous, although certain hints suggest one "merchant Sulayman" as the author.[79] The second, written by another citizen of Siraf, Abu Zayd Hasan ibn al-Yazid "al-Sirafi", in 916, is a commentary and supplement to the *Akhbar*.[80] Finally, there appeared, probably in 951, the *Kitab Aja'ib al-Hind* or "Book on the Marvels of India" by Buzurg ibn Shahriyar of Ramhormuz; both the name of the author and his place of origin are Persian.[81]

On the basis of this variety of sources, modern historians have been able to piece together a tableau of commercial seafaring between Iraq and China, or more specifically between Basra and Canton, as it existed in Abbasid times. Thus G. F. Hourani in his classic *Arab Seafaring* has traced the progress of a merchantman from Basra to Canton and back. The 1½ year round-trip, planned so as to exploit the seasonal rhythm of the monsoon winds, would start in September, when the ship sailed down the Persian Gulf. The *nakhuda* or captain had to watch out for pirates from Bahrain, Qatar and the Persian coast, as well as for treacherous reefs, as he strove to reach safely the first stop, Suhar or Masqat on the Omani coast, where the ship would replenish its water supply. Then the *nakhuda* made straight for the port of Kulam Mali, now Quilon on the Malabar coast of India. With luck and expert navigation he reached it within a month, and spent the last two weeks of December trading there and repairing and revictualing his ship. In January he resumed the voyage eastward, hoping to arrive within a month in Kalah Bar, probably the modern Kedah, on the western coast of the Malay peninsula. A few weeks later, the *nakhuda* sailed through the Strait of Malacca, in time to catch the southern monsoon, with which he hoped to reach Canton by early summer. After two to three months of trading and respite in the famous Chinese port, the ship set out on its return voyage with the northeast monsoon, hoping to reach

---

[79] Jean Sauvaget, ed. & tr., *Ahbar as-Sin wa-l-Hind: Relation de la Chine et de l'Inde, rédigée en 851*. Paris 1948.

[80] *Relations des voyages faits par les Arabes et les Persans dans l'Inde et la Chine dans le IXe s. de l'ère chrétienne*, texte arabe imprimé par les soins de feu Langlès, publié et accompagné d'une traduction française par M. Reinaud, Paris 1845. 2 vols.

[81] *Le livre des merveilles de l'Inde*, texte arabe publié par P.A. van der Lith, trad. française par L.M. Devic, Leiden 1883-86.

Malacca by December, and, crossing the Bay of Bengal, Kulam Mali by Feburary. The ship then crossed the Indian Ocean to Masqat, from where she sailed on the final leg of the voyage to Siraf, Ubulla or Basra, reaching the final destinations by early summer.

There grew up as a result of this traffic a large merchant colony in Canton consisting of Muslims (Arab and Persian), Christians, Jews, and Magians (Zoroastrian Persians). This prodigious commercial activity coincided with the apogee of power and prosperity of the Abbasid Empire in Iraq and the T'ang Empire in China. From the 870s on, however, both dynasties were assailed by rebellions symptomatic of their incipient decline. Among the victims were 120,000 foreign residents and their families, massacred in Canton during the disturbances of 878. This may have curtailed the sailings of Arab and Persian merchants all the way to China, but the trade, though reduced in distance, continued. A probably more cost-effective alternative traffic took its place according to the aforementioned 10th century geographer Masudi:

> "At this place [=Kalah, on the western coast of Malaysia] Muslim ships of the Sirafis and Omanis stop at the present time and meet the ships that have come from China. In earlier days it was otherwise, however: The 'marakib al-Sin' [ships of China] used to come to the land of Oman and Siraf and the coast of Persia and the coast of Bahrain and Ubulla and Basra, and conversely ships used to go from the places mentioned to China." [82]

Spectacular as this maritime trade with China was, it should not obscure the fact that the greatest volume of seaborne traffic occurred in the orbit of the Indian Ocean between the Persian Gulf, southern Arabia, and Ceylon, and that the Persians themselves may have played a leading role in it. First of all, the Arabic maritime volabulary is interlaced with Persian words, such as *nakhuda* (na[w] = ship, khuda = master) for captain or shipowner, and *rahmani* (rah = route, nama = text, a metathesis occurring in the loanword), for texts of sailing directions. Then

---

[82] Quoted by Hourani, *Arab Seafaring*, pp. 75-76.

there is the testimony of another 10th-century Arab author, the famous geographer Muqaddasi:

> "The language of the people of this area [= the coasts of Arabia] is Arabic, except in Suhar, where they speak Persian. Most of the inhabitants of Aden and Jedda are Persians, although they speak Arabic... Those who travel to Hajar and Abadan have to pass through the Bahr Fars ["Sea" of Fars, i.e. Persian Gulf]...Mark well that many people give the name Bahr Fars [to this sea all the way] to the Yemeni border, and that most of the shipwrights and mariners are Persians."[83]

---

[83] Muqaddasi, *Ahsan al-taqasim*, pp. 17-18 (*Bibliotheca Geographorum Arabicorum*, vol. 3)

Chapter 8

The Persian Gulf in the Later Middle Ages

After the decline of Abbasid Iraq as the center of the Islamic world, the center of gravity of maritime enterprise moved away from the shippers of Basra, Ubulla and Siraf eastward and southward to those of Hormuz and Oman. From this time until the 19th century, these two areas would alternately dominate each other or act in tandem when unified under the same sovereign.

With the new millennium, another shift within the Muslim world took place. The establishment of the young and vigorous Fatimid dynasty (909-1171) made Egypt (where the Fatimids had moved from Tunisia in 972), the center of gravity of the Muslim world, or at least of the Arab part of it. Following the almost natural evolution characteristic of most previous rulers of Egypt ever since Pharaonic times, the Fatimids in their heyday also conquered and controlled Palestine and Syria. The Fatimid rise coincided with the Abbasid decline, and one of the results was the swing of the Spice Trade away from the Persian Gulf toward the Red Sea. This shift, however, was only one of degree. Even in its periods of slump, Iraq conserved enough productivity to make overseas trade possible and desirable; the same can be said of the other Persian Gulf countries, and especially of Iran.

The Fatimids, who had first ruled in Tunisia, were an Arab Shiite dynasty, and claimed the caliphate for themselves.[84] This

---

[84] In contrast to the contemporary Shiite dynasty of the Buwayhids, who contented themselves with being the secular guardians of the Abbasid caliphs. See Claude Cahen, "Buwayhids or Buyids," *EIs* 1: 1350-57; Bosworth, *Dynasties*, pp. 154-57; for the Fatimids, see Marius Canard, "Fatimids," *EIs*, 2: 850-62; Bosworth, *Dynasties*, pp. 63-65.

put a seal of finality on the splitting up of the core of the Islamic world and the loss of its most valuable province, Egypt, by the once grandiose Abbasid empire. A different expression of Baghdad's helplessness was that a Persian Shiite dynasty, the Buwayhids, who had come to Iraq from Daylam in northern Iran, occupied Iraq itself and in 945 took the Sunni caliph under their tutelage. The fact that a century later, in 1055, the Seljuqs drove out the Buwayhids and reestablished Sunni secular rule beside the religious authority of the caliph, removed this anomaly but did not restore the Abbasids' and Iraq's former glory. The Seljuqs were Turks, recent converts to Islam who had moved in from Central Asia, and by the end of the 11th century they had spread their rule over the greater part of the Middle East, except Egypt and most of Arabia.[85] They eventually split into several branches to rule different provinces of their extensive empire. The so-called Great Seljuqs ruled in Iran and Iraq (1040-1194). They and smaller offshoot lines of their family thus dominated an area that included the northern fringes of the Persian Gulf and the Gulf of Oman. Theirs was a powerful sultanate; but characteristically, they showed little ambition seawards into the two gulfs or beyond. The southern, Arab coast of the Persian Gulf stayed outside their reach, except for a brief period when they exercized some degree of control over Oman. In the Persian Gulf and the Indian Ocean, there was no Seljuq navy and no merchant marine; there were no Seljuq privateers beholden to the sultan. In varying degrees and forms, this was the case with all empires fringing the two Gulfs, as we have already pointed out. Such activity as there was at sea during the centuries of their rule pertained to private individual enterprise or to smaller coastal principalities with, eventually, the notable exception of Oman. Trade, fishing, pearling, and piracy were their chief occupations.

Siraf, even in its heyday, was never the only port on the Persian coast, and as it began to decline, some of the other places stepped in with a vengeance. One of its early rivals and a base of naval activities was the island of Kish (Qais in Arabic), about 17 kilometers off the coast, half-way between Siraf and the Strait of Hormuz.[86] Much of this segment of the Persian coast had seen

---

[85] C.E. Bosworth, "Saldjukids," *EIs* 8: 936-59; idem, *Dynasties*, pp. 185-88.

[86] Le Strange, *The Lands*, p. 257; Schwarz, *Iran*, pp. 88-89.

intermittent immigration of Arab tribal elements from across the Gulf since Sasanian times, a counterpart to the above-mentioned opposite current of Persian elements settling in many parts of coastal Arabia from Bahrain all the way to Jeddah. Eventually an Arab dynasty, the Banu Qaisar, styling themselves *maliks* or kings, arose on this island; their domain comprised also the adjacent coastal strip known as Sif `Umarah. Kish had a rare combination of assets that made it for a time the foremost trading place on the Persian Gulf, until Hormuz began to surpass it in the first decades of the fourteenth century. The island functioned as the principal market for long-distance seaborne trade, usually characterized as trade with India and China but in fact fanning out in all directions, including Africa. It had no full-fledged harbor, but there was good anchorage, protected by the island and facing the mainland, for the larger ships; and the nearby coastal point of Huzu, a terminus of caravan routes, served as the channel for the transshipped goods going to or coming from Shiraz and other parts of the interior. At the same time, Kish was not devoid of water and had luscious palm groves, cornfields and pastureland, while on the neighboring sea banks there was a thriving pearl fishing activity. The island was thickly populated, chiefly by Arabs. The *maliks* of Kish not only grew rich from trade passing through their island, but acquired a fleet of their own and, as a naval mini-power, built a maritime domain comprising a good deal of the two gulfs, including the Arabian side from Bahrain to Oman. The Arab geographer Yaqut (d. 1229), who visited Kish more than once, gives a glowing account of the island:

> Qais, which is also called Kish, is an island in the sea of Oman [sic]; its circumference amounts to 4 farsakhs. It is a handsome city with gardens and excellent crop fields. Here is the residence of the prince of this sea, the ruler of Oman, who also receives two-thirds of the income from Bahrain. Ships from India cast anchor here... I have visited this place several times... The king enjoys great reputation and influence among the kings of India because of his merchant ships and fast sailers; he is a Persian, resembling with his appearance and clothes the princes of the Buwayhid dynasty. He has many Arab thoroughbreds

and obvious wealth: pearls are gathered there as well as on many islands around.[87]

And Hamd Allah Mustawfi al-Qazvini (d. 1339):

> The city has a wall and gates. Ships of the Indians and Persians anchor here; it is a transit port and mart of the Arabs and foreigners...The export from here is every precious product, coming from the Indies.[88]

Eventually Kish had to cede primacy to Hormuz, but the process was long and complicated. While the main trade routes from Kish led toward the province of Fars with its capital Shiraz, those from Hormuz did so toward the province of Kirman and its capital of the same name. The economic connection was paralleled by the political one: the rulers of Kish usually owed allegiance to Fars, those of Hormuz to Kirman. Thus when in 1229 the *malik* of Hormuz Sayf al-Din Aba Nadar seized Kish and, executing its ruler Malik Sultan[89], eliminated the dynasty of the Banu Qaisar, he was not to enjoy the conquest for long. The Salghurid ruler of Fars, Abu Bakr b. Sa`d b. Zangi, quickly intervened and in 1230 installed his own rule on the island.[90]

The conquest gave the Salghurids, initially a landlocked principality in the *sardsir* or "cold zone" to the north of the Zagros chain, the possibility of expanding overseas, and this they did. Renaming Kish as Dawlatkhanah, "The Auspicious Abode", Abu Bakr garrisoned it with a choice corps (*lashkar-i guzidah*)

---

[87] Yaqut ibn Abd Allah al-Hamawi, *Mu`jam al-buldan*, Leipzig: ed. F. Wüstenfeld, 1866-73, 4 volumes (henceforth cites as Yaqut, *Mu`jam*), vol. 4, p. 215; Schwarz, *Iran*, pp. 88-89.

[88] Hamd Allah Mustawfi al-Qazwini, *Nuzhat al-qulub*, ed. Wüstenfeld as el-Cazwini, *Kosmographie*, Göttingen 1848-49, 2: 161: 17

[89] We have here an illustration of the almost frustrating whimsicality of Arabo-Persian vocabulary and titulature. Sayf al-Din Aba Nadar, ruler of Hormuz, styled himself as *malik*, Arabic for king (a rather incongruous custom that for some reason took root on the Persian coast of the Persian Gulf); meanwhile the ruler of Kish, also claiming the title of *malik*, at the same time included the terms Malik and Sultan as parts of his personal name.

[90] C.E. Bosworth, "Salghurids," *EIs* 8: 978-79; Bosworth, *Dynasties*, pp. 207-208.

of Turkish, Lur and Kurdish troops as well as with an administration (*kuttab*). Settling there *savahil-nishinan* or coastal people (probably selected craftsmen), he stocked its harbor and
shipyard with victuals, weapons and ship-building materials, and
thus made Kish a naval base. This done, he launched campaigns
of conquest in the Gulf. Abu Bakr's first target was Uwal, the
largest island of the Bahrain archipelago, which his amphibious
force took in 1235; nine years later, in 1244, it was the turn of
Qatif on the Arabian mainland. This thrust of maritime expansion along the axis Fars – Bahrain – Qatif or other points on the
Arabian coast followed a historical pattern both from before and
after the events under discussion.

Chapter 9

Hormuz as the Great Emporium of Seaborne Trade in the Orient

Meanwhile a both parallel and inverse development occurred in neighboring Hormuz.[91] Hormuz was the name of a port city – the ancient Harmozia – on the lowermost course of the aforementioned Minab River, which flows from the northeast into the bay that delimits the Strait of Hormuz on the north. A local dynasty of originally Arab *maliks* had become established there, and at the time under discussion it recognized the suzerainty of the Qutlughkhanids or Qara Khitay of Kirman (1222-1307). In 1272 the *malik* of Hormuz Mahmud Qalhati attacked Kish, which by then was no longer under Salghurid suzerainty but under that of the Ilkhanids, the Mongols of Iran. Despite their status of vassalage toward Kirman, the *maliks* of Hormuz in turn dominated certain points on the coast of Oman – Qalhat, Mahmud's probable birthplace, being one of them. The contemporary Persian author Natanzi writes that Mahmud Qalhati *"conquered the islands and coasts of the sea of Oman such as Kish, Bahrain, and Qatif..."*[92] Marco Polo, who

---

[91] L. Lockhart, "Hurmuz," *EIs* 3: 584-86; D.T. Potts and Willem Floor, "Hormuz," *EIr* 12: 470-76; Schwarz, *Iran*, pp. 242-45.

[92] Our discussion of Hormuz during its rise and florescence as an emporium is chiefly based on the outstanding work of the French scholar Jean Aubin, especially his long articles "Les Princes d'Ormuz du XIIIe au XVe siècles," *Journal Asiatique*, tome 241 (1953), pp. 77-138, and "Le royaume d'Ormuz au début du XVIe siècle," *Mare Luso-Indicum*, 2 (1973), pp. 77-179. The aforementioned article by Monique Kervran, "Forteresses, entrepôts et commerce..." discusses Hormuz on pp. 345-49. Also excellent is Valeria Fiorani Piacentini, *L'Emporio ed il Regno*

visited Hormuz twice, states that "When the Sultan of Kirman wants to impose extraordinary taxes on the "melic of Curmos", his vassal, the latter takes to the sea and prevents the ships from India from entering the Gulf; the Sultan of Kirman suffers great loss; his customs revenues decrease, so that he ends up making peace without obtaining what he has demanded." Almost two centuries later, according to Abd al-Razzaq Samarqandi, the *malik* of Hormuz Sayf al-Din possessed an extensive overseas domain.

Be that as it may, the above-mentioned king of Hormuz Mahmud Qalhati (probable years of rule: 1244-1278) deserves our attention for being the ruler under whom Hormuz began to assert its ambition as the power that would for over two centuries, until the arrival of the Portuguese, play the leading role in the Persian Gulf. Mahmud Qalhati had influence over an extensive area of the Gulf of Oman, the Arabian Sea and even the Indian Ocean to the shores of Hindustan; to the northwest of the Persian Gulf, however, he met his match in an unlikely foe: the Mongols.

Mahmud Qalhati's rule coincided with the second generation of Mongol conquests, of which one wave overwhelmed Iran and Iraq. In 1258 Genghis Khan's grandson Hulagu with his troops stormed Baghdad, killed the caliph al-Mustasim and, extinguishing the Abbasid caliphate, put an end to what could be considered the first era of Islamic history. The transcontinental Mongol Empire, still fairly well united at the time of Hulagu's campaigns under the aegis of the Great Khan in Mongolia, evolved into four separate khanates by the end of the 13th century. Iran and Iraq became the appanage of Hulagu's descendants, who were known as *ilkhans* or "regional khans", and the state of which they were the rulers came to be known in historiography as "Ilkhanate".

This brings us back to the island of Kish and its final or best-recorded flowering as the principal center of long-distance trade in the Persian Gulf. The Ilkhans' usual headquarters was Ma-

---

di Hormoz (VIII – fine XV sec. d. Cr.): vicende storiche, problemi ed aspetti di una civiltà costiera del Golfo Persico, Milano: Istituto Lombardo di Scienze e Lettere, 1975 (Memorie dell'Istituto Lombardo – Accademia di Scienze e Lettere, Classe di Lettere – Scienze Morali e Storiche, vol. 35, fasc. 1.)

ragha in Azerbaijan, with their subordinates, Mongol or other, in charge of several provinces. The governor of Fars was for some time a Turk named Sughunjaq or Suyunjaq, who thwarted the Hormuzi *malik*'s seizure of Kish in 1272 by almost immediately driving him out. The grounds for this were, on the one hand, that Sughunjaq considered himself the successor of the Salghurids, who had been suzerains of Kish; and on the other, the tendency of the nearest power in the interior to exercize some degree of control – on the whole indirect – over the immediate littoral. Usually that was where the reach stopped, but the Mongol governor gathered a fleet in the port of Khurshif which then defeated that of Mahmud and restored the authority of Fars over Kish. Sughunjaq's ships had been requisitioned not only from the littoral of Fars, but also from Bahrain and the neighboring Arab coasts; besides the Arabo-Persian sailors and troops, Mongol archers are believed to have played a role.

The main interest of these developments, however, is the fact that they secured for Kish a competitive advantage over Hormuz for several more decades. In 1293 Jamal al-Din Ibrahim, also known by his *laqab* or personal title "Malik al-Islam" ("King of Islam"; possibly because of his original or additional function as *shaykh al-islam* or premier jurisconsult in the field of Islamic law) obtained a special lease for the province of Fars which included Kish and the other adjacent islands. Jamal al-Din was above all a merchant, whose base was Kish from where his trade extended all the way to India and China. His was a real commercial empire; if we are to believe the historian Vassaf, a brother of Jamal al-Din, Taqi al-Din Abd al-Rahman but best remembered by his title *Marzuban al-Hind* ("Margrave of India"), had the function of vizier at the court of a south Indian prince, where his main occupation may have been commercial: "When goods arrive from the Far East and from [other parts of] India, his delegates and agents prevent any business before those of Malik al-Islam have made their selection, especially of textiles. [Only after that has been done] can the other merchants proceed with their buying." One of the special and lasting articles of export to the Indian subcontinent was horses, sent overland from Central Asia and by sea from the Near East. Jamal al-Din owned extensive stud farms on both sides of the Gulf, and exported up to 1,400 head annually. When in 1304 his brother Taqi al-Din died in India, the king of Mabar (Coromandel) wanted to seize his property, but Jamal al-Din deflected the danger by presenting the king with 200,000 dinars, thereby assuring the passage of the inheritance to the deceased's son. By a poignant coincidence, the following year Jamal al-Din's son, who was returning from China, died just two days before the ship reached the coast of India, and was then buried by the side of his uncle in Coromandel.

Meanwhile a special event occurred that would play a decisive role in the rise of Hormuz as the great emporium of the Persian Gulf. The original city and port were, as we have seen, on the lower course of the Minab on the mainland. Although tributary to Mongol-dominated Kirman, the principality became towards the end of the 13th century increasingly exposed to raids by unruly bands of Chaghatay (Mongol) horsemen. It thus happened that by 1300 the *malik* of Hormuz Baha' al-Din Ayaz[93] had moved the government center and activities to a nearby island in the bay of Hormuz called Jarun. Eventually the name of Hormuz migrated to the island as well and substituted itself for Jarun; it was at first called "New Hormuz", while the original or "Old Hormuz" lost that appellation and became known by the name of the river, Minab.

Rivalry between Hormuz and Kish intensified in the first decades of the 14th century, and culminated in the definitive victory of the former when Qutb a-Din Tahamtan II (1325-1347), *malik* of Hormuz, conquered Kish and executed or deported the grandsons of Jamal al-Din Ibrahim. It was with Qutb al-Din Tahamtan II that Hormuz came into its own and became the center of a seaborne commercial empire spreading over much of the Persian Gulf and the Gulf of Oman. The island kingdom's primacy as the greatest single emporium in the Near East over the

---

[93] Although he is called *malik* in some sources, Ayaz was not a scion of the dynasty of *maliks* of Hormuz. A Turk serving Mahmud Qalhati and Sayf al-Din Nusrat as governor of Qalhat, he took advantage of discord in the royal family to seize power in 1296 and hold it until his death in 1311/1312. The sources present him as a remarkable personality, and it may have taken a person of his caliber to grasp the potential advantages of an insular location for a state bent on maritime trade. Instead of viewing Baha' al-Din Ayaz as a usurper, we might thus see him as a benefactor of the Hormuz princely dynasty.

next three centuries was chiefly based on its special geographical location: dominating the strait that both separated and united the Persian Gulf and the Gulf of Oman, Hormuz received and distributed the spices, silks and other products of the Orient on the one hand, and those of the Gulf itself such as pearls, horses, and dates, on the other. The island was almost barren, with little vegetation and drinking water but plenty of salt; but a short distance to the west of it lay the larger island of Qishm, which supplied it with the necessary victuals. And while Hormuz had no harbor in the usual sense of the word, anchorage on its northern side facing the mainland was safe and spacious for the busy traffic of merchant vessels.

There thus grew up a city on the island that was both the political capital of a maritime kingdom and a great cosmopolitan emporium teeming with resident as well as visiting merchants. The ruling dynasty of *maliks* was said to have Arab roots, but by the time of the prodigious upswing of Hormuz as an emporium it was quite Persianized – even the name of the eponym, Diramkub, was Persian. It was one of the longest-lived dynasties, if the approximate date of Diramkub's appearance on the scene, 1100, reflects reality, for it lasted over half a millennium. One of the reasons may be that the kings of Hormuz, while rulers of essentially coastal areas of the two gulfs, accepted the overlordship of stronger powers in Iran and finally from overseas. Until the beginning of the 16th century these powers were, as we have seen, mostly rulers in the Persian interior, at first those of Kirman, later those of Fars and eventually the first Safavid monarch of Iran; even after 1515, when the Portuguese, thus the Infidels, became the suzerains of Hormuz, the dynasty ruled on until the expulsion of the new masters themselves by Shah Abbas in 1622.[94]

Hormuz was thus a merchant maritime kingdom, but the ruling family does not seem to have actively participated in business ventures, in contrast to the family of Jamal al-Din on Kish. Here, the merchants were a separate group of wealthy citizens as well as temporary visitors from overseas. The native elite, Per-

---

[94] For whatever reason, neither contemporary nor modern historiography has managed or attempted to label this dynasty with a distinctive name. *Maliks* of Hormuz, Kings of Hormuz, Princes of Hormuz are the labels applied to it. Perhaps "Diramkubids" might serve the purpose?

sian or Persianized, maintained ties with their erstwhile home areas on the mainland, especially Minab, in whose surroundings they had summer homes. The Arab element was ever present, however. Government administration, religious culture, and human contacts all reflected the symbiotic amalgam of Persians and Arabs that distinguished this remarkable kingdom.

It may be worthwhile to mention a few of the many testimonies on the history of Hormuz while it was the dominant merchant kingdom of the Persian Gulf. The first is an account left by the Arab traveler Ibn Battuta, who visited it twice in the course of his extensive travels which took him from Morocco all the way to India and China. His visits occurred during the rule of the above-mentioned Sultan Qutb al-Din Tahamtan II (1325-47).[95]

> "Then I traveled from Oman to Hormuz. Hormuz is a city on the seacoast; it is also called Mughistan, and across from it is New Hormuz, an island whose city is called Jarawn…It is a handsome, large city, with busy markets, and its anchorage is the entrepot of India. Goods brought from India are exported to the two Iraqs[96], Fars, and Khurasan. The sultan's home is in this city. The island's length amounts to one day's march, and most of it is covered by brackish depressions and salt hills. This salt is called *darani*, and they make from it decorative vessels and columns on which they put lamps. Their food consists of fish and dates brought from Basra and Oman. They say in their language: 'Khurma wa mahi luti padishahi,'…, which means in Arabic "Dates and fish are the food of kings…"[97]

Ibn Battuta's travels eventually took him to India, Indonesia and China, and part of the trajectory was by sea. In Calicut, the principal port of India's Malabar coast, he boarded a Chinese junk to proceed east, and his account confirms the extremely active seaborne trade carried on by the Chinese. We have seen that

---

[95] *Voyages d'Ibn Battuta*, Paris, 1969, vol. 2, pp. 230-31.

[96] "Iraq al-Arabi" and "Iraq al-Ajami" of medieval Islamic literature, meaning present-day central Iraq and northwestern Iran.

[97] *Luti padishahi*. I have failed to identify the word *luti*. It may be the copyist's or printer's error for *kuti* (*kut*, "food" in Persian, with the izafet particle –i).

in the 10th century, ports on the western coast of Malaysia became the usual rendez-vous of Islamic and Chinese trade after the Arabs and Persians had ceased sailing all the way to Canton; by Ibn Battuta's time, the western coast of India had assumed some of this role. The Moroccan globe-trotter describes three categories of Chinese ships, of which the largest included vessels that dwarfed not only those of the Muslims but also anything built by Europeans for several centuries to come. It also seems that Chinese shipping was private enterprise, or at least that the government – like the governments of other oriental states – had no desire to build a seaborne empire, much less a naval one. There occurred one partial but remarkable exception, however: the seven sailings of large fleets from Nanking, the Ming Dynasty's imperial capital near the estuary of the Yang-tse River, to the Indian Ocean between 1405 and 1433. Hormuz was among the ports of call of the last four, and Ma Huan, a participant and the chronicler of the enterprise, includes it in his report known as "Ying-yai Sheng-Lan, "The Overall Survey of the Ocean's Shores." [98]

> Setting sail from the country of Ku-li [Calicut], you go towards the north-west; [and] you can reach [this place] after traveling with a fir wind for twenty-five days...Foreign ships from every place and foreign merchants traveling by land all come to this country to attend the market and trade; hence the people of the country are all rich. The king of the country and the people of the country all profess the Muslim religion; they are reverent, meticulous, and sincere believers; every day they pray five times, [and] they bathe and practice abstinence. The customs are pure and honest. There are no poor families; if a family meets with misfortune resulting in poverty, everyone gives them clothes and food and capital, and relieves their distress. The limbs and faces of the people are refined and fair, and they are stalwart and fine-looking. Their clothing and hats are handsome, distinctive, and elegant. In their marriage- and

---

[98] Ma Huan, *Ying-yai Sheng-lan, 'The Overall survey of the Ocean's shores' [1433]; Translated from the Chinese text...with introduction, notes and appendices by J.V.G. Mills*, Cambridge, 1970. The two passages quoted here are on pp. 165-72, with further references in the exhaustive annotation.

funeral-rites they all obey the regulations of the Muslim religion...

Ma Huan then proceeds to describe the lifestyle, customs, food and occupations of the inhabitants, as well as the products, plants, animals, and noteworthy peculiarities of the island kingdom. He concludes the chapter on Hormuz in the following manner:

> The king of this country, too, took a ship and loaded it with lions, giraffes, horses, pearls, precious stones, and other such things, also a memorial to the throne [written on] a golden leaf; [and] he sent his chiefs and other men, who accompanied the treasure-ships dispatched by the Emperor, which were returning from the Western Ocean; [and] they went to the capital and presented tribute.

Both Malacca and Hormuz were among the many places visited by several of the expeditions; they were flourishing trading emporia, and a Chinese seaborne empire might have come into being had the maritime enterprise received adequate official backing by converting them into permanent bases for further expansion. Far from that happening, however, the opposite took place. Not only were the expeditions discontinued; the accounts of their findings were removed from the archives and burned in 1477. By the 16th century, all major shipping from the ports of China was forbidden, and any infraction was treated as a criminal offense. This radical reversal was brought about by the victory of the conservative Neo-Confucian bureaucratic class. There thus occurred a total Chinese withdrawal from the world scene just as Renaissance Europe was preparing to launch its entry and domination of it. In the Indian Ocean and the Persian Gulf, as we shall see, the Portuguese were the trailblazers of this dramatic entry. Less than a century after the Chinese withdrawal, they penetrated these waters and built their seaborne empire whose maritime axis was Goa on the western coast of India, Malacca on the western coast of Malaysia, and Hormuz on the southern coast of Iran.[99] The success of the Portuguese, and after them of the

---

[99] Like Hormuz, Malacca or Melaka was a maritime merchant kingdom and had an international merchant community, consisting here both of

Dutch, English, and French, was a result of factors characteristic of modern Europe, and one of these was sudden growth of its military and naval strength. Determination to gain access to resources, dominate trade, and build colonial empires could bear fruit only because of this superiority and competitive spirit. Naval warfare deserves a special mention in this context. Seapower as a means of overseas expansion was an almost exclusively European phenomenon, and its roots may be sought in early Mediterranean history. Admittedly, we run here into an apparent contradiction when we identify the Persians as the earliest major representatives of such policies. Their navies, whose crews were chiefly Phoenician mariners, fought the first known major naval battles against the Greeks. This happened at the beginning of the 5th century BC, and from then on for many centuries to come the Mediterranean was a zone where sea battles often played decisive roles in contests between nations or even continents. Naval warfare led to a constant improvement in the military quality of ships, their armaments, and the prowess of naval commanders, and eventually it spilled over into the Atlantic and the other oceans. Later the Arabs and eventually the Turks participated in

---

native Malays and of resident foreign merchants, especially Gujeratis, Fukien Chinese, and Tamils. Seaborne trade was the main source of their wealth and success, a feature they shared with such distant and otherwise different polities as Aden, Venice, Genoa, Zanzibar, and Calicut.

They all presented a contrast to the land-focused agrarian states and empires; in the Orient, these were the empires of the Ottomans, Safavids, Mughals, Vijayanagara (in southern India), Ming (in China) and Mataran (in Indonesia), whose direct participation in maritime trade and overseas expansion for the sake of commerce or economic colonization (access to markets, valuable commodities, raw materials) was minimal or nonexistent. It was the five Atlantic nations of Western Europe – Portugal, Spain, England, France, and the Netherlands – that later evolved into a third and new type of state, the seaborne merchant and eventually colonial empire of the modern era. The maritime dimension became their distinguishing mark, and remained absent from the latecomer that was the colonial empire of Russia (in the Caucasus and Central Asia). The persistent and successful determination of Great Britain to deny Russia unhindered access to the Mediterranean, the Persian Gulf and the Indian Ocean was to maintain her naval dominance ensuring the security of her overseas possessions.

this contest, but with diminishing returns, and, barring a few desultory attempts by the latter, they hardly ever ventured out onto the oceans. Significantly, the Achaemenids launched grandiose war fleets against the Greeks, but never in the Persian Gulf or the Indian Ocean; so did the Arabs, but only in the Mediterranean. It was the Europeans who reaped the benefits of this "naval academy" that was the Mediterranean, and by the time the Portuguese had reached the Persian Gulf in 1507, they had a free hand to start building their maritime empire, of which Hormuz became the western linchpin.[100]

1515 was the year in which the Portuguese consolidated the subjugation of the Kingdom of Hormuz as a vassal state of the King of Portugal. This in turn represented the inception of Western presence in the Persian Gulf, a presence that would prove to be permanent, and eventually escalate to massive proportions in our own day. Accounts and descriptions by Europeans, from those of chance travelers to exhaustive government reports, would in due course appear and proliferate; it may be worthwhile to glance at the accounts written by two visitors at the inception of this new era. One is by the Bolognese Lodovico Varthema, who visited Hormuz in 1503, thus on the eve of the arrival of the Portuguese.

> Proceeding on our viage, we came to a citie named Ormus, very fayre. This is seconde to none in goodlye situation, and plenty of pearles: it is in an Ilande dystaunt from the continent twelue miles…Three dayes sayling from thence, are gathered those muscles which bring foorth the fairest and biggest pearles:…There are seene sometime almost three hundred shyppes, and other kynde of vessels, which come thither from many places and countreys. The Soltan of the citie is a Mahumetan. There are above foure hundred merchauntes and factours remaining here continually, for the trafike of merchandise which come from diuers other regions, as silke, pearles, precious stones,

---

[100] One of the reasons for the divergent evolution of the two components of mankind may be the fact that European overseas expansion was fuelled by essentially economic interests in which the ruling elites and governments had a stake and thus played a decisive role.

spices, and suche lyke. They lyue with Ryse for the moste parte, for they haue none other corne.[101]

The other is by the Portuguese colonial official and traveler Duarte Barbosa (d. 1521), who lived in India between 1503 and 1515. He visited Hormuz during that period and wrote his account by 1518, before joining Magelhães on his epic voyage around the world. Here is what he says about Hormuz:

> The Islands of the Kingdom of Ormus. The actual island on which stands the city of Ormus is between the coasts of Arabia and Persia, at the mouth of the Persian Sea, and within this sea are scattered many isles pertaining to the same King of Ormus and under his governance...[102]

> The Fair City of Ormus. Coming from this sea and from the Narrows, in the very mouth of these is an isle of no great size, on which stands the city of Ormus, which is not so great as it is fair, with lofty stone and mortar houses with flat roofs and many windows; and, because that country is very hot, all the houses are built in such wise as to make the wind blow from the highest to the lowest storeys when they have need of it. This city is very well placed and laid out in streets with many good open places. Outside in the same isle is a little hill of rock-salt, also some brimstone, but very little. The salt is in blocks as large as great rocks in rugged hills; it is called Indian salt, and is produced there by nature, and when ground it is exceeding white and fine. All ships which come to this city take it as ballast, for it is worth money at many places. The merchants of this isle and city are Persians and Arabs. The Persians are tall and well-looking, and a fine and up-standing folk, both men and women... They hold the creed of Mafamede in great honour...In this city

---

[101] Lodovico di Varthema (d. 1517), *The Itinerary of Ludovico di Varthema of Bologna from 1502-1508, as translated from the original Iralian edition of 1510, by John Winter Jones...* London: Hakluyt Society, 1863.

[102][Barbosa, Duarte] *The Book of Duarte Barbosa: an account of the countries bordering on the Indian Ocean...completed about the year 1518.* Translated, edited and annotated by Mansel Longworth Dames. London: Hakluyt Society, 1918-1921. 2 vols. (Hakluyt Society, 2nd series, vols. 44 and 49), vol. 1, p. 79.

are many merchants of substance, and many very great ships. It has a right good harbour where many sorts of goods are handled which come hither from many lands, and from here they barter them with many parts of India. They bring hither spices of all sorts, and divers kinds, to wit pepper, cloves, ginger, cardamoms, eagle-wood, sandal-wood, brasil-wood, mirobalans, tamarinds, saffron, indigo, wax, iron, sugar, rice (great store), and cocoa-nuts, as well as great abundance of precious stones, porcelain, and benzoin, by all of which they gain much money. They have also great plenty of Cambaya, Chaul, and Dabul cloths, and from Bengala they bring many syfabos, which are a sort of very thin cotton cloth greatly prized among them and highly valued for turbans and shirts, for which they use them. And from the city of Adem [= Aden] they bring to Ormus abundance of copper, quicksilver, vermillion, rose-water, many brocaded cloths, tafetas and ordinary camlets; also from the lands of the Xeque Ismail [= Shah Ismail] come a great quantity of silk, very fine musk and rhubarb of Babilonia. And from Barem [= Bahrain] and Julfar come seed pearls and large pearls, and from the cities of Arabia a great number of horses come, which they carry hence to India, whither every year they used to take one and at times two thousand horses, and each one of these is worth in India, taking good and bad together, three or four hundred cruzados, more or less according to the demand for them. And in the ships in which these horses are taken they carry also abundance of dates, raisins, salt and sulphur, also coarse seed pearls in which the Moors of Narsingua take delight.

...In this city of Ormus the king abides ever in a certain great palace which he has therein, hard by the sea, on a cape of the city, in which palace he always dwells and keeps his treasure. And this king keeps his governours and collectors of revenue at those place in Persia and Arabia and the isles which pertain to his seignory...[103]

---

[103] *Ibid.*, pp. 90-98.

Chapter 10

The Portuguese Century, 1507-1622

T he last decade of the 15th century witnessed two events which were to change the course of history: Columbus's voyage to what he thought was the Indies in 1492, and Vasco da Gama's voyage to what he knew was India in 1498. The latter also almost immediately affected the Persian Gulf.

Columbus died in 1506, embittered by the ingratitude of his Spanish sovereigns but conscious of the significance of his three voyages, though unaware of the magnitude and true nature of the discovery he had made. Meanwhile the Portuguese had been laying the foundations of their maritime empire by penetrating the Indian Ocean and its ramifications. In 1507 Affonso de Albuquerque, entering the Persian Gulf with a squadron of ships, seized the great commercial emporium of Hormuz.

The Spanish and Portuguese voyages were events symptomatic of a profound and radical transformation that was ushering in the modern age. Historians have used other dates or events to separate the Middle Ages from the Modern Era. Besides Columbus's 1492 voyage, the conquest of Constantinople by the Ottoman Turks (1453), and the almost simultaneous appearance of the first book printed from movable type by Johann Guttenberg (1454), are frequently cited. Such seemingly artificial yardsticks are useful as reminders of how vast and even contradictory the revolution was. The voyages of discovery and invention of printing blossomed from the surge of energy and inventiveness of Renaissance Europe, and were among the scientific revolution's achievements that would have immense consequences. The fall of Constantinople revealed Christian Europe's vulnerability to a powerful but alien Islamic empire, but also that empire's alienation from the revolution taking place in Europe.

These two latter aspects were to play capital roles in the 16th and subsequent centuries.[104]

Albuquerque's first descent on Hormuz ended inconclusively, for as a result of both native resistance and the discontent of the expedition's crews, he had to withdraw most of his forces. In 1515, however, he made a second and this time successful attempt at consolidating the Portuguese grip on Hormuz. The emporium-principality became a vassal kingdom tributary to the King of Portugal, and stayed so until 1622. A Portuguese garrison settled there, and the island also served as a base for the intruders' operations throughout the Persian Gulf. The 16th century in the Indian Ocean and the Persian Gulf was to be á Portuguese century. When they entered the Indian Ocean in 1498, the new-

---

[104] See S. Soucek, "Piri Reis and Ottoman discovery of the Great Discoveries," *Studia Islamica* 79 (1994), pp. 121-42. Our account of the global revolution wrought by Europe's scientific and technological revolution, voyages of discovery and penetration of the world's oceans has followed a hitherto accepted traditional pattern. A spate of recent studies have challenged this premise and proposed often quite revisionary interpretations. The latest thrust is the following: not much change really occurred as a result of Columbus's and Vasco da Gama's expeditions, especially in the Orient, where for almost three centuries European penetration and presence remained marginal. Only in the 18th century, when Europe's improving military technology gained the upper hand on the battlefield, could huge chunks of overseas real estate be conquered, and only in the 19th did technology, the industrial revolution and political power give the colonial powers the undisputed productive and commercial superiority with which they overwhelmed the world. I agree that in terms of territorial conquest, foundation of extensive colonial empires, and impact on the lifestyle and trade of non-Europeans, this is convincing (with the exception of central and southern America). Two qualifications are necessary, however. The conquest of the oceans was of crucial importance, and it began with the voyages of discovery, thus in the 15th and 16th centuries; although structurally different from the later conquest of the continents, it was a symptom and result of several features gaining momentum in Europe but declining or absent elsewhere: scientific curiosity, technological inventiveness (of which navigational techniques were a part), commercial aggressiveness, and maritime and naval superiority, all of which were prerequisites or incubation grounds for the transformations of the 18th and 19th centuries.

comers had no real naval rival. The predominantly Muslim, chiefly Arab, Persian, and Gujerati seafaring was of the peaceful, commercial type, although also fostering the inevitable plague of piracy; but war fleets of major powers were all but non-existent. This presented a sharp contrast to the Mediterranean, witness of epochal naval battles since antiquity.

The arrival of the Europeans in the Indian Ocean was going to change that, although even then in a one-sided manner. Eventually, they would wage naval wars, but only amongst themselves. There was one brief and partial exception that confirmed the rule. The Portuguese at first had no competitors; when they later encountered a serious challenge, it did not come from native navies but from the greatest military power of the time, Ottoman Turkey. The contest for the Persian Gulf in the 16th century was to be played out chiefly between Portugal and Turkey, or, put in starker relief, between the essentially seaborne Lusitanian Empire and the primarily continental Ottoman Empire.

When Affonso de Albuquerque first came to Hormuz in 1507, Dom Manuel I (1495-1521) was King of Portugal, eager to reap the benefits from the unprecedented opportunities opened up by his fleets penetrating the Orient. The ships brought to Lisbon spices which until then had had to make an overland crossing after being unloaded in the Persian Gulf or the Red Sea en route to the Mediterranean, and for some time the kingdom's capital functioned as Europe's principal market for this precious commodity; at the same time, Dom Manuel knew that the overseas expansion had great religious merit: his mariners searched for Christians – ideally, for the legendary Prester John – with whom they would join forces to combat the Mohammedans, and missionaries would endeavor to convert pagans to Christianity.

The first target of Vasco da Gama's voyage was India, and Goa on the subcontinent's western coast eventually became the headquarters of Portugal's Oriental empire. The port city was conquered and selected for that purpose by Albuquerque in 1510. As the second viceroy of the Indies, this great admiral was the real founder of the far-flung seaborne empire, a devoted servant of his king, Manuel I "The Fortunate", who assumed the proud title "Lord of the conquest, navigation, and commerce of India, Ethiopia, Arabia, and Persia". Albuquerque's letters to the king and memoirs edited by his son are a vivid testimony to his vision of the empire as a maritime one that should be founded on four principal naval and commercial bases: Goa in the western Indian Ocean, Malacca (Melaka) in the eastern Indian Ocean, Aden on the Arabian Sea, and Hormuz in the Persian Gulf.

The sudden appearance of a European Christian power in eastern waters which had hitherto been a mainly Arab, Persian and Indian preserve naturally caused alarm in some quarters of the Orient for reasons that were the inverse of jubilation in Lisbon.[105] Native maritime trade was harmed by the intruders, and the religion of Islam was threatened by the militant conquerors. This, at least, should have been the reaction among Muslims; and their leaders, one might think, should have joined forces to repel the invader and recover both wealth and security.

The reality, however, was more complex. Let us choose 1507, the year of the first Portuguese intrusion into the Persian Gulf, as a vantage point from which to review the situation.[106] The ruler of Hormuz, Sayf al-Din Abu Nasr, of the aforementioned dynasty endowed by Muslim historiography with the title of *maliks* (kings), possessed a fairly extensive kingdom of which the small island of Hormuz was the center and royal residence. The king's possessions included, in the first place, the larger neighboring island of Qishm, indispensable as a source of drinking water and of much of the food consumed in Hormuz. Then a strip of land along the mainland coast, the *sif* of the Arabs but also called in Persian *"birunat"* , the outlying territories, indispensable for another and perhaps most important reason: on its shoreline were the terminals of caravan routes for goods passing through the anchorage of Hormuz to be loaded on ships with various destinations. What is more, Hormuz also exercized intermittent control over a number of points across the Gulf on the opposite, Arab side, including the Omani coast. Such places as Qalhat, Masqat, Suhar, Khorfakkan, Julfar, and Bahrain formed part of a network engaged in vigorous local as well as overseas trade. Not unlike Venice, diminutive Hormuz was the hub of a great shipping and commercial enterprise. The fact that this kingdom vir-

---

[105] But consternation in Venice, which stood to lose by this deflection of trade routes as much as the Muslims did. The Serenissima quickly urged the Ottoman Porte to take action against the intruders.

[106]Arnold Wilson, *The Persian Gulf*, pp. 110-27 (Chapter 8: The Coming of the Portuguese).

tually straddled the Persian Gulf was a confirmation of long traditions of Perso-Arab symbiosis marking this branch of the Indian Ocean.

As he sailed with his squadron towards Hormuz in 1507, Albuquerque followed the Omani coast along the Arabian Sea until he reached the level of Ras al-Hadd, "The Cape of the Extremity [of the Arabian Peninsula]", where he entered the Gulf of Oman on a northwestern tack. The Arabian coast of the Gulf of Oman was studded with harbors bustling with commerce, whose ships sailed in three principal directions: northwest into the Persian Gulf; eastward across the Indian Ocean towards India; and southwestward towards Yemen, the Red Sea and East Africa. Besides merchantmen, the Gulf of Oman was also teeming with fishing vessels, and it was the latter that the Portuguese squadron, as it was rounding Ras al-Hadd, saw first. With his customary candor, Albuquerque narrates in his *Commentaries*[107] what then happened:

> '...And they found there...30 or 40 fishing vessels, which come thither from the city of Ormuz, Calayate [Qalhat], and all that coast to fish for bonitos and albeciras; for there is a great traffic in these fish to many parts...and they burned all these ships, and on the following morning set sail with a fair wind, and took the ships' boats with masts and sails.'

The squadron then proceeded along the Omani coast, on an almost straight line towards Hormuz. It stopped at the ports of Qalhat, Quryat, Masqat, Suhar, and Khurfakkan, before passing by Ras Musandam (Cape Musandam) and crossing the Strait of Hormuz towards the island kingdom. Imposition of Portuguese authority was Albuquerque's usual demand, promising that if the natives agreed to be tributaries of the King of Portugal they would not be harmed. This happened at Qalhat, where the squadron took in supplies, for which the admiral insisted on paying.

---

[107] Wilson, *The Persian Gulf*, p. 113, quoting Albuquerque's memoirs edited by his son Affonso (1500-1580), and published in English translation as *The Commentaries of the Great Affonso de Albuquerque* by the Hakluyt Society, London 1875 (new ed. 1978), 4 vols. (Hakluyt Society, New Series, vols. 53, 55, 62, 69).

The people of Quryat were less prudent, and the retribution was swift according to the Portuguese historian Faria e Sousa:

> '[Albuquerque] was ill received, and storming the town, met with a vigorous opposition, but entered with the death of 80 of the enemy, and loss of 3 Portuguese; after the plunder, the place was burnt, and with it 14 vessels that were in the harbor. Hence he sailed 8 leagues farther to Mascate, a place stronger than any of the others, and well manned with people, who resorted to it from all parts, hearing of the destruction of Quryat.'[108]

Masqat, the main prize before Hormuz, seemingly took to heart the example of Quryat, and when Albuquerque anchored before the city two 'Noble Moors' came out to meet him as representatives of the inhabitants. They begged him not to harm their city and declared readiness to become vassals of the King of Portugal, paying him the dues they had hitherto paid to the King of Hormuz. Negotiations dragged out, and the admiral, perceiving that the inhabitants were organizing resistance, ordered two of his ships to stand in to shore and bombard the town, preparing an attack. The defenders in the end surrendered, promising to pay 10,000 *xerafins* of gold before noon the next day. They failed to deliver the amount, however, and Albuquerque set fire to the town together with its mosque, and the ships in the harbor. Here is how he narrates the event in his *Commentaries*:[109]

> 'When the appointed hour was passed, he ordered the city to be set on fire, wherein were burned many provisions, and 34 ships in all, large and small, many fishing barks, and an arsenal full of every requisite for shipbuilding; and he ordered 3 gunners with axes to cut the supports of the mosque, which was a very large and beautiful edifice, the greater part of it

---

[108] Wilson, *The Persian Gulf*, pp. 113-14, quoting Manuel de Faria e Sousa (1590-1649), *Asia Portuguesa*. (1st Portuguese ed. 1666-75, 3 vols.); new edition: *Asia Portuguesa; com uma introd. por M. Lopes de Almeida*. Porto, 1945-47. 6 vols. Wilson quotes the English translation: *The Portugues Asia, on the History of the Discovery & Conquest of India by the Portugues. Trsl. By Capt. John Stevens*. London, 1695.
[109] Wilson, *Persian Gulf*, p. 114.

being built of timber finely carved, and the upper part of stucco. When the supports had been cut through, and the gunners were about to go, the building came down all at once upon them, so that Affonso de Albuquerque gave them up for dead; but thanks to Our Lord, they came forth alive and sound, without a wound or a bruise, just as they stood when cutting the supports of the mosque. Our people were frightened, and when they saw them gave many thanks to Our Lord for that miracle which He had done for them, and set fire to the mosque, which was burned, so that nothing remained of it.'

The example of Masqat was not lost on the people of the next port the Portuguese called at, Suhar, for, as we read in the Commentaries,[110]

'All the inhabitants thereof fled, except the Governour, and some of the principal Moors, who offered it to Albuquerque, and received it back to hold for King Emanuel, paying the same Tribute he had given to him of Ormuz.'

On the other hand, the final port Albuquerque called at before reaching Hormuz, Khurfakkan, tried to resist, and again his retribution was drastic: the town was pillaged and burnt, and captured combatants had their noses and ears cut off, as at Masqat.

Finally the Portuguese squadron, having doubled Ras Musandam, crossed the Strait and anchored in front of the city of Hormuz, situated on the northern side of the island. The rulers of the island kingdom were well aware of what was coming, and had made preparations for defense. Since the king himself was a boy 12 years of age, the man who ran the government was his chief counselor Khvaja Attar. To quote the above-mentioned historian Manuel de Faria e Sousa,[111]

'When Albuquerque arrived there, [Sayf al-Din], a youth of 12 years of age reigned, and over him his Slave Coje Atar, a man subtil and courageous. Who hearing what had been done by Albuquerque, made preparations, laying an embargo upon all the ships in the Harbour, and hiring Troops from the Neighbouring Provinces, Persians, Arabians, and others, so that

---

[110] *Ibid.*, p. 115.

[111] *Ibid.*, p. 116.

when Albuquerque came, there were in the town 30,000 fighting men, among them 4,000 Persians, most expert Archers, and in the Harbour 400 Vessels, 60 of considerable bulk, with 2.500 men.'

The king sent a messenger to ask Albuquerque what was the purpose of his coming, and here is how the admiral answered, according to the *Commentaries*:[112]

'Say to the King of Ormuz, that the King Dom Manoel, King of Portugal, and Lord of the Indies, desiring greatly his friendship, hath sent me to this port to serve him with his fleet, and if the King be willing to become his vassal and pay him tribute, I will make peace with him and serve him in everything he shall command me against his enemies; but if he be unwilling, let him know that I shall surely destroy all his fleet wherein he placeth his trust, and take his city by force of arms.'

The king – or rather his government – refused, and Albuquerque took Hormuz by storm. The locals had a far greater force than the attackers, and the battle was fierce:

'This battle which our men had with the Moors on sea, lasted from 7 o'clock in the morning until 3 in the afternoon, and in it there perished an infinite number of Moors, and our gunners so managed that day (for Our Lord was thus pleased to help them) that there was not a single shot fired that did not send a ship to the bottom and put many men to death.'

Hormuz became a vassal kingdom of the Portuguese Crown and pledged to pay an annual tribute of 15,000 xerafins. The agreement included a stipulation that goods imported by the Portuguese would enter duty free, while merchandise exported by them from Hormuz and its other ports would not pay more duty than the natives paid. Perhaps most important, the system of *cartazes* or passes imposed upon native shipping in the Indian Ocean was extended into the Persian Gulf – henceforth no merchant vessel could sail there without a document obtained from

---

[112] *Ibid.*, p. 117.

the Portuguese authorities for a specific fee.[113] The vassal status of Hormuz was then cemented by the building of a Portuguese fortification on the island. Albuquerque, who had selected its site, completed the construction of the principal tower by October 1507, and established a factory or Portuguese trading center in the city.

Hormuz, even with its *"birunat"*, of course possessed only a narrow strip along the large Iranian land mass, whose sovereign was Shah Ismail, the founder of the great Safavid dynasty (1501-1736).[114] Like most of their predecessors and successors who ruled Persia, the Safavids had a landward focus insofar as direct initiative or action was concerned. They applauded and encouraged the seafaring and trade of coastal provinces, but did not themselves engage in any maritime expansion or even defense. The farthest they were willing to go was to demand tribute from coastal principalities such as Hormuz. Thus at about the same time or soon after Hormuz had become Portugal's vassal, Ismail demanded from the King the payment of the customary annual tribute; the latter then asked Albuquerque what he should do, and the conqueror replied that

> '...the Kingdom of Ormuz belonged to the King of Portugal, gained by his fleet and his men, and that he might know of a certainty that if any tribute should be paid to any other King, except the King Dom Manoel, his lord, he would take the government of the Kingdom and give it to some one who would not be afraid of Xeque Ismael....'

---

[113] The system of *cartazes* in the Indian Ocean eventually foundered on a combination of three reasons: the resilience of the mostly Muslim maritime traders, the fact that the task of imposing it throughout the vast expanse of the ocean was beyond the capability of the Portuguese navy, and failure to seize, besides Hormuz, Aden. It remained effective, however, in the Persian Gulf because of the strategic advantage possession of the "choke point" that was Hormuz gave the Portuguese.

[114] R.M. Savory, "Safawids," *EIs*, vol. 8, pp. 765-74; Bosworth, *Dynasties*, pp. 279-80; H.R. Roemer, "The Safavid Period," *CHIr*, vol. 6, pp. 189-350; Laurence Lockhart, "European contacts with Persia, 1350-1736," *ibid.*, pp. 373-411; Ronald Ferrier, "Trade from the mid-14th century to the end of the Safavid period," *ibid.*, pp. 412-90.

He then sent to the ships for cannon-balls, guns, matchlocks, and grenades, and told the messenger to say to the king that

> 'he might send all these to the captain of Xeque Ismael, for this was the sort of money wherewith the King of Portugal had ordered his captain to pay the tribute of that Kingdom that was now under his mastery and command; he, for his part, would promise him that as soon as the fortress was completed, he would enter the Persian straits and render tributary to the King of Portugal, his master, all the places which the Xeque Ismael held on that shore...'[115]

As we have said, however, by the end of the year the Portuguese left Hormuz and Albuquerque left for India, half-abandoning the important conquest. The reasons for the withdrawal were complex, the principal one probably being the fragility of the young and still tentative Lusitanian Empire. Like Hormuz, Goa had been won and lost again, and uncertainty, disagreement and discontent were rampant among the captains of Albuquerque's fleet. Thus the initial conquerors of Hormuz sailed to India in two squadrons, one loyal to the commander and the other mutinous, bringing accusations against him to the viceroy, Almeida. Whether by a stroke of luck or thanks to foresight on the part of the King of Portugal, Albuquerque not only received official support but was appointed to succeed Almeida as Viceroy of Portuguese India. This happened in 1509, and almost immediately Albuquerque reconquered Goa and established it as the capital of the Portuguese overseas empire.

His post of supreme command induced Albuquerque to reassess the full range of the Portuguese maritime empire's promises and dangers, which at this point appeared especially acute in the Red Sea and the approaches to it. Much of the spice trade from the Orient to Europe had passed since Roman times along that route; and once the mostly Muslim ships brought the cargoes to the Red Sea ports, it was at this time the Mamluk sultans who reaped the benefits of their transshipment and sale in Egypt's Mediterranean ports, where the Venetians bought the cargoes and shipped them to Europe. The Portuguese irruption into the

---

[115] *The Commentaries*, quoted by Wilson, *The Persian Gulf*, p. 117.

Indian Ocean initially shattered this system, and the consternation in Egypt and Venice was extreme. Venice, with no direct
access to the other side of the isthmus of Suez, could do little
except trying to persuade those able to intervene to do so, and
the Mamluks did make some efforts. They were not a naval
power, however, and Egypt lacked the timber necessary for
shipbuilding. It was the Ottoman Sultan Beyazit II (1481-1512)
who sent the Egyptians both supplies and qualified mariners to
help them found an arsenal in Suez and build warships with
which to combat the Portuguese. An Egyptian fleet then confronted the intruders off the Indian coast in 1509 but was defeated and withdrew. Despite their victory, the Portuguese
seemed frightened by the prospect of an enemy coming from the
Red Sea to attack them. This may appear rather odd, since they
had witnessed Mamluk weakness at sea, and there was no other
naval power in the Indian Ocean to challenge them. The clue
may be found in one of Albuquerque's letters to King Dom
Manuel written in 1512:[116]

> 'The greatest of all evils to Goa is…the persistent and constant
> report that "the Rumes are coming". It is a great source of
> danger to India, and causes much disquiet and uneasiness
> among the natives and Christians alike. As regards these dam-
> aging remarks, I would respectfully submit to your Majesty
> that until we go to the Red Sea and assure these people that
> such beings as the Rumes are not in existence, there can be no
> confidence or peace for your Majesty's subjects in these
> parts.'

Who were these *Rumes*? Albuquerque, literally or figura-
tively, denies their existence. He must have been aware, though,
that local Muslims, whether Arab, Persian, or other, applied the
term *Rumi* to the Ottomans, both the Turks themselves and other
groups coming from the Ottoman Empire. The Ottomans were of
course the formidable military machine that made Europe trem-
ble, on land as well as at sea in the Mediterranean. Moreover, not
only the Mamluk sultan of Egypt and the doge of Venice, but
also the Ottoman sultan in Istanbul was upset by the irruption of
the Portuguese into the Indian Ocean and the deflection of the

---

[116] Wilson, *The Persian Gulf*, p. 118.

spice trade. Of the three, only the Ottomans should have been in a position to challenge the newcomers, provided they made the necessary effort to transfer some of their naval power to the Red Sea or the Persian Gulf. The prospect of such an undertaking appeared especially promising to the Muslims of India, who, like many other coreligionists, viewed the Ottoman sultan as the leader and defender of Islam against the Infidel. Significantly, the Muslims of the Indian subcontinent entertained hopes for many decades that Ottoman fleets would come and deliver them from Portuguese rule. These then must have been the *Rumes* that Albuquerque's contemporaries were talking about, whether they were the Muslim natives who rejoiced at the idea, or the Portuguese whom it frightened. Why, then, did *he* dismiss the danger? Perhaps because he was more perceptive that the others. Aware of the magnitude of the effort such an enterprise would require, Albuquerque doubted that the Ottomans would make it, and history proved him right. Nevertheless, the Ottoman and Lusitanian empires were to clash several times during the 16th century in the Indian Ocean, the Red Sea and the Persian Gulf.

Albuquerque worried even less about what Shah Ismail might do when in 1507 he encroached upon the Persian monarch's vassal domain, for the Shah not only ceased demanding tribute from the King of Hormuz but ended up concluding a treaty with the Portuguese. It is true that during the years of the Portuguese penetration into the Persian Gulf, graver dangers faced Ismail on the western and eastern frontiers of his young and schismatic kingdom. As the leader of Shii Islam, he had to confront the two great Sunni powers of the day, the Uzbek Turks in the east and the Ottoman Turks in the west. Ismail crushed the Uzbeks in 1510 but was defeated by the Ottomans in 1514. From then onwards, the Safavids were never averse to colluding with Christians – Portuguese in the 16th century, English in the 17th – against the Ottomans. Thus until Shah Abbas resolved to recover Hormuz for Iran, not the Persians but the Turks would challenge the Portuguese in the Persian Gulf.

That challenge came only after Albuquerque's death, however. The adversaries he had to contend with were, in 1509, the aforementioned fleet sent by the Mamluk sultan of Egypt to the Indian coast, and in 1513 the Arab defenders of Aden. Aden, a fortified port near the southwestern tip of the Arabian peninsula, was not only a great emporium but could also serve as an ideal base for controlling maritime traffic entering or leaving the Red Sea, provided the occupant had an adequate naval force. Albuquerque made an attempt to conquer it in that year, but the fortifications of the harbor proved too strong for his squadron, and he withdrew. It is somewhat of a mystery why the great conqueror-statesman, so acutely attuned to the role Aden could play as a Portuguese base, did not try again. One reason may be that he gave Hormuz priority. Had he lived longer, Albuquerque might well have made another attempt at Aden; but he died on 15 December 1515, as his fleet was entering Goa on its return from the second Hormuz campaign. This time the conquest was more solid, and the island kingdom remained Portugal's vassal until 1622.

One of the results was accommodation between the European power and Persia. Soon after the fortress was occupied by the Portuguese and their flag was hoisted over the royal palace, an ambassador from Shah Ismail arrived, and a definite agreement was entered into, whereby the local king was to be ruler of Hormuz *'in the name of King Dom Manoel, his lord'*. The agreement included stipulations that Portuguese ships would assist the Persians should they wish to invade Bahrain and Qatif, and that the two peoples would make an alliance against the Ottoman Turks. Albuquerque appointed his nephew Pero to be captain of the fortress, and gave him comprehensive instructions regarding its completion and arming. Having set the general affairs of Hormuz in order, he sailed for India aboard the *Flor da Rosa*, in poor health. He arrived at Goa only to die, soon after his ship had cast anchor in the harbor, on 15th December 1515. His last letter to his king, dated 'At Sea', reads as follows:[117]

> '... I leave the chief place in India in your Majesty's power, the only thing left to be done being the closing of the gates of the Straits. I beg your Majesty to remember all I have done for India and to make my son great for my sake.'

Albuquerque's letters to King Manuel and the instructions he received from him testify to the deliberate and planned manner of Portuguese oceanic expansion, and to the two men's aware-

---

[117] Wilson, *The Persian Gulf*, p. 121.

ness that they were founding, for Portugal, a great maritime commercial empire in the Indian Ocean and its ramifications. The 16th century was a Portuguese era in the East, just as it was a Spanish one in the West, although the two Iberian powers came near collision as they approached each other eastward through the Indonesian Spice Islands and westward across the Pacific and the Philippines.

The Portuguese expansion was a blow, as we have said, to Muslim shipping across a wide range of affected individuals and states. In the critical, formative period coincidental with Albuquerque and his immediate successors, the most prominent states in the Middle East were Iran, the Ottoman Empire, and Egypt. Both logic and the hope of many contemporaries fostered an expectation that the Turks would vigorously intervene and thwart the unprecedented threat. The response, however, was half-hearted, ineffectual, or none at all, and virtually collapsed by the end of the 16th century. To an observant witness or a perceptive historian, this may have come as no surprise. In order to successfully challenge the Portuguese, at least one of the three powers would have had to possess an adequate navy or to be able or determined to build and use one, but none did. To be sure, the Ottoman Empire had by 1501 become the major naval power in the Mediterranean; and the Mamluks of Egypt showed their concern over the Portuguese irruption by developing the abovementioned arsenal at Suez, where they built a fleet which in 1509 confronted the Portuguese off the Indian port of Diu. Moreover, the Ottoman sultan Beyazit II (1481-1512) shared the Mamluk sultan Qansawh II al-Ghawri's (1501-16) concern while also displaying some degree of Muslim solidarity by sending both naval supplies and expert advice to Egypt. All this proved too marginal, however; the aforementioned Mamluk expedition of 1509 ended in failure, as did the only two noteworthy attempts made by the Ottomans themselves, the first in 1538 and the second in 1552. As a naval power, Portugal continued to reign supreme in the Indian Ocean and the Persian Gulf throughout the 16th century.

The main reason for this outcome was that at the level of their governments and rulers, each of the three major Muslim powers in Albuquerque's time, Turkey, Egypt, and Persia, remained essentially alien to matters of naval warfare, maritime commerce and oceanic, colonial-commercial expansion in the Indian Ocean. The contrast becomes especially striking when we glance at the events on the Persian and Egyptian fronts. Although Albuquerque failed to take Aden in 1513, his successors made several attempts to penetrate into the Red Sea. This should have been alarming news to the Ottoman sultan Selim I (1512-20), but he had other things on his mind: As noted above, he waged a major war in eastern Anatolia against Persia, defeating Shah Ismail I at Chaldiran in 1514; and in 1516, he set out on a campaign to conquer Syria and Egypt, which he concluded with a triumphal entry into Cairo in April 1517.

The Mamluks had not quite expected the Ottoman attack, thinking that once more Persia was the target of the armies advancing eastward through Anatolia. They were preoccupied with the Portuguese penetration into the Red Sea, the Spice Route's final leg towards Egyptian ports, and welcomed any Ottoman help of the kind that Selim's father Beyazit had proffered. One of the Turkish captains in Mamluk service was Selman Reis, who had been made director of the Suez shipyard in 1514.[118] The next three years were spent on preparations to repulse the expected Portuguese attacks. Jeddah, the port of Mecca, had exceptional status both for religious and commercial reasons: serving thousands of Muslims coming to perform pilgrimage at Islam's holiest city; and functioning as one of the principal ports on the spice route towards the Ottoman Empire and the Mediterranean. Its dual role was seen in this light both by the Christian invaders and by Muslim defenders. Albuquerque wrote in one of his letters to the king :

> '...It is my intention to proceed to Massawa...and see what I can do at Jeddah...The voyage to the Red Sea will...be a profitable one on account of the valuable spices which come every year to those parts from India; and because I wish to exterminate the Rumes and...destroy Mecca...'[119]

Albuquerque did not live long enough to make this attempt, but his successor Lopo Suares did make it. He found the harbor

---

[118] S. Soucek, "Selman Re'is," *EI*s 9: 135-36.
[119] Wilson, *The Persian Gulf*, p. 120.

defended by a garrison ably commanded by Selman Reis and had to withdraw. That happened in April 1517, a historic coincidence with the Ottoman sultan's conquest of Egypt. Selim I summoned Selman Reis to Cairo, and did not treat him kindly. The worthy captain was thrown in jail, and then sent in chains to Istanbul. The charge, never made explicit, must have been that the sultan's subject had served a country with which the Ottoman Empire was at war at that moment. The intrinsic merit of Selman's case must have eventually prevailed, for not only did the authorities in Istanbul exonerate him but the sultan sent him back to Suez as commander of this now Ottoman naval base opening towards the Indian Ocean.

In his new, enhanced capacity, Selman Reis was both preoccupied with the ever present Portuguese danger and with what he thought were promising possibilities if the Ottomans picked up the gauntlet and entered the naval and colonial contest for the Indian Ocean. He expressed this in a memorandum (*layiha*) dated 2 June 1525 and presented to the grand vizier Ibrahim Paşa, who had come to Egypt on an inspection tour; the memorandum is anonymous, but internal evidence argues in favor of Selman Reis as its author. He describes the war fleet based at that moment in the harbor of Jeddah, and states that if an effort were made to make it battle-ready, the Muslims would not only keep the Red Sea safe from intruders, but could recover for Islam the fortresses and ports held by the Portuguese in India. Having discussed at some length Jeddah and the Red Sea, he describes the state of affairs farther east, and starts with Hormuz:

> This chapter tells how the godless Portuguese seized [certain] provinces in the country of Hindustan. At first they took the island of Hormuz, an anchorage pertaining to Persia, and built there a small fortress, garrisoning it with two hundred infidels. They levy from the fifty to sixty large ships that annually call there the tithe to the sum of one hundred thousand florins and send it to Portugal.[120]

The last ten years of Selman Reis's life, from 1517 to 1527, witnessed a series of desultory attempts on his part to break out

---

[120] Michel Lesure, "Un document ottoman sur l'Inde portuguaise et les pays de la Mer Rouge," in *Mare Luso-indicum*, 3 (1976), pp. 137-60.

of the Bab al-Mandab Strait and challenge the Portuguese in the Arabian Sea, followed by his governorship of Yemen, which had by then become an Ottoman province. The relevant fact for our purposes is that his appeal for a more forceful policy in the Indian Ocean did not stir much interest in Istanbul. Selman Reis's career and the response to the memorandum which he wrote on his own initiative, no doubt hoping that it would reach the highest quarters, present a sharp contrast to Affonso de Albuquerque and his correspondence with Dom Manuel. Moreover, he was not the only Turkish mariner who worried about the dangers incurred by Muslims in eastern waters and who deplored the cost of missed opportunities. There were others, and the most prominent among these was his younger contemporary Piri Reis.

Selman Reis was a native of the island of Midilli (Lesbos), Piri Reis of Gelibolu (Gallipoli), both places famous as maritime frontiers of the empire's Mediterranean realm and as incubation points producing great mariners. Seafaring in its manifold forms was their profession. During his years as a privateer and later as an admiral in the sultan's navy, Piri Reis garnered rich experience which he used to produce famous works of hydrography and sailing directions. The second version of his *Kitab-i Bahriye*, a book of sailing directions for the Mediterranean Sea (written by 1526), includes a long versified introduction in which Piri Reis describes the oceans as well as their ramifications such as the Persian Gulf and the Red Sea. He laments the loss of Hormuz and of its revenues to the Portuguese. What follows is our abbreviated prose paraphrase of the passage:

> "Now that you have heard about the situation of Bahrein, come and listen to what it is like at Hormuz. Know that it is an island. Many merchants visit it...But now, O friend, the Portuguese have come there and built a stronghold on its cape. They control the place and collect the customs – you see into what condition that province has sunk! The Portuguese have prevailed over the natives, and their own merchants crowd the warehouses there. Whatever the season, trading cannot now happen without the Portuguese..."[121]

---

[121] S. Soucek, *Piri Reis & Turkish mapmaking after Columbus*, London 1996, p. 97; idem, "Piri Re'is, " *EIs* 8: 308-9.

Piri Reis presented the *Kitab-i Bahriye* to Süleyman the Magnificent (1520-66), but there is no evidence that the sultan paid much attention to it. The sovereign was busy with one of his many campaigns in the Balkans, this time scoring the great victory at Mohács, which added Hungary to the Ottoman Empire. Three years later, in 1529, he laid siege to Vienna; although unsuccessful, this campaign displayed the vertiginous expansion of Süleyman's realm on land in Europe, which far outweighed, in the sultan's eyes, the importance of Hormuz, the Persian Gulf, and the whole struggle against the Portuguese in the Indian Ocean.

This contrast did not disappear even when in 1534 the Ottoman sultan turned his attention eastward to confront Persia. The adversaries of the 1514 war, Sultan Selim and Shah Ismail, were dead by then; and it was their sons, Süleyman and Tahmasp I (1524-76), who were now locked in a struggle that would lead to two wars between them. Following a pattern that had almost become the rule ever since the emergence of the early Iranian empires, Iraq was either under Persian domination or under that of the major Western power of the time, and wars between the two sides allotted it to the winner of the latest confrontation.[122] Shah Ismail, soon after he had asserted the rule of his Shii dynasty in Persia, eliminated the Turcoman Aqqoyunlu dynasty from eastern Anatolia and Iraq and by 1507 had added those areas to the Safavid Empire. We have seen that in 1514 Selim defeated Ismail and drove him out of Anatolia. Iraq, however, remained partly Safavid – this was especially true of the central segment, with Baghdad as its main prize – and partly under local rulers such as the Banu Mughamis of the Jaza'ir region,[123] with Basra

---

[122] The great Muslim empire of the Abbasids (750-1258), whose capital was Baghdad, was of course one of the major exceptions, a kind of throwback to the great Babylonian and Assyrian empires of Biblical times. Even it, however, eventually confirmed the general rule: after their supremacy during the first two centuries, the Abbasids came to be dominated by the Buwayhids and Seljukids, dynasties invading Iraq from Iran.

[123] A region mainly on the western side of the lowermost course of the Tigris and Euphrates rivers and their joint course, the aforementioned Shatt al-Arab, though which they flow into the Persian Gulf. In Arabic, the term *Jaza'ir*, "Islands," is the same as that of Algeria. The Iraqi

as the principal city and port. Süleyman the Magnificent's campaign of 1534-35 had the double purpose of defeating Tahmasp and conquering Iraq. In December 1534 he triumphantly entered Baghdad, and from then onwards until World War I this city was the easternmost metropolis of the immense Ottoman Empire, except for transitory periods of Persian reconquest.

Süleyman did not push all the way to the Gulf, but the local ruler, Rashid b. Mughamis, hitherto a vassal of Shah Ismail, sent his son Mani with the keys of Basra to the Ottoman conqueror as an expression of submission. Other Arabs hitherto tributary to the Safavids acted similarly: the tribal chieftains of the Jaza'ir, Garraf and Huwaida areas, the governors of Qatif and Bahrain all sent envoys with expressions of submission. This loyalty did not yet mean incorporation into the Ottoman empire, but rather represented the local chieftains' opportunistic diplomacy. Real conquest resumed with the acquisition of Basra in 1546, though not as a result of any large-scale imperial campaign, but rather through the action of the *beylerbeyi* or governor of Baghdad. Ottoman imperial campaigns against Iran would recur until the 19th century, but always along a latitudinal line farther north, skirting Iraq except when Baghdad had been seized by the Persians. Conquests and control of provinces farther south, beginning with Basra and proceeding into the Arabian Peninsula along the southern rim of the Persian Gulf, would invariably be "delegated" to local governors, usually those of Baghdad or Basra, or undertaken on their own initiative.

We have seen that the Kingdom of Hormuz straddled the two gulfs – the Persian Gulf and the Gulf of Oman – and controlled several ports or islands also on the southern, Arab side. When the Portuguese established themselves at Hormuz as the kingdom's suzerains, they assumed some of its prerogatives on the Arabian side. Thus in 1521 the Arab chieftain of Bahrain and Hasa, Mukrim, was defeated and killed, and the island and coastal province had to pay tribute to Hormuz.[124] In 1529, Bel-

---

"*Jaza'ir*" is so named because of its special terrain marked by a myriad canals and islets formed by the lowermost courses of the two great rivers, and is to a considerable extent synonymous with the geographical concept of the *Bata'ih*, "Marshlands."

[124] Salih Özbaran, "XVI. Yüzyılda Basra Körfezi sahillerinde Osmanlılar," *Tarih Dergisi* (Istanbul), vol. 25 (1971), p. 52. The foremost spe-

chior de Sousa Tavarez came with a small squadron to Basra, ostensibly to help Rashid ibn Mughamis, ruler of that port, against the ruler of Jaza'ir, but then demanded that seven fustas (a type of small galley) and fifty *Rumes* present there be delivered to him; upon refusal, he burned several villages before retiring. Also in the same year of 1529, the ruler of Bahrain, Reis 'Barbadim', neglected to send the tribute to Hormuz; the viceroy of India Nuño da Cunha sent his brother Simão with five ships and 500 soldiers to chastise the 'rebel' and perhaps even establish a permanent occupation on the island. The attempt failed through inadequate supplies, sickness, and stubborn defense of the fortress, but some time later Bahrain relapsed into tributary dependence on Hormuz, and a Portuguese fort was built a short distance to the west of the island's capital Manamah. These were episodes of no major importance in and of themselves, and probably ranked among many others that remained unrecorded or unnoticed, but they are suggestive of Portuguese naval dominance in the Gulf – a dominance that the Turks were going to challenge.

With the Turks established in Basra and the Portuguese in Hormuz, the scene seemed set for a historic confrontation of the Ottoman and Lusitanian empires in the Persian Gulf. As it turned out, barring one exception, the confrontation was minor and subsided well before the end of Portuguese rule at Hormuz.

The exception was an Ottoman naval assault on Hormuz, which confirmed the rule that in the Orient the Turks preferred to wage war on land. Again, this is not to gainsay those who favored mounting naval campaigns to break the Portuguese grip on

---

cialist on Ottoman-Portuguese relations, the author has combed not only Turkish but also Portuguese sources, both archival and literary. Here he refers to João de Barros (1496-1570), *Da Asia* (Lisboa, 1778): Decada III, Livro VI, p. 27; the latter also states that some of the ships owned by Mukrim had been built "*por industria de alguns turcos*". Özbaran's most valuable articles have been re-issued in two *variorum* volumes: *The Ottoman Response to European Expansion,* Istanbul: Isis Press, 1994 (including those originally in Turkish translated into English), and *Yemen'den Basra'ya Sınırdaki Osmanlı*, Istanbul: Kitapyayınevi, 2004 (those originally in English translated into Turkish).

emporia like Hormuz. Such was indeed the mission of an Ottoman squadron that sailed out of the Red Sea in April 1552. It was under the command of the aforementioned Piri Reis, who since 1547 had been commander of the Ottoman "Indian Ocean Fleet" based at Suez. The expedition consisted of 24 galleys and 4 sailing ships. Instructions to Piri Reis stipulated that once Hormuz was conquered, other points in the two gulfs that had belonged to it – in other words, at this time to the Portuguese – should be summoned to recognize Ottoman suzerainty; significantly, Bahrain was singled out as an especially desirable acquisition.[125]

The Turkish fleet's progress along the Arabian peninsula towards Hormuz proceeded somewhat as Albuquerque's had done 45 years earlier. As he was sailing along Arabia's southern coast, Piri Reis became fog-bound near the port of Shihr, and sent out a few scout ships under the command of his son Mehmet, while Dom Alvaro de Noronha, governor of Hormuz, sent out his scouts under Simão da Costa. The two sighted each other and hurried back with the news to their commanders. One can surmise that Costa's mission was more vital, for the Portuguese needed to know whether the Turks were really coming and how close they were. Once the approaching danger was confirmed, Noronha set about preparing for the probable siege.

The dating of the Ottoman fleet's progress before it reached Hormuz is uncertain, just as are the length and circumstances of its first enterprise, the siege and occupation of Masqat. The governor of this port, conquered in 1507 by Albuquerque, was in 1552 João de Lisboa. According to Portuguese sources, the fortress resisted for a month before surrendering; an Ottoman source mentions only a brief siege, with six days of bombardment by the Turkish ships; on the seventh day Masqat surrendered. Faria e Sousa states that Piri Reis, instead of releasing the commander as had been agreed among the conditions of surrender, took him prisoner, while throwing 60 Portuguese soldiers into galley service; the Turkish document talks about 128 soldiers being captured. Having accomplished the conquest of Masqat, the Turks, short of manpower, did not garrison the city but demolished its defences and proceeded directly to Hormuz.

---

[125] Cengiz Orhonlu, "Hint kaptanlığı ve Piri Reis," *Belleten* (Ankara), vol. 34 (1970), pp. 235-54.

At the time of the Hormuz expedition, Basra was a new Ottoman *eyalet* (province); we have seen that it had been conquered a mere six years earlier, and now its *beylerbeyi* or governor was one Kubad Paşa. This obscure individual was going to play a rather nefarious role in the subsequent events through actions – or in fact inaction – incongruous with the strategic role Basra should have played in the Ottoman struggle for the Persian Gulf. When exactly the Turkish fleet reached Hormuz the sources do not tell us, but it probably did so in October 1552 and proceeded to the siege forthwith. Bombardment both from the ships and from cannon set up on land caused considerable damage to the fortress, but not enough to enable the Turks to storm it or force the Portuguese garrison to surrender. It also seems that the problem of supplies of food and ammunition was worse on the Ottoman side – the fleet had been at sea for half a year and now was only indifferently helped from Basra by Kubad Paşa. The last straw was a report that a strong Portuguese relief fleet was coming from India. Piri Reis raised the siege and, after a brief raid on the neighboring island of Qishm, proceeded with his ships to Basra. Hearing of the Turkish withdrawal, the Portuguese commander reversed course and returned to Goa. Piri Reis, leaving the bulk of his fleet in Basra, then returned with two swift galleys to Cairo.

Had the Turks conquered Hormuz and maintained themselves there, the subsequent history of the Persian Gulf might have been different. First of all, their strategic position would have been excellent – with a base at its head that was Basra, and another at its entrance from the Ocean that was the Strait of Hormuz,[126] the Turks could have turned the Gulf into an Ottoman lake; with that, commercial exploitation of the area's economic assets, backed by Iraq as an Ottoman province, would have turned this part of the realm into one of the most lucrative possessions of the sultan. The strategic advantage presented by the "choke point" that was the Strait of Hormuz should have sufficed to maintain a naval force strong enough to police this branch of the Indian

---

[126] Or "choke point", a term favored by current historiography; among other examples, we could cite the Strait of Bab al-Mandab at the entrance to the Red Sea with Aden strategically located nearby, and the Strait of Melaka (Malacca) named after the port city and capital of the Sultanate of Melaka.

Ocean and to repel any attempt by outsiders to break in. And, needless to say, had the sultan chosen for once to add one more hat to his attire and become also a "merchant king" like his Portuguese counterpart, by launching a forward policy and sending his fleets to acquire trading posts and colonies around the Indian Ocean, then indeed the history of the Orient might have taken a different course. The chances of that were illustrated by the case of six Portuguese merchantmen sailing from Lisbon to Hormuz; once they heard that the Turks were besieging Hormuz, they changed tack for India.[127] Muslim shippers could have resumed using Hormuz as their emporium, and even the Europeans, in their own interest, might have felt compelled to frequent it on Ottoman terms.

But none of that happened, because the sultan and his military class remained what they had always been: land-bound conquerors and tax gatherers rather than maritime merchant kings and commercial entrepreneurs. Indeed, if the main purpose of the original expedition was to counter Portuguese dominance of the Persian Gulf, Basra could have served as an excellent base despite the failure to dislodge the enemy from Hormuz. With an expanded war fleet, and a well prepared campaign, the Turks could have made another attempt at Hormuz and, penetrating into the Indian Ocean, might have tried to gain a dominant position on this avenue of the spice trade. None of that happened, however. The year 1553 was the first year of the sultan's three-year campaign against his Safavid adversary, and the empire's resources and energy were concentrated, as usual, on land farther north. To Süleyman the Magnificent and his ministers the Persian Gulf was, in the last analysis, a backwater, and they paid only incidental attention to it. Instead of summoning Piri Reis to Istanbul or to the sultan's headquarters to probe the reasons for the failure at Hormuz and to plan a new and better campaign, they had him summarily executed in Cairo, and entrusted the fleet at Basra to another captain, Seydi Ali Reis.[128] The appointment occurred in November 1553, when the grand vizier Rüstem Paşa, the principal architect of imperial policy at the time, summoned Seydi Ali to Aleppo, where Süleyman the Magnificent

---

[127] Faria e Sousa, *The Portugues Asia*, vol. 2, pp. 164-65, cited by Orhonlu, "Hint Kaptanlığı...," p. 244.

[128] S. Soucek, "Sidi Ali Re'is," *EIs* 9: 535-36.

was going to spend the winter before launching the offensive planned for next spring against Shah Tahmasp. The mariner finally reached Basra in February 1554 and set about making preparations for the voyage.

By then Basra had a new governor, Mustafa Paşa, who asked Seydi Ali to help him with a few of the galleys under his command to mount a campaign against a rebel in the estuary of the Karun River in the neighboring province of Khuzistan. The captain, stymied for the time being by contrary seasonal winds in the Gulf, obliged Mustafa Pasha in his request, but the sidestep brought little result except some casualties among his men and ships. When he finally sailed out on 13 July 1554, he was in command of 15 vessels – attrition of various kinds had reduced to one half the number with which Piri Reis had left Suez two years earlier. Seydi Ali managed to slip out of the Persian Gulf, but on 5 September, as the Ottoman fleet approached Masqat, a Portuguese squadron sailed out, and in the ensuing clash the Turks incurred serious losses; what may have saved them was a storm that broke out and separated them from the enemy, but at a price: it drove their ships in the wrong direction, towards the coast of Makran and Baluchistan, where they rested at the port of Gwadar and then made a second attempt to sail back to the Red Sea. They crossed the Gulf of Oman; but as they approached the Ras al-Hadd cape, another and more terrible storm broke out and drove the Turks farther east, this time all the way to the Indian coast, where they landed at the port of Surat. From there, Seydi Ali and his men set out on an epic overland journey homeward that first took them to Ahmedabad, the capital of the Moghul Empire. The Moghuls were Muslim Turco-Mongols who originally hailed from Central Asia; in 1526, just as Süleyman the Magnificent was adding Hungary to the Ottoman empire, the Emperor Babur had won the decisive battle of Panipat near Delhi and was founding the greatest Muslim empire of Indian history. The language spoken at the court was still Chaghatay or Eastern Turkish when the Ottoman guests visited it; and Seydi Ali Reis, who stayed there several months, gained the monarch's heart by composing poetry in Chaghatay. The anabasis then took him and his companions to Central Asia and Iran, until they returned to Ottoman territory by reaching Baghdad in February 1557. From there they hastened to Istanbul, and Seydi Ali himself to Edirne, to report to the sultan. Süleyman received him graciously, and his interest in the extraordinary adventure inspired the mariner to write an account of it which he called *Mir'at al-Memalik* or Mirror of Countries.[129]

Seydi Ali's adventures in 1554 could be viewed as the closing chapter of the struggle – such as it was – between the Ottoman and Lusitanian empires for the Indian Ocean and its two ramifications, the Persian Gulf and the Red Sea. The 16th century was, as we have said, a Portuguese century. Henceforward the role played by the Ottoman Empire in the Persian Gulf hardly ever had a truly naval or even maritime dimension.[130] The same could be said of the Safavid Empire and its successors. The main players here would be, on the one hand, the Europeans: the Portuguese in the 16th century, English, Dutch, and French in the 17th and 18th, and almost exclusively the British[131] in the 19th and early 20th centuries; and on the other, the mostly Arab coastal principalities.

This is not to say that the Portuguese eliminated or paralyzed native shipping in the Indian Ocean, as we have already emphasized. After the initial shock, the resilient maritime traders, mostly Gujerati, Persian, and Arab, bounced back; and by the

---

[129] Seydi Ali Reis, *Miratul-memalik*. Ed. Mehmet Kiremit. Ankara 1999. For English translation, see A. Vambéry, *The Travels and Adventures of the Turkish Admiral Sidi Ali Reïs in India, Afghanistan, Central Asia, and Persia, during the years 1553-1556*, London, 1899. For a French translation, see Seyyidî Re'îs, *Le Miroir des Pays: une anabase ottomane à travers l'Inde st l'Asie Centrale, traduit du turc ottoman, présenté et annoté par Jean-Louis Bacqué-Grammont*, [Paris?], 1999.

[130] Several studies have emphasized this fact, mostly indirectly; for example Saffet Bey, "Bahreyn'de bir vak'a," *Tarih-i Osmani Encümeni Mecmuası* (Istanbul), vol. 3 (1328/1910); Cengiz Orhonlu, "1559 Bahreyn seferine âid bir rapor," *Tarih Dergisi* (Istanbul) 17 (1967), p. 1-18; Jon E. Mandaville, "The Ottoman province of al-Hasa in the sixteenth and seventeenth centuries," *Journal of the American Oriental Society* 90 (1970), p. 486-513.

[131] It was only the formation of the United Kingdom in the 18th century, when Scotland was recognized as a distinct constituent in the Union, that made the term British preferable to English in political and international parlance.

middle of the 16th century the flow of spices in native bottoms toward the Red Sea may even have surpassed former levels.[132]

---

[132] Frederic C. Lane, "The Mediterranean Spice Trade: Further evidence of its revival in the sixteenth century," *American Historical Review* 45 (1940), p. 581-90, reprinted in *Crisis and Change in the Venetian Economy in the 16th and 17th centuries*, ed. Brian Pullan, London 1968, p. 47-58; Charles Boxer, "A note on Portuguese reactions to the revival of the Red Sea spice trade and the rise of Atcheh, 1540-1600," *Journal of Asian History* 10 (1969), p. 415-28.

Chapter 11

The Age of Europe's "India Companies"

T he success of the Portuguese at Hormuz made possible
their dominance of much of the trade passing through the
Persian Gulf, and for the first few decades of the 16th
century they even managed to capture a sizable portion of the
spice trade that before their arrival had headed across the Indian
Ocean toward the Red Sea and the Mediterranean. It was now
carried in Portuguese bottoms via the Cape route to Lisbon,
which, as we have seen, became the premier spice market of
Europe. This was a terrible blow not only to the merchant republic of Venice, but also to the mostly Arab, Persian, and Gujerati
shipping and trade.

Before long, however, the native mariners and merchants had
recovered from the initial shock wrought by the superior ships
and firepower of the intruders and gradually learned to elude
them or defend themselves, so that by the middle of the 16th
century the spice trade had resumed its flow to the Red Sea. The
sheer magnitude of the challenge that faced the small nation of
Portugal, and the resilience of Muslim and Indian seamen, must
have been the principal reasons for this revival of the traditional
spice trade route: permanent patrolling of the long coasts and
vast expanse of the Indian Ocean was beyond Portugal's means.
An additional reason was Portugal's failure to conquer Aden or
some other strategically located harbor in or near the Red Sea.
The Portuguese needed here a base that would play a role comparable to that of Hormuz, and they had none.

Nevertheless, although the newcomers failed to prevent the
natives from recovering and the trade from swinging back to the
traditional route, they did succeed in capturing and keeping at
least some of the spice trade, and carried the precious cargoes in

their own ships via the Cape route to Lisbon. The Portuguese capital thus continued to function, if not as the chief spice market of Europe, at least as an important distributor of pepper brought from the Orient. For much of the 16th century, northern Europe was the principal customer of this outlet. Dutch shippers carried the merchandise from Lisbon to Amsterdam, whose merchants grew wealthy from this trade.

From about the middle of the 16th century, English merchants had been seeking ways to reach the Orient. They were already familiar with the Levant – Turkey, Syria, and Palestine – hence the name of the English association of merchants dealing with that quarter, the Levant Company. The countries and seas beyond the Levant, however – Iraq, Persia, the Persian Gulf, by now well known to the Italians and the Portuguese – were still beyond the horizon of the English, and London merchants resolved to send there an exploratory mission. In February 1583 Ralph Fitch and three other members of the Levant Company embarked in a ship bound for Tripoli[133] and then traveled overland to Aleppo and the Euphrates, which they descended to Fallujah; there they set out on a short overland trip to Baghdad, from where they sailed down the Tigris to reach Basra in July 1583. From Basra they sailed to Hormuz, where they were arrested by the Portuguese, who suspected them of being spies (which of course, in a sense, they were; it also seems that resident Venetian merchants – understandably averse to new competition from Europe – were at the root of this accusation). The Portuguese sent the Englishmen to Goa, where they stayed in prison from September to December, when they were released through the sureties procured by two Jesuits.[134] The party broke up, some returning home forthwith, but Fitch in April 1584 undertook an epic journey through India and several other countries before embarking in Malacca on his homeward voyage, which again led through Hormuz, the Persian Gulf and Basra. He ar-

---

[133] The party carried letters from Queen Elizabeth I to the King of Cambay and the Emperor of China. The trip is alluded to by one of the witches in *Macbeth*, act I, scene III: "Her husband's to Aleppo gone, Master o' th' Tiger."

[134] One of these monks was Thomas Stevens, who in 1579 had sailed to India by the Cape route – the first Englishman to do so. A Jesuit, he did so within the framework of the Portuguese system.

rived in London on 29 April 1591 and wrote a report[135] which became a cornerstone in the planning of the English commercial – and eventually colonial – enterprise in the Orient.

Meanwhile some of the Dutch had the opportunity of joining the Portuguese on their east-bound voyages and thus gaining knowledge that may have been worth the Lisbon spices many times over. One participant was Jan Huyghen van Linschoten (1563-1611), a native of Haarlem, who in 1583 came to India at the age of twenty and for the next six years worked as book-keeper to the archbishop of Goa. Upon his return to Holland, he wrote accounts of his travels that considerably increased the knowledge of the Orient and stimulated the desire to penetrate there not only among his countrymen but also among their peers and rivals, the English. The Dutch originals were published in three parts as *Itinerario: Voyage ofte schipvaert van Jan Huyghen van Linschoten naar Oost ofte Portugaels Indien, 1579-1592* (Amsterdam, 1596).[136] A mere two years later, an English translation appeared in London[137]: *Iohn Huighen van Linschoten his Discours of Voyages into ye Easte & West Indies.* The speed with which Linschoten's book was published in the original and then also in English translation is but one of the indicators of the ferment among the enterprising merchants of Amsterdam and London impatient to penetrate the Orient and gain access to the huge profits to be made from trading with it.

---

[135] Richard Hakluyt, *Principal Navigations*, London 1599, vol. ii, pt. I, pp. 245-71, included in Samuel Purchas, *Hakluytus Posthumus or Purchas His Pilgrimes*, Glasgow: James MacLehose, 1905, vol. 10, pp. 165-204.

[136] Jan Huygen van Linschoten, 1563-1611. *Itinerario, voyage ofte schipvaert, van Jan Huygen van Linschoten naar Oost ofte Portugaels Indien: inhoudende een corte beschryvinghe der selver landen ende zee-custen... Alles beschreven ende by een vergadert, door den selfden...voor alle curiese ende liefhebbers van vreemdigheden.* t'Amsterdam: By Cornelis Claesz. op't Water, in't schrijfboeck, by de oude brugghe, Anno M.D.XCVI. 3 v. in 1.

[137] *Iohn Huighen van Linschoten his Discours of Voyages into ye Easte & West Indies: deuided into foure bookes.* Printed at London: by Iohn Wolfe printer to ye honourable cittie of London, [1598]. A modern edition: *The Voyage of Jan Huyghen van Linschoten to the East Indies...* Ed. & tr. A.C. Burrell and P.A. Tiele, London 1885. 2 vols. Hakluyt Society no. 70-71.

Even before the appearance of the Dutch printing, the *Itinerary* in manuscript form served as a text of sailing directions for Cornelis Houtman, who led the first Dutch expedition to the East Indies. It left Amsterdam in April 1595 and returned two years later, bringing a valuable cargo and a treaty with the Sultan of Bantam (Java). Together with Linschoten's book, Houtman's voyage triggered a dramatic surge of Dutch expeditions to the Indies, and by 1602 at least sixty ships had sailed in quest of Oriental goods. This in turn further spurred English merchants to bestir themselves to seize their share of the unprecedented opportunities. They had already been alerted to the riches beckoning them from overseas when in 1587 Sir Francis Drake captured the *San Felipe*, a Portuguese carrack bringing a dazzlingly valuable cargo. The English translation of Linschoten's *Itinerary,* published in 1598, provided one more stimulus, and in September 1599 a group of London merchants formed an association for trade with the East Indies in order to better compete with the Dutch. On 31 December 1600 Queen Elizabeth I granted a charter for fifteen years to the "Governor and Company of Merchants trading into the East Indies," conferring on them a monopoly of the East Indian trade. This was the birth of the East India Company, the greatest of eight such associations established during the 17th and 18th centuries in Europe. Remarkably, the English company was chartered even before the Dutch one (De Verenighde Oostindische Compagnie or Unified East India Company, usually referred to by its acronym VOC), for the latter received its *octrooy* or charter from the Dutch Republic only on 20 March 1602. In subsequent decades, however, the Dutch won out in the coveted arena of the fabulously spice-rich Indonesian archipelago, driving out the Portuguese and shutting out the English after a series of often brutal and bloody clashes. Indirectly, English failure in Indonesia was one of the factors that would eventually lead to the creation of the "jewel in the crown," British India.

Hormuz was one of the places mentioned by Linschoten, and his description portrays the great volume of commercial traffic passing not only through the island port but also through the entire Persian Gulf, starting or ending at Basra, as well as the land routes connected with these two ports. This state of affairs which the Dutch traveler witnessed in the 1580s shows that the Gulf continued to function as one of the three maritime avenues of long-distance trade between the Orient and Europe, the other two being the Red Sea and the Cape route. Europe was of course not the only destination or source of trade; the greatest volume pertained to the countries of Asia and Africa themselves. Here is what Linschoten says:[138]

"...Every yeare twice there commeth a great companie of people over land which are called Caffiles or Carvanes, which come from Aleppo, ... , in the months of April and September. There is a Captaine and certain hundredths of Iannisaries, which connvaye the said Caffila until they come to the Towne of Bassora, from whence they travaile by water unto Ormus ...Hurmuz...has a great traffique, for it is the staple for all India, Persia, Arabia, and Turkie, and of all the places and Countries about the same, and commonly it is full of Persians, Armenians, Turkes, and all nationas, as also Venetians, which lie there to buy spices and precious stones, that in great abundance are brought thether of India, and from thence are sent overland to Venice, and also carried throughout all Turkie, Armenia, Arabia, Persia and every way. There are likewise brought thether, all manner of merchandises from the same Countries, that is from Persia... great store of rich Tapestrie which are called Alcatiffas: out of Turkie all manner of Chamlets: out of Arabia divers sortes of Drugges for Poticaries, as Sanguis Draconis, Manna, Mirre, Frankinsence and such like, divers goodly horses, that are excellent for breeding, all manner of most excellent Orientall Pearles..."

Basra was the principal port at the head of the Persian Gulf linked by a maritime route with Hormuz, which was the hub of trade between it and such ports in India as Diu, Cambay and Chaul. In this context it is instructive to read Fitch's description:[139]

"Basora standeth neere the Gulfe of Persia, and is a Towne of great trade of Spices and Drugs which come from Ormus. Also there is great store of Wheat, Rice, and Dates growing thereabout, wherewith they serve Babi-

---

[138] *Ibid.*, v. 1, pp. 47-48.
[139] Purchas, *op. cit.*, pp. 167-69.

lon[140] and all the Country, Ormus, and all the parts of India. I went from Basora to Ormus downe the Gulf of Persia, in a certaine ship made of bordes, and sowed together with Cayro, which is threed made of the huske of Cocoes, and certaine Canes or straw leaves sowed upon the seames of the bordes which is the cause that they leake very much. And so having Persia always on the left hand, and the Coast of Arabia on the right hand wee passed many Ilands, and among others, the famous Iland Baharim[141], from whence come the best Pearles which be round and Orient.

Ormus is an Iland in circuit about five and twentie or thirtie miles, and is the driest Iland in the world: for there is nothing growing in it but onely Salt; for their water, wood, or victuals, and all things necessary come out of Persia, which is about twelve miles from thence. All thereabout be very fruitfull, from whence all kind of victuals are sent unto Ormus. The Portugals have a Castle here which standeth neere unto the sea, wherein there is a Captaine for the King of Portugall, having under him a convenient number of Souldiers, whereof some part remaine in the Castle, and some in the Towne. In this Towne are Merchants of all Nations, and many Moores and Gentiles. Here is very great trade of all sorts of Spices, Drugs, Silke, cloth of Silke, fine Tapestrie of Persia, great store of Pearles which come from the Ile of Baharim, and are the best Pearles of all others, and many Horses of Persia which serve all India. They have a Moore to their King which is chosen and governed by the Portugals. ... Here very shortly after our arrival wee were put in Prison, and had part of our goods taken from us by the Captaine of the Castle, whose name was Don Mathias de Albuquerque; and from hence the eleventh of October[1583] hee shipped us and sent us for Goa uto the Vice-roy, which at that time was Don Francisco de Mascarenhas. The ship wherein wee were imbarked for Goa belonged to the Captaine, and carried one hundred twentie and foure Horses in it. All Merchandize carried to Goa in a ship wherein are Horses, pay no Custome in Goa. The Horses pay custome, the goods pay nothing; but if you come in a ship which bringeth no Horses, you are then to

---

[140] This name was in Fitch's time applied by Europeans to Baghdad.
[141] Bahrain.

pay eight in the hundred for your goods. The first Citie of India that wee arrived at upon the fifth of November, after wee had passed the Coast of Zindi[142], is called Diu, which standeth in an Iland in the Kingdome of Cambaia, and is the strongest Towne that the Portugals have in those parts. It is but little, but well stored with Merchandize; for here they lade many great ships with divers commodities for the straights of Mecca, for Ormus, and other places, and these bee ships of the Moores and of Christians. But the Moores cannot passe, except they have a Pasport from the Portugals...."

The Portuguese derived great profit from the customs levied on the trade passing through Hormuz, but the benefits did not stop there. The system of *cartazes* or passes issued upon payment of onerous sums which they imposed upon all native shipping, only imperfectly enforceable over the expanse of the Indian Ocean, could be applied more successfully in the Persian Gulf.[143]

It was only a matter of time before other European powers, especially the English and Dutch, would make their appearance in the Persian Gulf. When they did, the effects were, predictably, momentous. The English entered the arena in a manner that was dramatic and historic: with assistance to the Persians in the expulsion of the Portuguese from Hormuz and its recovery by Persia.[144]

Iran was at that time ruled by Shah Abbas the Great (1587-1629), who had resolved to develop a relationship with Europe that would benefit his country economically and make it stronger militarily. It was at first a slow process during the Shah's long reign, but by the second decade of the 17th century the circumstances had become more propitious and converged toward the

---

[142] Sind.

[143] One of the functions of the fort at Hormuz was alerting, by firing cannon, Portuguese patrol ships to any passing ship that refused to stop and pay the required fee; the recalcitrant merchantman would be given chase and forced to pay. See Ahmad Iqtidari, *Khalij-e Farsi*, Tehran 1966, p. 120.

[144] Laurence Lockhart, "European contacts with Persia, 1350-1736," *CHIr* 6: 373-409; Ronald Ferrier, "Trade from the mid-14th century to the end of the Safavid period," *ibid.*, 6: 412-90.

feasibility of the Shah's projects. The East India Company had been established at the Indian port of Surat, and its merchants wished to extend their commercial activities also toward Iran and the Persian Gulf. For the first time since their appearance in the Indian Ocean, the Portuguese encountered a rival whose naval strength matched theirs and gradually began to surpass it. Meanwhile Englishmen, as we have seen, had been reconnoitering the area, and soon two of them not only met the Shah but even became his trusted advisers and representatives abroad. They were the Sherley brothers, Anthony (1565-1630) and Robert (1571?-after 1627).[145] Their professed goal was an alliance with the Shah against the Turks, and establishment of commercial relations. The wishes were mutual. The wish of Safavid monarchs to ally themselves with the Europeans against the Ottoman Empire, as we have seen, had existed since Shah Ismail, and under Shah Abbas it became even stronger and was augmented by what would become a perennial desire of Oriental monarchs, the modernization of their military strength along European models and with Europe's help. Thus when in 1600 the two Sherley brothers arrived at Qazvin with a party of twenty-six men and presented themselves to Shah Abbas as English knights who had heard of the fame of the Persian monarch and desired the honor of entering his service, they found a friendly reception. The Shah employed the Sherleys in two ways: modernizing his troops, and sending them on missions to Europe. According to Anthony Sherley's own account,

> "The mightie Ottoman, terror of the Christian World, quaketh of a Sherly-Fever, & gives hopes of approaching fates: the prevailing Persian hath learned Sherleian Arts of War, and he which before knew not the use of Ordnance, hath now 500. Peeces of Brasse, & 60000 Musketiers; so that they which at hand with the Sword were before dreadfull to the Turkes, now also in remoter blowes and

---

[145] For the remarkable Sherley family, see Evelyn Philip Sherley (1812-82), *The Sherley brothers: an historical memoir of the lives of Sir Thomas Sherley, Sir Anthony Sherley, and Sir Robert Sherley, knights; by one of the same house*, Chiswick: Press of C. Whittingham, 1848; and David William Davies, *Elizabethans errant: the strange fortunes of Sir Thomas Sherley and his three sons...* Ithaca: Cornell University Press, 1967.

sulfurian Arts are growne terrible. Hence hath the present
Abas won from the Turke seven great Provinces, from
Derbent to Bagdat inclusively..." [146]

It was mainly Robert Sherley who spent prolonged periods in
Persia, at one point as Master-General of the Persian army. In
1609 Shah Abbas sent him, like his brother a few years earlier,
to Europe, and with a similar mission: to establish and confirm
relations of friendship between Persia and the West, and to announce his intention of destroying the Turks and bringing the
Persian frontiers in contact with those of Christendom. Robert
Sherley visited several countries in this capacity, and in 1611
came to England where he delivered letters from the Shah pro-
fessing "the Persian's great love and affection unto his Majesty,
with hearty desire of amity with the King of Great Britain, with
frank offer of free commerce unto all His Highness's subjects
through all the Persian dominions..."[147] He was knighted, and
returned to Persia in 1613 where he again served the Shah.

The activities and testimonies of the Sherley brothers are significant and revealing in several respects. On the military level,
they and their companions strengthened the Persian army, especially its artillery, which would then play a role in the reconquest
of Hormuz. On the religious level, the missions entrusted to them
by Shah Abbas confirm the deep chasm separating Iran's Shia
Islam from Turkey's Sunni Islam (although it may also tell us
something about the Shah's latent secularism and desire to catch
up with Europe, not unlike Kemal Atatürk's in 20th-century Turkey). On the economic level, these missions reveal the Persians'
desire to increase trade with Europe and their awareness that the
newcomers, especially England, would become better and
stronger partners than the Portuguese. They are also suggestive
of the fact that the Persians would have preferred to deflect their
commerce with the West from the frequently war-ravaged route
through Ottoman territories, and this of course meant chiefly
maritime routes, which in turn meant further enhancement of the
importance of the Persian Gulf and the Gulf of Oman.

---

[146] Purchas, *op. cit.,* p. 376.
[147] Wilson, *Persian Gulf,* p. 132. The author does not cite here the location of these letters, and his quotation contains an anachronism:
"Great Britain" came into being only a century later.

Most of these projects gradually came to fruition. Although the Sherleys, especially Robert, had made an important contribution, the catalytic factor to emerge on the Europeans' side was not an individual but the above-mentioned East India Company with the British government in the background. From 1600 onwards it had been sending 'trading fleets' to India. In 1608 one of these ships arrived at Surat; its captain, William Hawkins, was the bearer of a letter of recommendation from King James to the Great Mughal Emperor Jahangir. Four years later Thomas Best, arriving with three ships, obtained a trading agreement from the local authorities at the same port, which was then confirmed by a *firman* (imperial order) from Jahangir. As a result, a trading factory was set up at Surat. The process culminated in the establishment of a permanent accredited ambassador at the Court of the Great Mughal in 1615. Sir Thomas Roe was the first incumbent.

In the same year Richard Steele and John Crowther, factors of the Company, were sent from Surat to Isfahan to procure information about the possibilities of trade. The Factory furnished them with letters of recommendation to Sir Robert Sherley, and instructed them to visit the harbors of the Gulf to see which were best suited to receive the Company's ships. The mission was a success. In 1616, Shah Abbas issued a firman by the terms of which his subjects were enjoined 'to kindly receive and entertain the English Frankes or Nation who might present themselves.'[148]

The two factors examined several ports, Bahrain among them, but chose Jask, because it was 'a little within entrance of the Gulf of Persia...and not so much in danger of the Portuguese as Bareen [Bahrain]'. The time was right, and Jask proved to be the right choice. War between Persia and Turkey blocked the overland routes, and in consequence there was an abundance of silk – one of the most valuable Persian exports – and a dearth of cloth – one of the most profitable English imports – in Persia. There was a surplus of goods at Surat, and new markets had to be found. Things moved fast. That same year (1616) the first English ship, the *James*, left for Jask and arrived there in December after 27 days' sail. The goods were landed in January 1617, and this shipment marked the beginning of the British

---

[148] Wilson, *The Persian Gulf*, p. 136.

maritime and trading activity in the Persian Gulf and in Iran itself. Edward Connock, who directed the venture in Jask, proceeded to Shiraz and Isfahan, where he established factories. Shah Abbas issued a firman granting highly satisfactory privileges to the English, which included the perpetual residence of an English ambassador at the Persian court, and the right of buying and selling freely in the Persian dominions. In 1618 Thomas Barker succeeded Edward Connock as the Company's agent in Persia, and obtained from the Shah an agreement that all silk leaving Persia should be sold to the English and none should be sent to Europe by way of Turkey or be disposed of to the Spanish or the Portuguese.

The successful entry of the English into the Persian Gulf and their trade agreements with Iran contrasts with the initial Portuguese entry, which was not accompanied by any attempt to create a cooperative relationship with a major regional state. In the course of the 17th century, the increasingly laborious maintenance of Portuguese presence would turn into an irreversible retreat. Initially Shah Abbas seemed willing to deal with the King of Spain Philip III (1598-1621) – then also King of Portugal – on a correct business basis, especially with respect to the export of Persian silk. The Iberians, however, lacked the practical commercial methods and the diplomatic tact that worked to the benefit of the English. Too often, it seems, the King of Spain sent ecclesiastics as his representatives, which elicited a remark the Shah made in a letter to him that 'he was weary of receiving Friars as Ambassadors,' and asked him to send him some 'Spanish Gentleman of Note'…' Philip obliged but, alas, the lay envoy was a downright disaster. Don Garcia de Silva Figueroa arrived in Hormuz in 1617, and in 1618-19 was received by the Shah at Qazvin and Isfahan. During the final audience Figueroa presented letters demanding restitution of Gombroon and other territories lately conquered by the Persians, which were claimed by the Portuguese on behalf of their vassal (in fact puppet) the king of Hormuz; moreover, these letters also included a demand that the English and all other Europeans be excluded from the Persian trade. Shah Abbas tore up the letters and swore that he would drive the Portuguese from their fortress at Hormuz, and ordered a firman to be made out granting the sole trade in silks by the sea route to the English.[149]

As we have remarked, the 16th century had been a Portuguese century in the Persian Gulf. In 1600 they still possessed the key points of Hormuz, Qishm, Masqat, and Bahrain, and were present in Basra. The first retreat was their loss of Bahrain to Shah Abbas in 1602.[150] By the middle of the 17th century, they had lost most of their possessions in the two gulfs. Internal weakening of Portuguese power was no doubt one of the causes of this collapse, but equally important may have been the rapid growth of stronger rivals – the East India Company, Iran under Shah Abbas, and the new Yarubi dynasty in Oman. By far the most severe blow, however, would be the loss of Hormuz to Iran in 1622.

A harbinger of this calamity was the Portuguese loss of Gombroon in 1615. Shah Abbas had built a fortification at Shilu, originally a small coastal village to the northwest of Hormuz, a few years before, and it began to function as a port known to the Europeans as Gombroon. In 1612 the Portuguese made a descent on it and wrested it from the Persians. Three years later, however, the Shah's troops, now better equipped with artillery, invested Gombroon and took it after a lengthy siege. Recovery of Hormuz was the principal goal, and its achievement was only a matter of time and adequate preparations. However, there was a problem: Hormuz was an island, and Persia had no war fleet capable of confronting the Portuguese. It was the East India Company that provided the indispensable naval support.

Initially it had not been the intent of the English to engage in any such enterprise. England and Spain-Portugal were not at war with one another, and the Company wanted to trade, not to make war. But trade also meant competition, and when the protago-

---

[149]*Ibid.*, p. 140.

[150] The Persian force in the conquest of Bahrain was under the command of Imam Quli Big, who then sent valuable trophies to Shah Abbas. The monarch rewarded him with the title of *khan* and soon afterwards with the governorship of Laristan. This was the beginning of the brilliant career of Imam Quli Khan, the main architect of the reconquest of Hormuz twenty years later. See Ahmad Iqtidari, *Khalij-e Farsi*, Tehran 1966, pp. 125-26.

nists were Europeans in their armed merchantmen vying for the best or even exclusive deals, conflict was unavoidable. This was especially the case with the Portuguese, whose approach was less commercial and more predatory than that of the English: conquest of commercially lucrative sites (such as Hormuz and several other points in the Persian Gulf, in contrast to the English and Dutch who only exceptionally and briefly resorted to such a practice), imposition of onerous customs duties in the ports under their control, hamstringing those that were not, and the practice of *cartazes* were, besides trade, their methods of enrichment. They had worked – up to a point, as we have seen, for over a century – as long as native shipping and ports had been their chief victims; now with the English and Dutch entering the game, the naval superiority that had enabled the Portuguese to apply these methods disappeared and with it, eventually, the Portuguese seaborne empire.

In 1602, as we have seen, the Portuguese had lost Bahrain; in 1615 they lost Gombroon, and in 1620 Julfar[151], all three to Persian forces sent by Shah Abbas. Nevertheless, they still possessed Hormuz and Masqat and had a strong presence in Basra. Their use of these three sites was of crucial importance and meant that shipping in the Persian Gulf remained under Portuguese control. Understandably, they viewed with apprehension the appearance of two English vessels approaching the port of Jask on the Persian coast of the Gulf of Oman in 1620, and a Portuguese squadron prevented them from entering it. The ships sailed back to Surat but returned, reinforced with two more units, and after a skirmish with the enemy managed to enter the harbor; the Portuguese squadron retreated to Hormuz to refit and reappeared in greater strength off Jask; another battle was fought in which the English prevailed. The Company's ships then loaded a cargo that included 520 bales of silk for transmission to England, and returned to Surat.

---

[151] The reader may have noticed a seeming contradiction here. We have mentioned the lack of Persian naval power as an obstacle to conquering Hormuz, an island, before the English provided that force. The conquest of Bahrain and Julfar, both on the opposite side of the Gulf, of course also could be done only through an amphibious operation. The answer is that these two sites were less vital to the Portuguese, who did not bother to mount a naval defense of them.

With the success of this commercial as well as naval expedition, which happened at the end of 1620, the Company made plans to send a larger fleet. It coincided with a request by the Persians for naval help in their effort to expel the Portuguese from Hormuz, accompanied by a warning that in case of refusal the shah would withhold from the English their commercial privileges such as exportation of silk.[152] This put the EIC in the aforementioned quandary: England was not at war with Portugal,[153] and compliance with the request would be a violation of international law besides causing trouble for the Company's directors at home. The fact that they ultimately acquiesced in the shah's demand shows how much they valued trade with Iran.[154]

Meanwhile the Portuguese had their war fleet under Ruy Freire made ready to defend the island possession. The Shah then sent a message to the English, whose fleet of nine units had arrived in Jask, requesting them to join him in the planned assault on Qishm and Hormuz. Despite the misgivings of some members of the Company at the Surat Factory, the invitation was accepted, and a formal agreement was drawn up and signed. On 19 January 1622 an English squadron sailed from Jask and on the 22nd anchored off Hormuz. They were faced by a Portuguese fleet consisting of five galleons and a number of frigates which rode under the shelter of the castle. The English had hoped that the enemy ships would come out and give battle, but they did not, so the fleet passed on to Qishm and anchored off the Portuguese fort, which was under the command of Ruy Freire. The garrison was already besieged by the Persians on the landward side; now also attacked by the English who landed five guns and constructed a battery, it surrendered. Don Freire and his chief subordinates were taken prisoner, and dispatched to Surat. A Persian garrison was installed in the Qishm fort, and the fleet moved to Gombroon to prepare for the siege of Hormuz itself.

On 9 February 1622 the English squadron, accompanied by 200 Persian boats, sailed from Gombroon and anchored off

[152]Iqtidari, *Khalij-e Farsi*, p. 128.

[153] Or rather Spain and Portugal; this was the period of the union of the two crowns, 1580-1640.

[154] For the Persian conquest of Hormuz and English participation, see Wilson, *The Persian Gulf*, pp. 144-49; and a slightly different and quite detailed account in Iqtidari, *Khalij-e Farsi*, pp. 125-34.

Hormuz City. On the 10th, a large force of Persian soldiers under Imam Quli Khan was landed, took possession of the island, and drove the Portuguese into the Castle, which stood in a strong position on a spit of land projecting northward into the sea. On 24 February the large galleon *San Pedro* was set ablaze by a fire-boat. An assault by Persian soldiers was repulsed, but the siege took its toll on the Portuguese; on 23 April they surrendered to the English, who had guaranteed the safety of their lives and promised to send them to Masqat or Goa, thus to Portuguese bases. The success at Hormuz prompted Imam Quli Khan to propose a follow-up with a conquest of Masqat, but the request was turned down. The English fleet left and on 1 September 1622 arrived at Surat.

The conquest of Hormuz by Shah Abbas was a milestone in the history of the Persian Gulf, but the immediate degree and nature of its impact is less clear-cut. A contemporary observer might have expected or predicted consequences some of which took place while others did not. One was the collapse of Portuguese dominance in the two gulfs, which was consummated within a generation; another was its replacement by English dominance, which occurred but gradually, to be consummated by 1820, and in a form different from that of their predecessors; yet another consequence that might have been expected was the creation and growth of Persian naval power and its assertion throughout the Gulf. That, however, did not take place.

We have seen that the Persians wished to follow up their conquest of Hormuz by taking Masqat, which was a logical and highly sensible idea. Historically both sides of the two gulfs were intimately linked, and controlling Masqat and with it the coast of Oman would have given the Persians a chance to do what the Portuguese had been doing, only better and more justifiably than they, since those were the Persians' home waters. More than that, Persia was ideally positioned to grow as a seaborne empire bent on gaining a dominant position throughout the Indian Ocean.

For that, however, Persia would have had to develop a strong navy and conceive a forward mercantile policy comparable to that of the Western powers. Neither happened, for reasons akin to those we have been mentioning since the early pages of our book. The Shahs kept welcoming foreign ships and merchants into their ports, and Persian and Arab shippers and merchants continued to sail and trade; but the state itself did not attempt to participate or undertake a maritime commercial expansion overseas.[155] To build or acquire a navy would admittedly have been, at least initially, difficult, but not impossible. Timber could have been imported from India, or the ships themselves could have been purchased there.

The Persian conquest of Hormuz also meant the end of the island city and port as the great emporium of the Persian Gulf. That role was now assumed by the above-mentioned port known to the Europeans as Gombroon but which the conquering Shah Abbas renamed after himself as Bandar Abbas or Bandar Abbasi. It grew quickly and soon began to receive praise as a great emporium similar to that until then lavished on Hormuz. Its clientele was both native shippers and Europeans, no longer Portuguese but mainly English and Dutch. Unlike their predecessors, however, they did not install themselves as conquerors and masters but as guests, always endeavoring to receive favorable trading and customs conditions from the Persians. The East India Company established a factory at Bandar Abbas as early as 1623, and received considerable privileges from the grateful Shah. The Dutch almost immediately made their appearance as well and established their factory, and intense competition arose between them and the English that would abate only at the end of the century. By the 1640s the Dutch were winning.[156] They came with more ships and richer cargoes, much of it pepper and spices from the Spice Islands (Moluccas), where they had established their dominance. In exchange, they obtained a license to purchase silk in any part of Persia they might please, and to export it free of customs duties. On the other hand, they failed to drive out the English, who in fact after the fall of Hormuz remained, at least on paper, the most favored nation. Remarkably, their agents succeeded in maintaining a footing at Bandar Abbas and in real-

---

[155] Except for the brief efforts of Nadir Shah to make Iran a naval power; see below, p. 133.

[156] For a special episode in this context, see Willem Floor and Mohammad H. Faghfoory, *The First Dutch-Persian Commercial Conflict: The Attack on Qeshm Island, 1645,* Costa Mesa: Mazda Publishers, 2004.

izing their moiety of the customs, granted by Shah Abbas, despite the ascendancy of the Dutch.

In 1639-40 the East India Company sent a ship to Basra with the object of exploring the possibility of trade there. Basra, as we have seen, was with Hormuz and then Bandar Abbas the leading port in the Persian Gulf, and the desire of the English to gain a footing there was more than just a matter of finding alternatives to Bandar Abbas or other places. The fact that Basra had in 1546 become part of the Ottoman Empire made little difference with respect to its function as the indispensable maritime and caravan center at the head of the Gulf, especially for trade heading toward Aleppo and the Mediterranean ports. The Turks did not develop it as a major naval base, which they could and would have done had they been bent on overseas expansion,[157] and the Ottoman government's hold on it often was tenuous. But this did not prevent the port city from continuing to function as a major commercial port and caravan terminal. When the English agents of the East India Company made their first appearance there, the license they received to land their goods did not come from an Ottoman official but from Ali Pasha, the second ruler of the virtually independent dynasty Al Afrasiyab (1612-1668). In 1643 the English returned and established their first factory in Basra. Two years later, they sent the Company's property at Bandar Abbas to Basra, possibly because they considered it more secure from Dutch hostilities. Rivalry between the Dutch and the English here partly reflected major events in Europe, which included two wars between England and Holland (1652-54 and 1665-67). The two countries had become the foremost naval powers of their time, and their fleets fought several dramatic battles in the North Sea; only toward the end of the 17th century did the English begin to assert their superiority, and the confrontation was similar in the Persian Gulf. In a battle fought off Hormuz in 1654, five Dutch ships sank one English ship and captured another. The situation at Bandar Abbas and in the entire Gulf ap-

---

[157] By mid-17th century, Portuguese dominance in the Persian Gulf was broken. The entry of the English and Dutch was one obvious and well-known cause; Omani renaissance was the other. This meant that the question of who was the dominant power or even important participant in the Persian Gulf never involved the Ottoman Empire, and that even its impact on Basra itself remained minimal.

proached what may have appeared as Dutch dominance. Here is
what Jean de Thevenot, who wrote in 1663, says:

> "The English and Dutch have each of them their Houses
> very well built by the Sea-side, with the Flag of their sev-
> eral Nations upon a high Pole on their Terrasses. The
> Dutch are absolute Masters at Bender. They have so great
> Credit there, that some days before, the Scheich Bender
> having displeased the Dutch Commander, this Com-
> mander caused the Dutch Flag to be torn down, and made
> the Scheich humbly beseech him, nay and give presents
> too, to put up another. I stayed but a week at Bender
> Abassi, and then was obliged to turn back again, there
> being no probability that I could embark there for the In-
> dies, seeing I must have run too great a danger if I stayed
> longer for a favourable occasion. There were but six ves-
> sels there, which were bound for the Indies, four Dutch
> ships, one Armenian, and a Moor: as for the Dutch there
> was no thinking to go with them, for they have taken Oath
> to Transport no Franck thither, and that by express Com-
> mand from the Company; because (they say) the Francks
> discoursing with the Sea-men, inform themselves com-
> monly of what concerns the Trade, and they are willing
> that that should be a hidden mystery, unknown to any but
> themselves."[158]

Jean Chardin (1643-1713), who visited Bandar Abbas in
1674, mentions the high standing of the Dutch at the Persian
court:

> "It is a strange thing how prejudiced Orientals are in fa-
> vour of the Dutch. The Persians and Indians, basing their
> reasoning on the matter of their commerce, which they
> see ever flourishing, while that of other nations only
> crawls along, so to speak, believe them to be the Kings of
> Europe. Thus remarked the Governor of Bandar to the
> Chief of the Frenchy Company: "You say that your king
> has captured the Country of the Dutch; nevertheless, here

---

[158] *The Travels of Monsieur de Thévenot into the Levant (1687)*, pt. ii,
p. 137 ff., cited by Wilson, *The Persian Gulf*, p. 166.

come seven of their ships, whereas to you and to the English not one arrives."[159]

An Englishman, Dr. J. Fryer, who visited Bandar Abbas in 1677, also testifies to the superiority of the Dutch position over that of the English:

"This Port receives most ships going or coming from Busserah, as they find the Markets answer their designs: But the greatest Traffick, next Indian Cloth, comes from the Spice Trade; which the Dutch engross, beside Sugar and Copper formerly; from which they carry off Fifty thousand Thomands worth of Velvets, Silk, Raw and Wrought, with Rich Carpets, besides many Tunn of Gold and Silver, Yearly; so Great and Absolute is their trade from the Muluccoes, and South Sea, hither, that they are reported to have brought Six Ships laden with Spice, which the cunning Merchants thought to make advantage of; but the Hollanders, being Crafts-Masters, sent for the Cargo on shoar of Two Ships, and piled it up before the Factory Gate, where they not coming to their Price, immediately, set Fire thereto, and consumed it all; which the Buyers neglecting, or laughing at, they caused other Two to be served in the same manner, knowing so great a quantity had caused a Glut, when they asked the same rate for the remaining Two;... whereby the Persians were Taught, that their Extravagance was not Madness, but Policy, they being obliged to Bid Higher for fewer Commodities; the Hollanders being well assured none could furnish them with others than was brought by them.... The English Company's Trade is but small here, only carrying off some few Drugs, Carmania Wool, Goats, Dates and Horses; though they make it worth their while to keep their Agent in good Port, as well from the Allowance from the Sahbunder as by Consulage of 2£ and ½ percent for all Foreign Goods, that seek their Protection."[160]

---

[159] *Voyage du Chevalier Chardin en Perse et autres lieux de l'Orient.* Nouvelle edition par L. Langlès. 10 vols. 1811, quoted by Wilson, *The Persian Gulf,* p. 167.

[160] Wilson, *The Persian Gulf,* pp. 166-67, quoting John Fryer, d. 1733. *A New Account of East-India and Persia, in Eight Letters. Being Nine Years' Travels, begun 1672, finished 1681.* 1698. Hakluyt Society, 1909-15. 3 vols.

The success of the Dutch may be attributed to their possession of the richest source of spices – the aforementioned Moluccas, known then as the Spice Islands but now subsumed under the present-day Indonesian archipelago – and to the fact that their Dutch East India Company, the VOC, was at the time more united, better organized, and unstintingly backed by their government. These advantages enabled the VOC to drive their European rivals from Indonesia and convert an extensive area under its control into a colony, the first European power to do so. In other words, the VOC not only acted as a commercial company but also assumed the political role of an extension of the Dutch government, and its ships acted likewise for the Dutch Navy. The English East India Company would move in the same direction with respect to India, but that evolution bore fruit only in the 18th century.

The Dutch presence and success in the Persian Gulf in the 17th century may thus have appeared considerable, especially when compared with the travails of the English, the collapse of the Portuguese, and the virtual absence of the French. The seeds of the ultimate English victory had been sown, however. Perhaps the catalytic factor was geo-strategic and geo-economic. The Dutch may have possessed the richest colony at the time, but Indonesia was remote; commercial contacts with it did exist, as we have seen, but the greatest part of maritime traffic in the Persian Gulf since antiquity had been with India and Sri Lanka, Arabia, and East Africa.

Much of what would later happen in the Persian Gulf was thus being decided on the northwestern coast of India during the 17th century. The first step was the establishment of a factory at Surat in the course of the century's second decade; the second was the move of one part of the East India Company's headquarters to Bombay in 1687. Although the creation of the Raj, British India, did not occur until the 18th century and would proceed initially from the Company's colony in Bengal with its headquarters at Calcutta, the Bombay Presidency – with London as the ultimate authority in the background – would always be the place where Anglo-Indian policy toward the Persian Gulf would be planned and directed.

The discussion of the Portuguese, English, and Dutch fortunes in the Persian Gulf should not make us forget that much of what went on there was an affair of native mariners and merchants, and thus remained less well documented in European sources. One of the reasons was the fact that on the official, governmental level, the two main non-European powers – Iran and the Ottoman Empire – kept out of the race. The first case of active participation of a major state was, as we have pointed out, Oman after the rise of the Yarubid dynasty; in fact, Oman remained the only such case. Masqat, although not the sole Omani port, came to symbolize the Omani seaborne empire.

Trade, and thus the life and functioning of ports, were always to a considerable degree affected by a number of factors, especially the safety of the shipping lanes and the situation in the regions and countries they served. Pirates, wars, the plagues came in turns or combined to place the English, Dutch and French commercial presence in the Persian Gulf on a kind of roller-coaster, and necessitated frequent reexamination and change of the policies to pursue and ports from which to operate. Bandar Abbas, as we have seen, functioned for almost a century as the site of the English and Dutch factories and their shipping; the most typical articles of import were English and Dutch woolens, and those of export were Persian silk and "Carmanian wool", an especially prized goat's hair from the province of Kirman that came in black, white, and red colors and was used for making shawls in England. With the advent of the 18th century, however, problems appeared. The Safavid dynasty lost its earlier vigor, and invasions from Afghanistan plunged the country into a turmoil that affected its economic strength, trade with foreign countries, and the safety of its ports. Eventually the Afghans were driven out, but the decline and fall of the Safavids ushered in a period of insecurity and uncertainty that would end only with the rise of the Qajar dynasty at the end of the 18th century. Thus in 1721 a segment of the invaders – a force of 4,000 Baluchi horse – attacked Bandar Abbas, where the East India Company's factory was defended by some 50 British seamen and Company servants. The defense of the factory – as well as that of the Dutch factory – succeeded, but a warehouse was plundered and the town sacked. Although the factories were saved, the sack of the town and the devastation of the hinterland province of Kirman set in motion an inexorable decline of Bandar Abbas and its eclipse by other places as sites of European factories.[161] Thus E. Ives, a British surgeon who visited Bandar Abbas in 1758, found it almost in ruins:[162]

> "At present it is a place of no kind of importance, except what it receives from the English and Dutch factories. The two factory houses are the only buildings remaining of any importance; the whole city besides is almost one entire scene of ruins, which...once flourishing...but wars and anarchy...have deprived the English of almost all their commercial advantages..."

Just one year after Ives's visit, in 1759 a French squadron of four ships under the command of Count d'Estaing attacked Bandar Abbas, which was defended by sixteen Company seamen and a detachment of Sepoys, all commanded by the Company's chief Agent, Alexander Douglas. The French left after burning the Factory and a ship. This action, taken in the context of the Seven Years War then raging in Europe (1756-1763), was one of the rare instances of notable French presence in the Persian Gulf. The *Compagnie des Indes Orientales,* founded in 1664, never approached the English and Dutch Companies in importance, and was dissolved in 1769.

The fact that the British and Dutch factories were still there is both surprising and suggestive of the intrinsic value of trade with Persia, despite such adverse circumstances. But a more suitable place was now sought by the East India Company, and the East India Company agent Douglas, after examining several possibilities, wrote in 1762 a report recommending Bushire. Before discussing the installation of the British in this port, however, it may be useful to glance some two decades back at events in Iran relevant to our story.

In 1736 Nadir, originally a tribal chieftain from Khurasan, shoved aside one of the last Safavids, Tahmasp II, whom he had served for several years in the struggle against the Afghans, and

---

[161] Bandar Abbas rose again in the 19th century, and today is the premier port of Iran, for which see below.
[162] Wilson, *The Persian Gulf*, pp. 176-77, quoting Edward Ives, d. 1786. *A Voyage from England to India, in the year MDCCLIV. ...* London 1773.

formalized his *de facto* rule by proclaiming himself Shah.[163] He then ruled Iran until his assassination in 1747. Like most Iranian monarchs, Nadir Shah wanted his country to be militarily strong, but unlike them, he included in this ambition a determination to turn Iran also into a naval power. Nadir Shah had to start from scratch: Persia had no navy, no naval base, and little know-how in this area. True, the Arabs and Persians on both sides of the Gulf were heirs to a millennia-old seafaring and boatbuilding tradition; and the shaykhs ruling most of the Iranian coastal points usually possessed ships and even fleets that could perform various functions, naval among them; but the navy Nadir Shah wanted was something different, close to what the great naval powers of Europe had. The first thing he knew he needed was a naval base, and his choice fell on Bushire. It was a small fishing village situated at the northern end of a low-lying peninsula, parallel to the mainland coast. Here in 1734 Nadir Shah established the base for his projected Persian Gulf fleet, and he renamed it Bandar-e Nadiriyah, or Nadir Port. He then proceeded to put together a war fleet – a laborious, expensive, and pathetic effort that lasted thirteen years. Nadir Shah himself was neither a seaman nor did he have time to spare on the coast or at sea, swamped as he was on the mainland with military campaigns east and west. But he had made his choice for a naval base, and now he also needed ships (and, of course, experienced mariners to sail them). In May 1734 he sent Latif Khan, one of his commanders, to Bandar Abbas as "Admiral of the Gulf", with the purpose of buying two ships from the English and the Dutch. They refused but suggested that the Persians place orders for new ships to be built at Surat, a port with a long shipbuilding tradition. This the Persians did, and eventually their war fleet was some 30 units strong. Historians have commended Nadir Shah for his vision unprecedented among Persian monarchs, in recognizing that Iran should and could become a naval power. His early death prevented him from carrying out the ultimate projects he may have conceived of, and they died with him; their main legacy was the growth of Bushire as the principal port of Iran until, in the 20th century, that distinction returned to Bandar Abbas. Another legacy was the selection of Bushire by the Brit-

---

[163] Peter Avery, "Nadir Shah and the Afsharid legacy," *CHIr* 7: 3-62; Laurence Lockhart, *Nadir Shah*, London 1938.

ish as the new site for their factory. That process started in March 1763 when the East India Company left the old factory at Bandar Abbas, and an agreement was entered into with Shaykh Sadun of Bushire for the establishment of a factory and trade there; it was then confirmed by a *firman* from Kerim Khan, the ruler of Iran (1751-1779), and a British factory was established in 1765. Britain's privileged position would grow with time until in the 19th century Great Britain's Political Resident in Bushire became a special kind of supervisor of the Persian Gulf. Meanwhile Bandar Abbas went into a decline, and was eclipsed by Bushire until reclaiming primacy in the 20th century.

For over half a century, however – roughly between the establishment of their residency at Bushire in 1765 and the conclusion of the General Treaty of Peace on 8 January 1820 with the Arab shaykhdoms on the Arabian coast of the Persian Gulf – the British still had to struggle through a number of vicissitudes in various parts of the area. The events of this period were unprecedented, and they gave rise to a state of affairs that would last until World War I, and in some respects till our own day.

A special constant was the lasting importance of Basra, where, as we have seen, the East India Company had had an intermittent presence since 1640. In 1764, its factory was recognized by the Turkish government as a consulate, and, being in Ottoman territory, it could function as a kind of alternative base for the British if they had difficulties with the Persian authorities. For their part, the only real rivals of Britain, the Dutch, had between 1753 and 1766 withdrawn from Basra, Bushire, Bandar Abbas and the island of Kharg, and by doing so had ended their effective presence in the area. With the Dutch gone, and the French, though not always absent, never strong enough to pose a serious challenge, the British became in the final decades of the 18th century the sole European power to play a role in the Persian Gulf. This role would continue to increase during the 19th century to the point where one might have considered this body of water a British lake.

The main reason for Britain's determination to extend her control over the Persian Gulf – and to some degree, we might add, the Gulf of Oman and even the Arabian Sea – was her possession of India. First of all, trade between the Gulf and India had existed since Sumerian times, as we have seen, and it was vigorous in the days of the Raj. Once in possession of the sub-continent, Britain both drew benefits from this trade and felt responsible for the safety of Indian merchants trading in the ports and cities of the two gulfs. Another factor, and in the long run perhaps the most important one, was that the Persian Gulf lay on the line of overland communication between India and Britain.[164] It thus became an area of vital interest to the colonial power, and Britain was determined to maintain it as her preserve both with respect to possible European rivals – who, in the course of time, would be French, German, and Russian – and local powers, chiefly Persian, Turkish, and Arabian.

With respect to local powers, a characteristic feature was that they never had sufficient naval strength to challenge Britain at sea in a full-fledged confrontation – with one dramatic, though again only partial, brief, and parasitical exception: the Arab pirates of Ras al-Khaimah. Piracy had never disappeared from the Indian Ocean and its gulf extensions, and it was something seaborne trade had learned to live with. As long as the buccaneers refrained from attacking the East India Company's shipping and that of Indian maritime commerce, the British were unwilling to take any action against them.

---

[164] Overland of course between Basra and the Syrian ports of the Mediterranean. The alternative all-maritime Cape route nevertheless held primacy, but it in turn was replaced by the Red Sea – Mediterranean route after the building of the Suez canal in 1869. At about the same time, however, the Persian Gulf regained crucial importance as the conduit of telegraph lines linking India with Great Britain.

Chapter 12

Establishment of *Pax Britannica* in the Persian Gulf[165]

The Arabs of Ras al-Khaimah were – and still are – ruled by a family of chieftains known as the Qawasim, which is the plural of Qasimi, derived from the name of their eponym, Qasim, who lived at the end of the 17th century.[166] The tribe the Qawasim pertained to, the Huwala, had in the past migrated across the Gulf to the Persian side, as a number of other Arabs had done in the course of history. Some of the Qawasim moved back to the Arab side and settled in the coastal region. Ras al-Khaimah, a place strategically located on a spit of land with a *khawr* or inlet that could function as a harbor, was their headquarters. The sea was their main source of livelihood, a feature that was characteristic of virtually all the riparian inhabitants of the Persian Gulf and Gulf of Oman: fishing, trade, pearling, boat-building, and piracy were in varying degrees their leading

---

[165] This chapter is based chiefly on Lorimer, 2: 658-77; John Barrett Kelly, *Britain and the Persian Gulf, 1795-1880*, Oxford: Clarendon Press, 1968 (henceforth cited as Kelly (1968), pp. 139-92; Charles Edward Davies, *The Red-Blood Arab Flag: an Investigation into Qasimi Piracy 1797-1820*, Exeter: University of Exeter Press, 1997, pp. 210-215 and passim; idem, "Britain, trade and piracy: the British expeditions against Ras al-Khaima of 1809-10 and 1819-20," in *Global Interests in the Arab Gulf*, ed. Charles E. Davies, Exeter: University of Exeter Press 1992, pp. 29-66; and Patricia Risso, "Cross-Cultural Perceptions of Piracy: Maritime Violence in the Western Indian Ocean and Persian Gulf Region during a Long Eighteenth Century," *Journal of World History* 12 (2001), 292-319.

[166] G. Rentz, "al-Kawasim," *EIs* 4: 777-78.

occupations; crops from the nearby date palm groves were an additional source of income. In 1719 the Portuguese, who still had a factory at Kung on the Persian coast, retaliated for Qasimi attacks on their shipping by driving Qasimi vessels into the harbor of Ras al-Khaimah and enslaving the prisoners they took. The first identifiable Qasimi ruler, Rashid b. Matar (possibly a grandson of Qasim), built a port at Basidu at the northwestern tip of the island of Qishm, which drew trade away from the East India Company's factory at Bandar Abbas; as a result, in 1727 the British agent forced the Qasimi ruler to make good the loss suffered by the East India Company. Trade, not piracy, thus was for a long time the major pursuit of Qasimi shipping, and it was only in the final decades of the 18th century that the predatory form became prominent. The shift may have been partly a result of a new religious current in Arabia that by 1792 had also reached the Persian Gulf coastlands: the militant Wahhabi sect and its political and military expression, the Saudi state. Some Qasimi Arabs converted to Wahhabism, and the hitherto peaceable traders and occasional freebooters turned into practitioners of that special kind of piracy that was at the same time a fierce maritime *jihad* or holy war. When Indian maritime trade and the Company's own ships began to be victims of the pirates of Ras al-Khaimah, the British decided to intervene. In three successive campaigns, Britain's Indian navy reinforced by units of the Royal Navy during the first two decades of the nineteenth century sailed from Bombay in order to curb the pirates. Only the third campaign, a major undertaking in 1819-1820, achieved the goal of satisfactory pacification of the turbulent area.

The campaign began on 3 November 1819 when the first division of the fleet sailed from Bombay, to be followed by the second a few days later. The total force comprised 1,453 Europeans and 2,094 sepoys. The transports were convoyed by the three largest units of the naval force assigned to the operation, including H.M.S. *Liverpool* (50 guns). Eight units were already in the Gulf, including H.M.S. *Eden* (26 guns). The expedition's commander, Sir William Grant Keir, was aboard the *Liverpool*. When the convoy reached the Gulf of Oman this ship broke away from the main body, which continued to the rendezvous at Qishm, and made for Masqat, to enable Keir to confer with Sayyid Said, the Sultan of Oman, who had promised to participate in the campaign. The encounter confirmed the alliance. Sayyid Said's assistance was useful not only for intrinsic reasons but also because of the strategic and logistical help it provided, for Bandar Abbas and Qishm were then under Omani control through a lease arrangement with the Persian government. When on 2nd December 1819 the British fleet hove to off Ras al-Khaimah, it was accompanied by two Omani frigates with Sayyid Said and 600 tribal levies on board. The town and its fort and towers were defended by some 4,000 men. The initial British landing was made on 3rd December at the base of the peninsula on which Ras al-Khaimah is located, and during the next few days artillery from the ships was brought ashore to pound the fort. The Qasimis fought bravely, but the cannon fire proved too much for them and when on 8 December the troops advanced to the assault they found the fort deserted. The next day Hasan ibn Rahmah, the Qasimi shaykh, came with his surviving fighting men to surrender. Besides Ras al-Khaimah, another Qasimi base had to be reduced: Rams, 12 kilometers further up the coast. It was the seat of Husain (or Hasan) ibn Ali, another notorious Qasimi chieftain who had several years previously acted as Wahhabi vice-regent over the Pirate Coast. Two of the Marine's cruisers had been blockading Rams during the siege of Ras al-Khaimah, and after its fall Keir sent troops there. When they arrived, they found the town empty, Husain ibn Ali having retreated with his men to Dayah some three kilometers inland in the hills. There was a strong fort at Dayah, and Keir felt obliged to summon reinforcements including artillery from the *Liverpool*. By 22 December the battery was in position to commence firing on the fort, and a breach was effected after a two-hour bombardment. As troops were about to advance to the assault, a white flag was run up over the fort, and Husain ibn Ali marched out with his fighting men. They were taken on board the warships and landed as prisoners at Ras al-Khaimah.

The fall of Ras al-Khaimah and Rams / Dayah signified the end of the naval and military operations, but the real challenge for the British was only beginning: devising a political settlement with the Arabs that would permanently suppress piracy and ensure undisturbed seaborne traffic in the Persian Gulf. The authority for that was invested in the Bombay Presidency, where lively debates on this matter were still going on as the expeditionary force was leaving with the fleet for the Persian Gulf in October 1819. The ultimate arbiter would have been Sir Evan Nepean, Governor of Bombay, but his instructions had not yet reached Keir while he was drawing up the treaty with the Arabs in January 1820. The British commander had thus no choice but to act on his own without delay, because weather conditions were soon going to worsen and endanger his fleet. According to most observers, this delay was fortunate. Nepean wanted to impose rather drastic conditions and penalties on the shaykhs, whereas Keir, while firm and resolute, was also guided by a profound humanitarian concern. By early January 1820 all the leading shaykhs of the Coast had arrived in Keir's camp to tender their submission and proffer friendship: Sultan ibn Saqr, the Qasimi Shaikh of Sharjah; Shakhbut ibn Dhiyab, father of Tahnun ibn Shakhbut, the Al Bu Falah shaykh of Abu Dhabi; Muhammad ibn Hazza, the nine-year-old shaykh of Dubai in company of his uncle; and the shaykhs of Ajman, Umm al-Qaiwain, and Jazirat al-Hamra.

Keir had meanwhile drawn up, in consultation with his staff, a draft treaty of peace[167] which came to be called 'General Treaty of Peace with the Arab Tribes', and all the shaykhs signed it between 8 and 28 January, the last one to do so being the uncle of the child shaykh of Dubai. Its opening words were:

> 'In the name of God, the merciful, the compassionate! Praise be to God, who hath ordained peace to be a blessing to his creatures. There is established a lasting peace between the British Government and the Arab tribes, who are parties to this contract, on the following conditions…:"

---

[167] C.U. Aitchison, comp., *A Collection of Treaties, Engagements, and Sanads relating to India and Neighbouring Countries*. 5th ed., Calcutta, Government of India, Central Publication Branch, 1929-33 (henceforth cited as Aitchison), 14 vols., vol. 11, pp. 245-49; Jacob C. Hurewitz, *The Middle East and North Africa in World Politics: a documentary record*, New Haven: Yale University Press, 1976-79, 3 vols., vol. 1: 217-19 (henceforth cited as Hurewitz). This is an expanded edition of the author's *Diplomacy in the Near and Middle East*, Princeton University Press, 1956.

The treaty consisted of 9 articles; no. 1 and 2 are the most trenchant.

> Article 1: 'There shall be a cessation of plunder and pi-racy by land and sea on the part of the Arabs, who are parties to this contract, for ever.'

> Article 2: 'If any individual of the people of the Arabs contracting shall attack any that pass by land or sea of any nation whatsoever, in the way of plunder and piracy and not of acknowledged war, he shall be accounted an enemy of all mankind and shall be held to have forfeited both life and goods...'.

A special and important feature of the treaty was a pair of articles, 3 and 10, which included a stipulation about the obligation of Arab ships to carry a special flag and accorded the resulting privileges:

> Article 3: The friendly Arabs shall carry by land and sea a red flag, with or without letters in it, at their option, and this shall be in a border of white, the breadth of the white in the border being equal to the breadth of the red, as rep-resented in the margin (the whole forming the flag known in the British Navy by the title of white pierced red), this shall be the flag of the friendly Arabs, and they shall use it and no other.

> Article 10: The vessels of the friendly Arabs, bearing their flag above described, shall enter into all the British ports and into the ports of the allies of the British so far as they shall be able to effect it; and they shall buy and sell therein...

On that same day (8 January 1820) Keir received instructions from Bombay, issued not by Nepean but by his successor as Governor, Mountstuart Elphinstone. They were a legacy of Ne-pean's time, and included conditions that were both harsher and fraught with unnecessary risks. For example, the Governor de-manded that the present shaykhs be deposed and replaced by those chosen by the British. Keir, who already had concluded the process, let the treaty stand and returned to Bombay. Faced with criticism, he pointed out that all the shaykhs, except Hasan ibn

Rahmah and Husain ibn Ali, had submitted voluntarily; if he had replaced them with his own nominees, the British Government would have been committed to the support of these nominees, and consequently, to further interference in the future. On the other hand, before leaving, Keir did not take any chances either. To enforce the agreements, he made the squadron search every port from Ras al-Khaimah to Dubai. Fortifications were destroyed and several dozen vessels were impounded.

The memorable campaign can be bracketed between 3 November 1819, when the first division of the fleet sailed from Bombay, and 16 March 1820, when Keir weighed from the Pirate Coast for the last time and set course for Bombay. The campaign had achieved its momentary purpose – curbing the centers of piracy and setting up a political structure designed to prevent its recrudescence and allow the enforcement of maritime peace. What remained was to devise the method of this enforcement. The approach seemed obvious: the British should acquire a naval base somewhere in the Persian Gulf, and introduce a system of regular patrols by units of the Indian navy. The island of Qishm was the choice of most observers, for two reasons: its proximity to the strategically vital Strait of Hormuz, and the fact that it was under the jurisdiction – or so the British thought – of the Sultan of Oman, their ally.

The British, while targeting the Qasimi Arabs of Ras al-Khaimah and several other shaykhdoms on the Gulf's southern coast, were not forgetting those on the northern, Persian side, in particular Lingah, Charak, Asalu, and Mughu. They suspected them of being implicated in piracy as well, but there was a problem: although Lingah was an Arab Qasimi shaykhdom, this port as well as the others were Persian territory and their suzerain was the Shah of Iran, who would without a doubt emphatically oppose any attack on them. Nevertheless, Keir had been instructed that whatever the Persian Government's attitude, he was to proceed against those ports whose participation in piracy could be proved. Captain Henry Willock, the chargé d'affaires of the British mission at Tehran, was given the task of reconciling the Shah to the expedition's operations on the Persian coast. He ran into stiff opposition on the part of practically everybody: the Shah, his ministers, and his son Husain Ali Mirza, governor of Fars. The Prince had initially seemed to hold a positive view of the expedition to the Gulf, for on its arrival he wrote a letter to Keir expressing pleasure at the proposed punishment of the Qawasim and even offered to supply provisions; after the fall of Ras al-Khaimah, however, as it became clear that the British intended to deal with the "Persian" Qawasim as well, he sent a letter to Keir stating that

> '...The port of Linga is one belonging to the Province of Fars,...the inhabitants are subjects of the Persian Government and have in no way acted contrary to the subjection they owe as dutiful subjects.... You will, therefore, as long as you remain in the Gulf, be pleased to order that none of the inhabitants belonging to any of the seaports of Fars, and of Linga in particular, shall in any way be molested...'

Keir decided in the first week of February to make a reconnaissance of the Persian coast before commencing operations, but before he could leave Ras al-Khaimah news arrived that part of the naval force had already been in action on the Persian coast. Captain Lock of H.M.S. Eden had been ordered to Bahrain on 3 January, in company with two other cruisers, to hunt down any Qasimi pirate vessels which might have taken refuge there. He first sailed along the Persian coast and seized and burned several ships whose armament made him suspect that they were pirates, among them two armed vessels from Lingah. Keir suspected that Lock had not adequately established the piratical character of the ships concerned before destroying them, and he asked Commander Bruce, the Resident at Bushire, to make a thorough investigation of the charges. Bruce's report confirmed the commander's apprehension: only two minor cases could be ascertained, one in 1814 and the other, the plunder of a vessel by Arabs from Lingah, in 1815. The latter, moreover, happened under the rule of Sultan ibn Saqr, not under that of its present Shaykh, Muhammad ibn Kadhib. Keir thus ruled out any further action against Persian ports. He was supported in this decision by the above-mentioned new Governor of Bombay, Montstuart Elphinstone, who ordered that steps be promptly taken to compensate those Persians whose vessels had been destroyed by Captain Lock's squadron.

Lock's principal mission was to search for piratical Qasimi vessels at Bahrain. The Al Khalifah shaykhs of that archipelago, although not Qasimi, had long been under suspicion of occasionally practicing piracy or harboring Qasimi vessels. While planning the Ras al-Khaimah campaign, Sir Evan Nepean, the Governor of Bombay, and his Council debated the fate of Bahrain, and Nepean leaned toward placing the island under the control of Sayyid Said, the Sultan of Muscat. No firm decision had been made by the time Keir was on the way toward the Gulf, however, and when Elphinstone succeeded Nepean in December 1819 he reached the conclusion that a policy of neutrality as advocated by the Chief Secretary, Warden, was the correct one. As he put it,

> '...We should abstain from all interference in the pretensions which are advanced to the occupation of Bahrain, under a distinct explanation to the Shaykh of that Island that so long as he restrains his tribe from the prosecution of acts of oppression on the high seas, and carries on those commercial pursuits in which they would appear to have formerly engaged, the ports of India shall be open to his vessels, and that he may rely upon experiencing from the British Government every degree of encouragement and of friendly intercourse; but that, on the contrary, if any indications of a piratical spirit should manifest themselves, we shall be compelled to adopt those measures of coercion which we are prosecuting against the Joasmees.'

Salman ibn Ahmad and Abd Allah ibn Ahmad, the Al Khalifah brothers, then conjointly ruling the archipelago, were eager to cooperate. Alarmed by the arrival of Captain Lock's squadron in Manamah Roads on 17 January 1820, they promptly handed over the ten Qasimi dhows present in the harbor, which Lock burned, and they promised not to trade with pirates or allow them to use their harbors. Then they dispatched a *vakil* or representative to Keir to offer submission and ask if they might be admitted to the General Treaty of Peace. Acting upon the Governor's instructions of 15 December 1819, that the Al Khalifah should be treated in a friendly fashion so long as they refrained from piracy on the high seas, Keir granted the request. After obtaining from the vakil a written assurance that any Indian prisoners in Bahrain would be released, and that consorting with pirates or trading in stolen property would cease, the commander allowed him to sign

the treaty on behalf of the shaykhs on 5 February 1820. Later
that month Salman and Abd Allah signed the treaty at Bahrain.
The shaykhs had good grounds for welcoming Bahrain's inclusion in the General Treaty of Peace. Historically, the archipelago
was too weak to resist stronger neighbors bent on conquering it,
and too lucrative as a major trade entrepot and center of pearl
export to make the neighbors resist the temptation to conquer it.
As we have seen, the foremost and most persevering of these
neighbors, since antiquity, was Iran; in the 18th and 19th century,
Oman, Saudi Arabia, and Ottoman Turkey took turns or simulta-
neously joined this fray. During the period under discussion –
that of the British expedition against the Qawasim and its aftermath – Iran and Oman were jockeying, sometimes in tandem, for
possession or at least suzerainty over Bahrain. All these and later
attempts failed, thanks to the steadfast though mostly low-key
moderating effect of the new *Pax Britannica* spreading through
the Persian Gulf. A curious episode in this context was an
agreement made between the already mentioned Captain William Bruce, the British Resident in Bushire, and Husain Ali
Mirza, the Shah's son and governor of Fars. In June 1822 the
Resident received a letter from the Prince inviting him to Shiraz
"to discuss matters of mutual concern to their respective government." Bruce complied, and on 30 August he concluded a
written agreement with Mirza Zaki Khan, minister to the Prince
of Shiraz. It consisted of a preamble and five articles embracing
all the issues then in dispute between the Government of Bombay and the Persian Government. The second article asserted
Iran's right to Bahrain: '...the Island of Bahrain...has always
been subordinate to the Province of Fars...', and demanded the
withdrawal from the Al Khalifah of the flag issued to them under
the third article of the General Treaty of 1820. As it turned out,
neither the Resident nor the Prince had the authority to hold such
discussions or conclude the agreement. Montstuart Elphinstone,
far from accepting it as valid, dismissed Bruce from his post and
recalled him to Bombay; and Fath Ali Shah expressed his extreme displeasure and refused to ratify the agreement.[168]

---

[168] Elphinstone's rejection of the agreement was inevitable for two reasons: the Resident had no authority to engage in such negotiations, and
the agreement itself was unfavorable to Britain. In one sense, the consequences of the Prince's success were real and lasted for a long time:

The campaign was followed by the above-mentioned attempts of the British to acquire a permanent base for their fleet near the Strait of Hormuz. The site chosen was the island of Qishm, partly because it could be considered a possession of the Sultan of Oman, a British ally. The Persian government, however, held a different view. While conceding that the island, together with Bandar Abbas and a few other points was controlled by the Al Bu Said, Tehran never swerved from the assertion that that control was only a lease, and that the entire coastal and insular littoral of Iran was Persian territory. The project thus was ultimately abandoned; the troops that had been landed in July 1820 were evacuated in January 1823, "much to the relief of the Supreme government and the Court of Directors [of the East India Company]... From now on the protection of British-Indian trade in the Gulf would have to depend upon naval means alone, and the Directors were confident not only that this would suffice to prevent piracy but also that the upkeep of a cruiser squadron over a period of years would be less costly than occasional military expeditions."[169]

The General Treaty of Peace was a watershed in the history of the Persian Gulf, for it signaled the beginning of the era of British dominance and spread of the *Pax Britannica*.[170] Suppression of piracy was the justification Britain always advanced for her action against Ras al-Khaimah. Here too critics proposing differing views have appeared in recent historiography. The British, some say, may have had the best intentions, but they had little comprehension that what seemed to them to be "piracy" was in fact a local naval and trade war that had been raging between the Omanis and the emerging Arab principalities of the upper Gulf. By imposing a permanent maritime peace, the Brit-

---

until 1968, successive Persian governments had recourse to it as proof that Bahrain belongs to Iran. See for example Feridun Adamiyat, *Bahrein Islands: a Legal and Diplomatic Study of the British-Iranian Controversy*, New York, 1955, and Gholam-Reza Tadjbakhche, *La Question des Iles Bahrein*, Paris 1960.

[169] Kelly (1968), pp. 191-92. A minor and lasting exception to this policy was the maintenance of a supply depot for the British navy at Basidu, on the sufferance of the Persian government.

[170] Hurewitz, 1: 217-19.

ish upset the context and dynamics of traditional life in the Gulf, an thus inadvertently struck the first real blows against the established system of Persian Gulf life.[171] Others, especially the Arab historians, have gone farther and questioned the sincerity of the motivation itself, pointing out the ubiquity of pirates from Masqat to Kuwait (including that of the notorious Rahmah bin Jabir, who operated in various parts of the Gulf and used Qatif as his frequent base without ever being molested by the British). The real reason, they say, was the very success of Qasimi maritime commerce and the competition it represented.[172] It does appear, however, that the other Arab pirates avoided attacking British and Indian shipping, whereas the Qasimis could not always resist the temptation. If anything, the ensuing improved conditions for seaborne trade and protection of all shipping benefited the coastal Arabs in the first place. This seems to be the conclusion of J.B. Kelly in his magisterial *British and the Persian Gulf, 1795-1880*: "The undertaking from Kuwait, the non-alienation bond from Muscat, and the Exclusive Agreements with Bahrain and the Trucial Shaikhdoms, were the final tier in the treaty structure erected by Britain in the Persian Gulf in the nineteenth century...There is no doubt that the treaty basis is a narrow one, but the British position in the Gulf has never rested solely, or even largely, upon the restricted ground provided by the articles of the treaties. It has rested as much, if not more, upon precedent and policy, and upon the responsibility which Britain has borne for the maintenance of maritime peace, for the security of commerce and navigation, for the suppression of the slave trade and the arms traffic, and for the upholding of the independence and territorial integrity of the maritime states. Above all, it has rested upon the exertions and sacrifices of the men who brought peace, justice, and the rule of law to the Gulf in the nineteenth century, and in so doing wrote one of the most honourable pages in the history of the British Empire."[173] The thorough analysis by Charles E. Davies on pp. 277-295 of his book

---

[171] Robert Gerald Landen, *Oman since 1956: Disruptive Modernization in a Traditional Arab Society*, Princeton University Press 1967, pp. 26-27.
[172]Sultan bin Muhammad al-Qasimi, *The Myth of Arab Piracy in the Gulf*, London: Croom Helm, 1986.
[173] Kelly (1968), pp. 836-37.

The Blood-Red Arab Flag ("Afterword: The Motivation behind Britain's Two Expeditions Against Ras al-Khaima in 1809/10 and 1819/20") reaches essentially the same conclusion: British motivation was to protect all shipping (though especially that of Indian merchants); and the consequences were beneficial for maritime trade in general, including that of the Arabs.[174]

---

[174]The excellent article "Cross-Cultural Perceptions…" by Patricia Risso is especially helpful by placing this episode of the history of the Persian Gulf in a wider context.

Chapter 13

The Wahhabi Movement and the Rise of Saudi Arabia[175]

In 1740 there appeared a new preacher among the Arabs of Najd, a region in central Arabia. Its inhabitants adhered to Hanbalism, the strictest of the four principal schools of worship in Sunni Islam. Like the Prophet himself, the preacher was named Muhammad; his father's name was Abd al-Wahhab (a partly theoforic name; *wahhab*, "the munificent one," is one of the 99 epithets for God found in the Koran, so that he himself also became known as Ibn (son of) Abd (the slave of) al-Wahhab. They were a family of professional theologians and jurisprudents, and Muhammad received a thorough religious education, of which the Koran is the centerpiece: the young scholar had apparently memorized the holy book by the age of ten. Both his family background and the education he received were nothing unusual; there were many others like him. It was his exceptional personality and inner drive that made him rise as the founder of a religious movement striving to cleanse Islam of all accretions that violated its essential doctrine of monotheism. The parallel between the foundation of Islam and its renaissance as Wahhabism is indeed striking. Like the Prophet, Muhammad ibn Abd al-Wahhab preached, as the main tenet of his message, *tawhid*, the oneness or uniqueness of God, and condemned any worship that does not focus on God alone as *shirk* (polytheism). His followers thus called themselves *Muwahhidun*, "Those who

---

[175] H. Laoust, "Ibn Abd al-Wahhab," *EIs* 3: 677-79; Esther Peskes and W. Ende, "Wahhabiyya," *EIs* 11: 39-47.

recognize the unity of God", "Unitarians".[176] In this, he was not
the first nor the only one. Among his predecessors the most famous and articulate had been the Syrian Ibn Taymiyah (1263-
1328). What distinguished Muhammad ibn Abd al-Wahhab was
his determination to transform his religious message into a political reality – just as the Prophet had done over a millennium
earlier. Similarly, Muhammad ibn Abd al-Wahhab at first met
with little acceptance in his home town; he had to leave Uaynah,
but again he found a responsive community elsewhere – in the
oasis of Diriyah, which for the next three generations became the
headquarters of the Wahhabi movement. Diriyah, situated in the
eastern part of Najd, was the possession of Muhammad ibn Saud
(ruled 1746-1765), a local chieftain.[177] Welcoming the preacher
from western Najd, Ibn Saud converted to Wahhabism, and the
result was a theocratic state determined to enforce the austere
doctrine internally and to propagate it abroad through military
conquests if necessary. As in the time of the Prophet, *dais*
(proselytizers) and letters inviting conversion and submission
were sent out, and those refusing to comply were considered infidels. Gradually, the small shaykhdom of Diriyah expanded to
the point of comprising the greater part of the Arabian peninsula.
In the east, it was the tribes and shaykhs along the Persian Gulf
coast from al-Ahsa, whose rulers, the Banu Khalid tribe, submitted in 1793, to Ras al-Khaimah, where the Qawasim chiefs
did likewise soon afterward. In the west, the holy cities of Mecca
and Medina were conquered between 1803 and 1806, and Ghalib
b. Musaid, the Sharif of Mecca (1788-1813), eventually had to
acknowledge Wahhabi suzerainty. For the first time in history,
Arabia was not only a geographical concept but also a political
one, a monolithic state governed from a polity in the interior and
strong enough to attempt further expansion beyond its confines.
The only comparable parallel could be found in Arabia at the
time of the Prophet and of his immediate successors, and not
only in political terms: it was indeed the rekindled religious zeal

---

[176] *Muwahhidun,* "Unitarians," was the early canonical term for the
movement; today, the name preferred by the Wahhabis themselves is
Salafiyyun or *Salafiyyah,* "The Original Ones," meaning Muslims who
practice the original pure Islam of the Prophet's time.
[177] Elizabeth M. Sirriyeh, "Saud, Al," *EIs* 9: 903-905.

of Wahhabism that again drove the conquering hosts of Muslims on their campaigns. But the earlier phase – that of the first century of Islam – soon moved its center of gravity to the peripheral areas of Syria and Iraq, becoming ever more cosmopolitan, whereas the Wahhabi-Saudi state has retained its essential Arabian character and location to our own day.

For our purposes, the noteworthy fact is that a major part of the Persian Gulf's southern coast came directly or indirectly under the rule of a powerful state in Arabia. The new emirate could have chosen to act as a Gulf state, by taking advantage of the many economic assets accruing from this situation: trade, fishing, and pearling would have brought considerable gains to the desert shaykhs through various taxes and customs fees; or the Saudi emirs could have taken part in these industries and developed a merchant fleet of their own. Moreover, alongside the considerable military power the Saudi state had mustered, it could also have sought to create a navy in order to safeguard and expand its coastline and compete with other shipping in the Persian Gulf and beyond. In other words, a new power would have appeared in the Persian Gulf and striven for dominance there. This, however, did not happen. The psychological focus and practical energies of the desert kingdom remained centered on expanding its domain on land and propagating the rigorous Wahhabi form of Islam.

The only native naval power in the full sense of the word was Oman, but its geostrategic situation and the main thrust of its maritime activities and expansion was towards the Arabian Sea and the Indian Ocean; the Omani naval presence in the Persian Gulf itself was intermittent and brief. Meanwhile the coastal or insular principalities or ports like Ras al-Khaimah, Bahrain, Qishm, Qatif, and Kuwait, although engaged chiefly in commerce, fishing, boat-building, and pearling, at times and in varying degrees also fought each other and resorted to piracy. Neither Oman nor any one of the other Gulf states was able to gain a dominant position in the Gulf and impose its form of peace. Nor was Iran or the Ottoman Empire able or willing to do so. In the case of Iran, this was a paradox; its long coastline along the two gulfs placed it in a unique position to become the major naval power there, with all the benefits of trade and access to the Indian Ocean, but the new Qajar government, like most of its predecessors, displayed little initiative in that direction. As for the Ottoman Empire, the days of its control of the al-Ahsa province – thus of the time when it could claim to be one of the Gulf's powers – were long past; if in the final years of the 18th and first years of the 19th century it still ranked among the members of that consortium, it was by virtue of its possession of Basra. Although this tie was often tenuous, and the coastline which the empire could claim was exceedingly short, the potential of this vital port remained great; and the Turks could have made their bid for a share of the Persian Gulf and its shipping. This would have required, however, a radically different, forward-looking commercial and maritime policy, a concept alien to the Sublime Porte.

Saudi Arabia had thus by 1800 become the third major state along the Persian Gulf, and could have become a Gulf power, had it chosen to do so. It did not, for, as we have said, not economic but religious inspiration guided the Saudis. After their conquest of al-Ahsa, their campaigns remained land-bound, and the prime targets were the sacred sites of both Sunni and Shia Islam: Mecca and Medina, Kerbela and Najaf. The Wahhabi puritans were fiercely opposed to any form of veneration except that of God, and not even the shrine tombs of Ali in Najaf and Husayn in Kerbela escaped destruction by them. The human toll of their raids was equally terrible, especially among the Shia population of southern Iraq.

The Saudi hosts seemed to be unstoppable, even though both critical areas of their attacks – the Sunni Hijaz and Shia Iraq – were nominally part of the once mighty Ottoman Empire. However, Istanbul was in no position to organize a major military campaign against the new threat from the desert. The Porte's authority in Baghdad was represented by a semi-independent governor, Sulaiman Pasha, whom it exhorted to curb the Saudis. Two campaigns were undertaken, one in 1797 and the other in 1798-99, but neither succeeded. Basra was the staging area, and both confrontations occurred in the al-Ahsa territory of the Banu Khalid. The attempt of 1798 had the oases of Hufuf and Mubarriz as the objective; but it failed, and the Turks retreated to Basra and Baghdad. It was chiefly after these failures of the Ottomans that the Saudi-Wahhabi forces became aggressive in southern Iraq and in 1803 sacked the Shia shrines of Kerbela and Najaf.

Then they turned their attention to the Sunni shrines of Hijaz, seizing Mecca. They withdrew, but came back in 1806 and took both Mecca and Medina. These defeats and losses were especially humiliating for the Ottomans, whose sultan claimed the distinction of being the protector of Sunni Muslims, and in particular of the Haramain, "The Two Sacred [Cities"]; their ruler, the above-mentioned *sharif* of Mecca Ghalib b. Musaid, was thus an Ottoman client. Here again, the level of impotence to which the Ottoman Empire had fallen became apparent. Conversely, the possession of the Haramain bestowed on the Saudi emirate a special distinction, besides giving it a unique position in that its territory now reached from the Persian Gulf across the Arabian peninsula to the Red Sea, with a potential of access to such Gulf ports as Qatif and Uqair and to those of the Red Sea such as Jeddah and Yanbu.

Once more, the Porte resorted to a measure it had tried, unsuccessfully, in Iraq: in 1807 it ordered a local governor to subdue the dangerous Wahhabi-Saudi rival. The man in question was Mehmet Ali Pasha, who had been appointed two years earlier to the important post of governor of Egypt. The accident of personality made all the difference. Mehmet Ali was a man of exceptional energy and vision, determined to revitalize the country under his trusteeship, and one of the measures he undertook was military strengthening and modernization. Thus in 1811 Egyptian troops landed at Yanbu and launched a campaign that freed the Haramain and gradually drove back the Saudi forces through Najd all the way to Diriyah, which fell in September 1818. The emir, Abd Allah b. Saud, taken prisoner, was sent to Istanbul, where a year later he was executed. The repression was thorough: the emir's brother Ali was executed in Diriyah, and many other members of both the Saudi and Wahhabi families were deported to Cairo. Diriyah was destroyed, and when the Egyptian troops left Arabia in 1819, the Wahhabi-Saudi state and movement appeared dead.

They were not dead, however, and by 1824 Turki b. Abdallah, an uncle of his unfortunate predecessor, had begun to reconstitute the emirate from a new center, the oasis town of Riyad. He could do so because the Wahhabi ideology and movement had survived and now again infused the Saudi state with religious fervor.

The prodigious energy displayed by the young theocratic state enabled it to reach, as we have said, the southern coast of the Persian Gulf, but again the Saudis did not pursue any of the advantages accruing from this situation. They did not become a Gulf power, and the power vacuum existing there practically since the withdrawal of the Portuguese still persisted after the successful conclusion, from the Saudi point of view, of the Ottoman-Saudi confrontation in al-Ahsa. Meanwhile Great Britain was being drawn into the Persian Gulf ever more strongly because of what it meant for her as a geostrategic area of prime importance. Her destruction of Ras al-Khaimah's sea power in 1819-20 may have been provoked by the pirates' depredations against Anglo-Indian commerce, as the British claimed, or such claims may have been a pretext for the extension of British control into the Gulf, as many Arabs now say. The fact remains that not Iran, not Turkey, not Arabia came to fill this power vacuum, but rather, as before, a European power. Thus in 1820 began what we might call the long British century in the Persian Gulf. It lasted until World War II, or in a special sense even until 1971.

Chapter 14

The Emergence of the Modern Persian Gulf

In 1820, Iran was under the rule of Fath Ali Shah (1797-1834), the second sovereign of the Qajar dynasty. Bushire was the country's principal port, and also the residence of the chief Political Resident of Great Britain in the Persian Gulf. Bandar Abbas had slipped back, but nevertheless remained active and would eventually regain primacy in the second half of the 20th century. Among the other ports on the Persian coast or connected with it, Lingah and Muhammarah – the present Khurramshahr – come first to mind. A noteworthy feature of these and other coastal places was the pronounced presence of Arab tribal groups despite the admixture of the Persian element: the Al Mazkur in Bushire, Qawasim in Lingah and Qishm, Banu Ma`in in Qishm and Hormuz, and Banu Ka`b in Khuzistan were the foremost among them. These Arabs had not quite lost the memory of their original homeland on the opposite side of the Gulf, but otherwise they were independent of it and most of the time acknowledged the authority of the Persian government. Meanwhile the Sultanate of Oman extended its influence across the Gulf in the 1790s, during the final stage of its maritime expansion, when between 1784 and 1795 Bandar Abbas and several other ports were leased to the Al Bu Said sultans by the Qajars. Gradually, however, the Persian government asserted their control over these ports and formations, and in 1868 they refused to renew the Omani lease of Bandar Abbas.[178]

Despite its long coast, numerous ports, active fleets, and able mariners and merchants, Qajar Iran still did not exploit this po-

---

[178] Lorimer, *Gazetteer*, 4: 2046-47; Hurewitz, 1: 322-24.

tential by engaging the sea and the ocean. The dichotomy between Iran's interior and its coastal strip, characteristic throughout much of this country's long history, continued. Naval power and merchant marines were those of the coastal formations, not of the central government, which remained, as always, psychologically landlocked or landward oriented. This is all the more anomalous since Tehran was well aware of the benefits of maritime trade and eager, in certain cases, to embark on expansion in the Persian Gulf. It did not give up its claims to Bahrain. Nevertheless, Iran's claims to this archipelago did not represent a policy of seaborne expansion, either in the commercial or naval sense. It was rather a desire to recover a patrimony, memories of which, consciously or subconsciously, went back to pre-Islamic times. Native seafaring in the Persian Gulf had become, for all practical purposes, Arab. On the other hand, whether it emanated from ports and principalities on the Persian or Arab side, it never rose to a level that could lead to the establishment of a major naval power; for that, none of the players was strong enough.

Besides Iran, Ottoman Turkey and Saudi Arabia were states with enough reservoir of inherent strength to create and project a naval expansion into the Persian Gulf and beyond, but neither ever attempted to do so. In 1820, Basra, the great port of Ottoman Iraq, continued to function as a busy crossroads of seaborne and caravan trade, but not as a base for a Turkish navy. Even during the eventual campaign to reconquer the important province of Lahsa – al-Ahsa or al-Hasa of the Arabs – a fleet of Kuwaiti ships had to help the Turks ferry their troops to Ras Tannurah in May 1871.

Saudi Arabia lay prostrate in 1820, felled by the Ottomans through their Egyptian proxy, but the resilient Saudi-Wahhabi alliance made the young state soon rise again and resume its push towards the Gulf. As before and again later, however, the desert colossus never translated his land-based strength into maritime power. The Emirate eagerly advanced forward to the coast but stopped there, contenting itself with trying to bring the coastal shaikhs under its control. In this respect, the Saudi policy was similar to that of the Qajars.

The seaborne empire of the Sultanate of Oman was, up to a point, an exception. In 1820, Said bin Sultan (1806-1856), the fifth ruler of the Al Bu Said dynasty (whose thirteenth member,

Qabus, rules Oman today), was enjoying the fruits of the victory at Ras al-Khaimah. The sultan had been Britain's ally in the campaign against the Qawasim, and their pacification rid his shipping in the Persian Gulf of a bothersome rival[179]. Masqat was the Omani capital and main port, and one of its trading partners was Basra; merchantmen, some 400 to 500 tons each, loaded with bales of coffee brought from Mocha, plied this route and returned with shiploads of dates. Bandar Abbas was not only another commercial partner of Masqat, but a temporary Omani possession through the aforementioned lease agreement. The most remarkable maritime venture of the Omanis, however, was the resumption of the expansion across the Indian Ocean started by the Al Bu Said's predecessors the Yarubids. Trade flourished with India, and parts of the east African coast were colonized. Between 1828 and 1840 Said bin Sultan transferred his main residence from Masqat to Zanzibar.

While the bulk of Omani trade moved within the orbit of the Indian Ocean and the Persian Gulf, Said bin Sultan welcomed the proposal of an American businessman made in 1828 for a treaty of friendship and commerce, which was then concluded in 1833;[180] it reflected the growing number of American ships visiting Zanzibar – 32 ships between September 1832 and May 1834, compared with seven ships from Britain, one from France and one from Spain. In 1837 the first American consul arrived in Zanzibar, four years before the British one. It does not seem that Omani ships themselves made reciprocal voyages, except for two colorful and quite endearing missions carried out by the sultan's corvette *Sultanah* to New York in 1840 and to London in 1842. This 14-gun square-rigger had been built in the ship-

---

[179] The slightly earlier defeat of the Saudi-Wahhabi emirate by the Ottoman-Egyptian expedition (1818), while facilitating the Anglo-Omani action against Ras al-Khaimah – a Saudi vassal – also freed Oman from Saudi encroachments and Wahhabi propaganda. The resilient Saudis would eventually resume these attempts, which then intermittently continued, in various forms, into the 1950s. Great Britain, ever desirous of having friendly relations with Saudi Arabia, nevertheless played a low-key but effective role in assisting Oman.

[180] The text of the treaty is in Hurewitz, 1: 255-56 (Document no. 75: Treaty of amity and commerce: the United States and Masqat, 21 September 1833).

yards of Bombay – the standard provenance of Oman's main naval units – in 1833, and remained in service until 1855. The Sultanah sailed from Zanzibar in February 1840, carrying Said bin Sultan's secretary Ahmad bin Numan al-Ka`bi as his special envoy to president Van Buren; after a voyage of 87 days, the ship reached New York in May. She docked in a wharf of the United States navy as its guest, and the visitors proceeded to sell the wares they had brought and which consisted of such articles as dates, coffee, ivory, copal, cloves, and hides, and to buy merchandise in their turn. They also brought from the sultan a letter of good wishes to the American president and gifts consisting of two Arabian horses, pearls, gems, rosewater, a Persian silken prayer rug, a cashmere shawl, and a gilded sword. Martin Van Buren reciprocated with his own letter and gifts, among which was a rifle with the inscription "From the President of the United States of America to the Imam of Masqat." One of the appealing byproducts of the visit is a portrait of the envoy, Ahmad bin Numan, by the American painter Edward Mooney,[181] with a small representation of the Sultanah in the background. The ship left New York in August and reached Zanzibar by the end of the year. The second diplomatic-commercial voyage took the Sultanah to England. She left Zanzibar on 11 February 1842, and sailed into the Thames on 12 June. The envoy was Ali bin Nasir, bringing letters from Said bin Sultan to Lord Aberdeen and Queen Victoria, with gifts for the latter. The main purpose of this mission, a request for a modification of the commercial treaty between the two countries, was not achieved. In other respects, however, the visit was a success, especially on the personal level. The queen, who received the envoy on 29 June, was happy with the gifts (they included pearl and emerald necklaces, shawls, rosewater and four thoroughbreds), and the Omanis stirred interest and curiosity among the natives (indeed, the *British* natives). The 18 June issue of the *Illustrated London News* included in its report a picture of the Sultanah.[182]

Upon Said bin Sultan's death in 1856, two of his sons divided the patrimony, with one branch ruling in Masqat, the other in

---

[181] Edward Ludlow Mooney (1813-1887), a New York painter especially esteemed as a portraitist.

[182] *Uman wa-tarikhuha l-bahri*, Masqat, Wizarat al-Ilam wa l-Thaqafah, 1979, chapter 17: Rihlat al-safinah "Sultanah", pp. 179-85.

Zanzibar. The strife that at first threatened to afflict the relations between the brothers was averted in 1861 through the mediation of the Viceroy of India, Lord Canning, who stipulated that the Sultan of Zanzibar would pay an annual sum to the Sultan of Masqat in return for recognition of Zanzibar's henceforth separate line of rulers (the so-called Canning Award).[183] The arrangement was also symptomatic of Masqat's economic decline, which set in after Said bin Sultan's death. More than this remarkable monarch's demise,[184] changed conditions in shipping caused Masqat's retreat. Foremost was the growth of steamship navigation, against which the Omani trading fleet of sailing ships could not compete; an additional cause was the opening of the Suez Canal in 1869, which siphoned off some of the traffic that would otherwise have used the Gulf of Oman-Persian Gulf route.

Great Britain's role in Omani affairs, which we might date as starting in 1798, when an agreement opening Bandar Abbas to a British presence was signed between the East India Company and the sultan, would grow and last until at least 1959.[185] Its goals were in most respects comparable to the goals of agreements made with the other Arab states, but without a formal treaty. The busy trade between Oman and India created in Masqat a colony of resident Indian Banyan merchants, subjects of the Raj and thus entitled to British protection. Britain strove, most of the time successfully, to maintain a privileged position

---

[183] Wilson, *The Persian Gulf*, p. 234; M. Rheda Backer, *Trade and Empire in Masqat and Zanzibar: Roots of British domination*, London and New York: Routledge, 1992, pp. 191-93.

[184] The remarkable personality and rule of Said bin Sultan has received considerable attention in scholarly literature, but two popular books deserve special mention; one is by his daughter Emily Ruete (1844-1924), who married a German diplomat: *Memoirs of an Arab Princess*, London 1888 and a new printing: Princeton, Markus Wiener Publishers, 2000; the other is by her son and thus the sultan's grandson, Rudolph Said Ruete, *Said bin Sultan (1791-1856), ruler of Oman and Zanzibar: his place in the history of Arabia and East Africa*, London 1929.

[185] The Bandar Abbas agreement coincided with Napoleon's occupation of Egypt, and its avowed purpose of challenging the British in the Indian Ocean and India itself. The determination of thwarting the French designs became one of the cornerstones of Britain's policy in Oman and the Persian Gulf.

in Oman and the Persian Gulf to the exclusion of other European powers, although France, Russia and Germany had begun to challenge that monopoly. In 1862 London and Paris jointly guaranteed the independence of both Oman and Zanzibar.[186] This somewhat futuristic declaration strengthened the validity of the Canning Award, a quintessential expression of yet another form of Pax Britannica now spreading over the Indian Ocean, and thus of the colonial power's imperial might; but it also admitted the limits of this power by sharing some of it with France.

As in the Persian Gulf, in Oman and the Indian Ocean too the British presence had a stabilizing effect. On land, it helped the Al Bu Said dynasty withstand Saudi expansion and dominance, and weather the dangers presented by the reappearing dichotomy between the Ibadite imams of Oman, a name now designating the interior, and the sultans of Masqat, this name now denoting the coastal domain of the Al Bu Said. British authorities also strove to eliminate two plagues afflicting the Indian Ocean and the Gulfs, one traditional and the other new: the slave trade[187] and arms traffic. The Omanis were the main practitioners of these occupations; the slave trade was a time-honored institution, the arms traffic a recent phenomenon engendered by the appearance of modern rifles, which were in great demand among the tribesmen all over the Gulf area.[188] East Africa was the chief source and supplier of slaves; Europe was the producer and supplier of weapons. Britain's main motivation remained of course the preservation of the benefits her colonies, especially India, brought her; and pacification of the area – of which curbing piracy and the arms traffic was a component – was in her interest. This fact has cast a pall on British efforts to curb the slave trade as well; some observers, both local and Western, have branded these efforts as a subterfuge to dominate and control native shipping. There may have been some of that, but at the core of these efforts was, beyond a doubt, a sincere recognition of human rights.

---

[186] Hurewitz 1: 349-50 (Document no. 114: Declaration by Great Britain and France guaranteeing the independence of Masqat and Zanzibar, 10 March 1862).

[187] Wilson, *Persian Gulf*, pp. 213-30.

[188] Ibid., pp. 269-71.

The overseas expansion of Oman under the Al Bu Said dynasty was thus based on a vigorous merchant fleet and navy, but the latter never rose to a level competitive with that of the two great naval powers of Europe – Britain and France – nor did it really need to do so. No sizable local rivals could challenge it at sea after the defeat of the Qawasim, and Britain did not stand in the way of the establishment of an Omani presence in East Africa; eventually, she even spread her protective shadow there as well (against the designs of Germany, which from her recently acquired colony of Tanganyika – now the continental component of the Republic of Tanzania – was casting covetous eyes on Zanzibar). In this the Al Bu Said differed from their predecessors the Yarubids, whose navy had confronted the Portuguese and projected its power in the Indian Ocean. The general rule was now reaffirmed: European mastery of the oceans and their ramifications.

On the naval level, Britain's involvement in the Persian Gulf with Iran went through a gamut of phases and aspects. British India loomed in the background as a factor inseparable from the Gulf. The colony played a capital role in British policy, but this policy in turn differed with respect to the countries in question. In the case of Iran, a dimension emerged at the dawn of the 19th century that would affect the Iranian side of the Gulf but spare the Arabs: the "Great Game", an almost century-long defense of India against an expected attempt by Russia to invade and conquer Britain's most valuable colony. Britain considered Afghanistan a buffer zone against Russia, and any weakening of it was deemed dangerous. Thus when in 1838 Muhammad Shah Qajar, advised by the Russians, laid siege to Herat, its fall had to be prevented, and the quickest and most economical way to do so was to put pressure on Iran through the Persian Gulf. In June of that year a naval squadron landed troops on the island of Kharg, implicitly threatening Bushire; by September the siege of Herat was lifted and the Shah's troops were withdrawn. Britain followed suit with her withdrawal from Kharg in 1842, although she maintained a coaling station there for two more years. This lingering occupation revealed a wish in some Anglo-Indian quarters to retain Kharg as a naval base; the fact that the final decision was against it again shows Britain's reluctance to acquire territory, however strategically advantageous, in the Persian Gulf, and her inverse conviction that patrols by the Anglo-Indian navy were sufficient.

In 1856-57 a replay of the 1838 drama occurred, but on a larger scale. Again abetted by Russia, the Persians invaded Afghanistan and this time succeeded in capturing Herat (October 1856). Britain declared war on Iran, and in December of that year troops were landed on Kharg and at Bushire, preparing for penetration inland. No substantial action took place there, but a deeper thrust occurred in Khuzistan, where an amphibious opertion penetrated via the Shatt al-Arab and the Karun as far as Ahvaz. Skirmishes with Iranian troops took place at Khushab in February and at Muhammarah in March 1857. By then, however, Tehran agreed to withdraw its troops from Herat; peace between the two countries was secured at the Treaty of Paris, and British troops in turn were withdrawn.

The use of the Shatt al-Arab and the Karun in the 1856-7 events reflected the growth of steamship navigation in the Gulf and on the Tigris-Euphrates and Karun rivers. Muhammarah, located on the eastern bank of the Shatt al-Arab at the juncture with the canal leading to the Karun, was made a free port in the 1830s, and commercial traffic flourished. The Karun provided an alternative to the Tigris for Anglo-Indian trade with western Iran, and the province of Khuzistan benefited from this situation.

Throughout the 19th century and until World War I, Bushire functioned as the principal port of Iran;[189] this and its strategically important location was why the British Political Resident in the Persian Gulf was stationed there. The post made him the superior of all the other British political agents in the area, a kind of implicit governor of the Persian Gulf. He made annual inspection tours of the other ports and islands, visiting the political agents and local rulers. Although Bushire was not a British naval base, naval units as a rule had permission to frequent it and use its anchorage.

It may be worthwhile to quote several excerpts from a book on Persian Gulf ports and islands by Muhammad Ibrahim Ka-

---

[189] Laurence Lockhart, "Bushahr," *EIs*, vol. 1 (1960), pp. 1341-42; Xavier de Planhol, "Bušehr," *EIr*, vol. 4 (1990), 569-72; Lorimer, *Gazetteer*, 7: 330-50.

zaruni,[190] a government official active during the reign of Muhammad Shah Qajar (1834-48). Kazaruni portrays a situation that evolved in the course of the century from the reign of Nadir Shah to that of Muhammad Shah, thus, using the wider brackets, from 1730 to 1848. This period witnessed a continued influx of Arabs to the Persian littoral; in the case of Bandar Abbas and several other sites on the coast, it was sanctioned, at the end of the 18th century, by the aforementioned lease granted by the newly established Qajar shahs to the Al Bu Said sultans of Oman. Here is what Kazaruni writes about Bushire (pp. 47-48):

> The blessed port of Abu Shahr is of recent construction; its buildings were erected at the beginning of Nadir Shah Afshar's reign. This is how it happened: A certain Arab, Shaykh Mazkur, came from Arabia to the Persian coast and settled in Rishahr, a village which is now considered to be one of the dependencies of Abu Shahr. With some of the villagers he then worked hard, and on this spot which is now known as Abu Shahr he built several houses with palm tree wood and mats, and took up fishing to earn his livelihood.
>
> Now this Arab had several alert, brave nephews, efficient especially in the matter of seafaring and captainship, so that the fleet of Nadir Shah was entrusted to them. The command of this fleet was at the origin of the rise of Al Mazkur.
>
> To the east of their new home [i.e. of Abu Shahr] there was an inlet (khawr) the like of which is only rarely seen, a harbor providing shelter against winds from the east, west, north, and south, in all kinds of stormy weather. Moreover, this inlet is connected with Abu Shahr in such a way that vessels can approach within a few steps the gates of caravansaries, depots and warehouses, and be unloaded ...This salt flat thus turned into a Garden of Eden, and worthy seafaring merchants come there from every quarter for the sake of trade. ...The governor of this province built there lofty buildings and high mansions. Gradually, the area of Abu Shahr in the time of the late Shaykh Abd al-Rasul Khan, the *daryabigi* (governor of

---

[190] Muhammad Ibrahim Kazaruni *mutakhallis bih* Nadiri, *Tarikh-e banadir va jazayir-e Khalij-e Fars dar zaman-e Muhammad Shah Qajar,* ed. Manuchihr Sutudah, Tehran, 1367/1988.

the maritime march) no longer sufficed, and the *daryabigi* expanded it southward where now the citadel of this city is located...

Here is what Kazaruni tells us about Hormuz (pp. 127-128):

The island of Hormuz has a circumference of eight far-sakhs.[191] A low mountain extends from the east of this island toward the west; rock salt and copperas is found in this mountain. On its eastern side there are no settlements, and the sea reaches its foot. Toward the west of the island the mountain descends into a level and broad plain; about one quarter of a farsakh [is covered by] what used to be lofty buildings, high mosques and remarkable baths, all of which are now ruined. By the sea side there are several wondrous monuments. On the eastern[192] side of the is-land there stands a solid fortress, an admirable engineer-ing feat built by a master architect.... Its circumference is three hundred paces. There are three cisterns in this for-tress, filled with rainwater; and there is also a well with sweet tasty water. The brother of the Shaykh of the Litto-ral (*Shaykh-e Sif*) – named Shaykh Muhammad – is the guardian of this fortress. Some two hundred families live outside the fortress; most of the men came from Oman as riflemen of the above-mentioned Abu l-Jam` Shaykh Mazkur. Large ordnance has been placed in the towers of the fortress: fourteen guns. In one of these towers lives the family of Shaykh Muhammad. ... In the area where buildings had existed outside the fortress, still now after rain women and girls of the island come and search among the ruins for fragments of gold and silver objects and rubies and emeralds, which have been washed up from the soil by the downpour. These women have to pay each winter one tuman; if they don't, the authorities pre-vent them from this activity. In this settlement there are three hundred cisterns, most of them still functioning. ...The island of Hormuz lies in such a location that who-ever controls it, watches over Qishm and Bandar Abbas.

---

[191] From the ancient Persian *farsang*, which was also loaned by Greek and passed into other Western languages as *parasang;* approximately 6 kilometers.

[192] This seems to be an error for "northern".

Thus Hormuz, though not deserted, had become a virtual archaeological ruin since the expulsion of the Portuguese two centuries earlier.[193] The case was different with Bandar Abbas. Although outstripped by Bushire, it did retain much vitality, according to Kazaruni's account (pp. 124-26):

> Bandar Abbas is a populous and prosperous port, with two thousand houses built with mortar and stone, and cabins built with mud brick. It has a strong fortress, with houses inside it. Outside there are some one thousand dwellings made of palm tree wood. ... Naranj Qal`ah is in the middle of the [above-mentioned] fortress by the sea shore; it was built by the Dutch,[194] who had previously lived in this port. They constructed a solid building of several storeys, with rooms and openings, so that in summer there is no better structure with respect to fresh air and moderate heat. The Shaykh of the littoral lives in this mansion. There is a mighty fortification wall around this port, with sixteen towers and two gates; one of these faces the sea on the south, one faces the west, and one faces the east. Four mosques have been built in this port; two inside the fortified part, the other two outside; one of the two inside, and both of those outside pertain to the Shia population. There is a bazaar with shops, fifty in number... The tax collector gathers three hundred *qrans* each year from these shops. ...There are four well-kept caravansaries, occupied by merchants. There are also various [other] shops selling haberdashery, fruit, cucumbers etc. among the quarters and also outside the fortress, all paying specified sums to the government each year. The rent for the camel bazaar brings in a revenue of 5000 *qurush* annually, that for the donkey bazaar, 3000 *qurush* annually.
>
> The custom of the people of this port is the following: At the beginning of *jawza* (Gemini, May/June), they lock (lit. seal) their houses and disperse in the district of Minab and its surrounding villages. Their health improves in the midst of sweet running water and a balmy breeze under the trees in the fresh air, while the brunt of the [summer] heat is tempered [lit. broken]. The people of this

---

[193] Lorimer, *Gazetteer*, 8: 747-50.

[194] "Hazarat-e Valandiz"; this could be translated as "Their excellencies the Dutch"; it may sound sarcastic, but the author's admiration appears sincere.

port thus stay in the villages around Minab from *jawza* till *mizan* (Libra = September/October) or *sunbulah* (Virgo = October/November). At the conclusion of this period, which is also the end of harvesting fruit from orchards, they return to the port. ...From the middle of *seretan* (Crab = July), the heat becomes so intense that eggs can be hardboiled [by exposing them to the sun, and] staying [in the port] is impossible. The Governor of the Littoral and the tax collector also leave for the port of Minab. Rain comes in the middle of *sunbulah*.

Two thirds of this port's population adhere to the Twelver Shia sect, and have a large diaspora abroad, especially in Bahrain and Lar, while one third belongs to the Shafii sect. The governor (*hakim*), however, and the two to three hundred men who are his troops and hail from Oman, adhere to the Ibazi[195] sect; their founder (lit. *mujtahid*, exegete) was Ahmad ibn Ibaz. They are [so] called because of their prevalent wearing of white garments (lit. whiteness, *bayazi*). This sect recognizes the caliphate of the two shaykhs – Abu Bakr and `Umar – but rejects that of Usman, because of the squandering (lit. expenditure) and raiding of the treasury that he had done; as for the Lord of the Pious [=Ali], it does not consider him caliph [either], because of the Holy War and killing of the infidel Quraysh and others like them [he had engaged in][196]. All Omanis recognize the caliphate of the two shaykhs and pertain to the Ibazi sect.[197]

---

[195] Persian pronunciation of the Arabic Ibadi; see below for further comment on this question.

[196] The author speaks here as a Shia Muslim, for whom Ali was the legitimate successor of the Prophet and his opponents were infidels, even if they claimed to be Muslims of Muhammad's own tribe, the Quraish.

[197] The correct Arabic form of the name is Ibadi. The Persian author seems to conflate here the name of the sect with the Arabo-Persian word for white color, *bayazi*. It is true, however, that the Ibadites of Oman were also called Bayadi or Bayazi, and both these words can structurally be linked with the Arabic word *bayad*, whiteness. On the other hand, it could also be linked with the name of the sect's founder, Abd Allah ibn Ibad al-Tamimi (fl. in the second half of the 7th century). The text suggests that the Ibadites of Bandar Abbas chose the more literal interpretation.

Another port worthy of notice was the above-mentioned Lingah, situated on the Persian coast facing the island of Qishm.[198] Like many other places on the coast, it had a predominantly Arab population and was usually under the rule of one or another type of Arab shaykh; its rise coincided with the decline of the neighboring port of Kung, which until 1711 had been held by the Portuguese. In 1760 Lingah was seized by the Qasimi Arabs, and may have benefited from this association despite the stigma of piracy that came with it, for trade was the other, less publicized but more vigorous, occupation of all concerned. As a trading center, it became the residence of Persian and Indian merchants, importing such articles as textiles destined for Iran and exporting tobacco and pearls, the latter chiefly to India. One traditional type of trade became a serious issue in the 1840s and 1850s: the aforementioned slave trade, which Britain was trying to eradicate from the Indian Ocean and its ramifications. The main theater of operations was along the coasts of eastern Africa, Arabia, and Oman, and Persia was a relatively minor recipient of this special merchandise. Nevertheless, the British, as everywhere else, mounted a tremendous pressure on the Persian government to join them in their efforts to curb the slave trade when it headed towards its ports or was carried in Persian ships. The campaign, somewhat reminiscent of the earlier one at the beginning of the century to stamp out piracy, occurred chiefly in 1840s and 1850s. It again ran into a similar problem of how to carry out the task without infringing upon Persian sovereignty or hurting Persian feelings. The British managed to persuade the Shah to issue *firmans* banning the slave trade, but since he had no navy and his Arab vassals on the coast were virtually autonomous, he could not enforce them. Delegating this task to British cruisers patrolling the Gulf should have been the answer, but that of course ran into the aforementioned problem. Ultimately, the British succeeded in arranging for Persian officers to accompany the cruisers, and the campaign began to bear fruit. Colonel Arnold Kemball, the Resident at Bushire, wrote toward the end of his tenure in 1855:

---

[198] C.E. Bosworth, "Linga," *EIs* 5 (1986), p. 765; Lorimer, *Gazetteer*, 8: 1088-1100.

'It was the reproach of Persia that she had been the last to follow the example of Turkey and other Mahommedan states in making concessions to Great Britain with a view to the abolition of the Slave Trade. It is but justice now to record to her credit that her obligations once accepted, she has been the first, nay the only one, to conform to their spirit as well as to their letter. The effect of the examples made of some of the Persian Chieftains during the past 3 years are already apparent. On my last tour of the Gulf I was assured by the Agent at Lingah that he had been unable to trace one single instance of the importation of slaves on that Coast during the current season; nor did the enquiries generally instituted by myself on the spot permit me to question the accuracy of the inference to be drawn from his statements.'[199]

It may be worthwhile in this context to quote Kazaruni's chapter on Lingah in its heyday at the time of Muhammad Shah Qajar, thus between 1834 and 1848 (pp. 115-118):

Lingah is an extremely prosperous place, the most prosperous of all the ports on the coast of Oman.[200] About five thousand notable Arab merchants and wealthy shipowners live there, and constantly trade with Oman, Yemen, and India. There are tall buildings (*imarat*) made of mortar and stone, and [houses that have] rooms (*ghuraf*) with wind tunnels and equipped with furnishings. Shaykh Sa`id, of the Qasimi tribe, resides here as the governor (*hakim*), and possesses great wealth. ... The people who live in this port confess the Wahhabi doctrine, except for some four hundred households that pertain to the Twelver Shiah denomination and pratice *taqiyah* (pious dissimulation);[201] most members of this group are of the Imami sect

---

[199] Kelly (1968), chapter XIII: The Attack on the Slave Trade, 1842-1873.

[200] Lingah, like Bandar Abbas and Hormuz, was leased to the Al Bu Said sultans of Oman, and the author has thus used a political instead of a geographical concept.

[201] This remark illustrates the relative independence of the Qasimi Arabs from the central government. Twelver Shia Islam was Iran's official religion; yet its adherents had to exercize caution in a territory controlled by the Qasimis who were Wahhabi Muslims, although they also were vassals of the Shah.

and came from Bahrain. ...There   is a mountain [range]
at a distance of two farsakhs from this port; the foothills
of this range, nine farsakhs long and one farsakh wide, are
covered with date palms and have   many villages,   ...
Shaykh Sa`id Jawasimi,[202] who is the governor
(*amil*) of this port, collects a levy of ten shahis of the old
gold standard per palm tree. .. There is an abundance of
female and male slaves in this port, so much so that each
househould has ten to twelve such boys and girls – so
many that the language most commonly spoken there is
Sudanese ("*zaban-e Sudan*"; this could also simply mean
"language of the Blacks")... Now on the northeast of this
port there is a fortress... the late Shaykh Muhammad bin
Qazib, who was the brother of Shaykh Sa`id, had built it
and lived there. When Shaykh Sa`id's turn [to govern]
came, he built several mansions on the seashore, [some of
them] within the city; he himself lives in these installations and is constantly busy with ship repair and construction of many *baghalas*.[203]

By the beginning of the 20th century, the Qajar authorities had
tightened the customs administration of their ports, sometimes
raising tariffs to the detriment of trade. Thus when in 1902 Lingah was especially badly hit by these measures, many of the
merchants – including the Persian ones – and most business
transactions moved across the Gulf to Dubai, giving this port a
further boost toward becoming the most successful emporium in
the eastern part of the Gulf.

Meanwhile Great Britain worked to confirm, modify or expand
the treaty of 1820 with the sheikhdoms whose domains lay along
the southern coast from Qatar to Ras Musandam. Collectively,
this stretch had previously lacked any specific geographical or
political appellation, except for its occasional and misleading
inclusion in the broader concept of Oman, and the rather de-
rogatory name of Pirate Coast given it by the British. The treaty
of 1820 and the subsequent ones outlawed piracy preying on
Anglo-Indian shipping, but only partially banned it when it came

---

[202] Regional pronunciation of Qawasimi.

[203] A large type of sailing ship created in this period by a combination of
native traditions with elements adopted from European ships. See
Uman wa-tarikhuha l-bahri, pp. 118-22.

to relations between these sheikhdoms; the treaties at first did no more than impose regular periods of mutual truce on the warring factions – hence the names Trucial Coast, Trucial Shaikhdoms, or Trucial Oman, by which this part of the Persian Gulf coast came to be known.[204] Britain then made similar treaties with Bahrain, Kuwait, and Qatar. The main purpose remained the same: preservation of peace and unmolested commerce, safeguarding these seafaring Arabs from absorption by Iran, the Ottoman Empire, and Saudi Arabia, and keeping European rivals out.

This string of treaties can be bracketed between 1820 and 1916, signifying a process that converted the originally independent sheikhdoms into British protectorates.[205] The most noteworthy were:

1820: The General Treaty of Peace, a series of agreements between Great Britain, the Trucial Shaikhs, and Bahrain.[206]

1853: The 'Perpetual Maritime Truce', under which the Shaikhs agreed to observe a 'perfect maritime truce…for evermore'.[207]

1868: An agreement that was the inception of the creation of Qatar as a new sheikhdom.[208]

1892: The 'Exclusive Agreement' by which the Trucial Shaikhs pledged not to enter into any agreement or correspondence with any power other than Britain, not to consent to the residence

---

[204] In Arabic, *al-Sahil al-Mutasalih* and its variants. Another appellation was *al-Shamal*, "the North" [of Oman].

[205] Donald Hawley, *The Trucial States*, London 1970, chapter 6: The Treaties with Britain, pp. 126-41; Malcolm Yapp, "British Policy in the Persian Gulf," chapter 4 of *The Persian Gulf States*, pp. 70-90.

[206] Hurewitz, 1: 217-19 (Document no. 60: General treaty suppressing piracy and slave traffic: Great Britain and the Arab tribes in the Persian Gulf, 8 January – 15 March 1820; based on Aitchison, *Collection of Treaties..relating to India* (5th ed.), 11: 245-49)..

[207] Hurewitz 1: 306-307(Document no. 99: Perpetual maritime truce concluded by the Shaikhs of the Pirate Coast, 4 May 1853; based on Aitchison, 11: 252-53).

[208] Kelly, *Britain*, p. 675; based on Aitchison, *Collection of Treaties…* (3rd ed.), 10: 138-9.

within their territories of any agent of another government, and on no account to cede, sell, mortgage or otherwise give occupation of any part of their territory to anybody but the British Government; this agreement was signed by the individual Shaikhs between 5 and 8 March, ratified by Lord Curzon, the Viceroy of India, on 12 May, and approved by Queen Victoria later that year.[209] A similar agreement was signed by the Shaikh of Bahrain on 13 March.[210]

1899: An agreement between Great Britain and Shaikh Mubarak, the ruler of Kuwait, which placed this sheikhdom under her protection in return for a promise similar to the Exclusive Agreement: not to cede, sell, lease, mortgage, or otherwise dispose of territory to a foreign government or national without specific permission from the British government.[211]

1914: A treaty that transformed Bahrain into a British protectorate.[212]

1916: A similar treaty with Qatar. [213]

Somewhat paradoxically, Britain was not averse to accepting the presence of the Ottoman Empire and Saudi Arabia almost as partners in her efforts to preserve the peace and safeguard commerce, as long as they did not seek to absorb these principalities and did not challenge her dominant position in the Gulf itself. This led to occasionally contradictory situations such as that in

---

[209] Hawley, *The Trucial States*, pp. 138-39, 320-21.

[210] Hurewitz, 1: 465 (Document no. 153: Exclusive agreement: the Bahrayni Shaikh and Great Britain, 13 March 1892; based on Aitchison, *Collection of Treaties...* (5th ed.), 11: 238).

[211] Hurewitz, 1: 475-77 (Document no. 156: Exclusive agreement: the Kuwayti Shaikh and Great Britain, 23 January 1899; based on Aitchison, *Collection of Treaties...* (5th ed.), 11: 262); Lorimer, *Gazetteer*, 1: 1048-50; R.M. Burrell, "al-Kuwayt, *EI* 5: 574.

[212] Hurewitz, 2: 6-7 (Document no. 4: The United Kingdom's recognition of Kuwayt as an independent state under British protection, 3 November 1914; based on Aitchison, *Collection Treaties*, 11: 265-66).

[213] Hurewitz, 2: 75-76 (Document no. 19: British treaty with the Shaikh of Qatar, 3 November 1916; based on Aitchison, *Collection of Treaties*, 11: 258-60).

Kuwait in 1899 and 1913: despite his 1899 agreement with
Great Britain – analogous to the 1892 Exclusive Agreement between Britain and the Trucial Shaikhs – the Shaikh of Kuwait,
wary of the landlubber giant, his Ottoman neighbor, whose
proximity as possessor of Iraq to the north and of the recently reconquered Lahsa to the south may have seemed menacing,
thought it prudent to placate him by accepting the nominal title
of *kaymakam* or governor, and the Ottoman flag. This allegiance
was even sanctioned by an agreement between Great Britain and
the Ottoman Empire in 1913. We shall never know what the
long-term effects of this triangle might have been, for the Balkan
War and then World War I forced the Turks to leave Lahsa and
eventually also Iraq, making Britain an even more exclusive arbiter in the Persian Gulf.

While during the 19th century Great Britain was consolidating
her grasp on the Persian Gulf, the Ottoman Empire, defying the
cliché label of being 'The Sick Man of Europe', strove to carry
out a number of reforms, collectively known as *tanzimat*, (re-
structuring, reforms, not unlike the *perestroika* of the Soviet
Union), meant to restore Turkey's social and economic health
and military strength. Midhat Pasha, appointed governor of
Baghdad, brought the same ambition to his new position. One of
his goals was to recover the above-mentioned province of Lahsa,
and he succeeded in doing so despite his relatively brief tenure
of office (1869-1872) in 1871.[214] Lahsa had been Ottoman territory between 1550 and 1672, but afterwards local Arab tribes led
by the Banu Khalid regained independence until conquered by
the Saudi-Wahhabi state in the 1790s. As we have seen, Ottoman
attempts at a counteroffensive had failed, and this was thus the
second – and last – successful Turkish expansion into eastern
Arabia. It proved to be relatively easy. Saudi power was collapsing amidst a quarrel between two brothers – Abdallah and
Saud – and the expedition launched from Basra on 10 May 1871

---

[214] Stephen Hemsley Longrigg, *Four Centuries of Modern Iraq*, Oxford
University Press 1925, pp. 302-303; Frederick F. Anscombe, *The Ot-
toman Gulf: The Creation of Kuwait, Saudi Arabia, and Qatar*, New
York: Columbia University Press, 1997, pp. 29-31; Zekeriya Kurşun,
Necid ve Ahsa'da Osmanli hakimiyeti, Ankara: Türk Tarih Kurumu,
1998, p. 79 ff.

landed the Ottoman troops, unopposed, at Ras Tannurah on 26 May. The Saudi governor of Qatif soon surrendered, Dammam fell, and the Ottoman troops set out for the provincial capital Hufuf, which they took at the end of July.

The British were concerned because of the naval dimension that this new expansion seemed to acquire. On 27 August 1871 the Turkish steam corvette *Lübnân* and the gunboat *Iskenderiye* called at Aden on their way to the Gulf. Commodore Arif Bey told the Political Resident that he had been ordered to take charge of a station extending from Mukalla on the Hadhramaut coast to Basra. A few days later he touched at Masqat, where he informed the Political Agent, Captain Ross, that ten ships were eventually to be assigned to the station. Already, he said, there were three steamers and one corvette in the Gulf, and docks and a powder magazine were being built at Basra for their use. What the Turks seemed to have in mind was little short of a challenge to the whole British position in the Gulf. At least, this is how it appeared to the Earl of Mayo, the Viceroy of India, when he heard the news. He wrote to the Duke of Argyll, the secretary of state for India, towards the end of September:

> "Your Grace will readily comprehend the difficulty which the continued presence of a Turkish naval force would throw in the way of our maintaining that position in the Persian Gulf which the British Government has, with the best results, come to occupy... In view of the many possible contingencies in the neighbouring parts of Asia, we conceive that at no time was the maintenance of our position in the Gulf of more material importance than at present to British interest, to the encouragement of trade, and to the preservation of the peace of the Indian Seas..."[215]

Mayo concluded his message with the opinion that if it were found to be true that the Turks intended to establish a squadron in the Gulf permanently, they should be induced to give up the idea. A related issue was the question what the Ottoman expansion could mean for the Trucial Coast principalities, Qatar, Bahrain, and Oman, all of which had special relations with Britain.

---

[215] Kelly (1968), pp. 730-31.

Especially Bahrain was a matter of concern, for hints were being received that Midhat Pasha might wish to add the archipelago "as a jewel to the [Ottoman] imperial diadem."[216] For a while the situation seemed critical. Colonel Lewis Pelly, the British Resident at Bushire, had at the moment only two warships at his disposal, the *Lynx* and the *Magpie*, but Sir William Fitzgerald, the Governor of Bombay, doubted whether the ships' armament was good enough, especially as the two Turkish corvettes in the Gulf were new. He concluded that the *Bullfinch*, then at Bombay, and the *Nimble*, at Aden, should be ordered to proceed immediately to the Gulf. On 11 November 1871 Pelly himself arrived at Bahrain, and expected an imminent crisis when he heard that Midhat Pasha was on board a Turkish steamer en route from Qatif to Uqair. The Turkish challenge never materialized, however. Midhat Pasha remained on the Lahsa coast until he sailed for Basra on 16 December, and the case was closed.[217] Clearly, the Viceroy of India had exaggerated the Turkish resolve. As always in the past, the Ottomans lacked the economic underpinning of dynamic maritime trade and enterprise necessary for adopting an effective forward policy on the high seas. The British soon sensed that, and ceased worrying about the presence of a Turkish squadron in the Persian Gulf. When in December 1871 Server Pasha, the foreign Minister, told Sir Henry Elliot, the British ambassador at Constantinople, that the Turkish Admiralty had 'always' regarded the Gulf as one of its naval stations, and that warships had to be kept there for purposes connected with the internal administration of Turkish Arabia, the Government of India asked the India Office whether it would not be to the satisfaction of everyone concerned if the Turkish naval squadron in the Gulf were to be kept to a strength commensurate with its professed task, so as to avoid the British Admiralty's being put to the trouble and expense of maintaining an unnecessarily large squadron in the Gulf.[218]

From then until 1913, this important province of eastern Arabia was an Ottoman *sanjak* or district. The British watched the Turks with a wary eye, but felt reassured when it became clear that the Ottoman naval presence would not turn into a challenge

---

[216] Ibid., p. 731.

[217] Ibid., p. 735.

[218] Ibid., p. 739.

to their dominance. By the turn of the century, the situation in the Persian Gulf thus seemed stabilized to the satisfaction of Great Britain, and, in varying degrees, to that of the other partners. Despite the competition of the Red Sea, which had benefited from the recently opened Suez Canal (1869), seaborne trade through the Gulf continued, and the area functioned as an artery of telegraphic communications between India and Europe. Beginning in 1864, telegraph lines and underwater cables crisscrossing the area were being laid, and by 1905 they linked a number of places in Iran, Oman, and Iraq, all part of the vast network stretching from Karachi to Constantinople and London.

In 1903, the whole world seemed to be enjoying the spread of civilization radiating from Europe, whose great powers – and even some of the small ones – possessed colonial empires around the globe and reaped substantial profits in return for the pacification and law and order they were propagating. The foremost among these was Great Britain, convinced of the righteousness of the imperial cause. This conception was expressed by Lord George Nathaniel Curzon, the Viceroy of India, while on an inspection tour of the Persian Gulf, in a famous speech that he gave before an assembly of the Trucial Coast Shaikhs during a *darbar* ceremony aboard H.M.S. *Argonaut* off Sharjah on 21 November 1903. It is worth quoting:

> 'Chiefs of the Arab Coast who are in Treaty relations with the British Government , – I have come here as the representative in the great Empire of India of the British authority which you and your fathers and fore-fathers have known and dealt with for more than a hundred years; and my object is to show you, that though you live at some distance from the shores of India, you are not forgotten by the Government, but that they adhere to the policy of guardianship and protection which has given you peace and guaranteed your rights... Chiefs, your fathers and grandfathers before you have doubtless told you of the history of the past. You know that a hundred years ago there were constant trouble and fighting in the Gulf; almost every man was a marauder or a pirate; kidnapping and slave-trading flourished; fighting and bloodshed went on without stint or respite; no ship could put out to sea without fear of attack; the pearl fishery was a scene of annual conflict; and security of trade or peace there was

none. Then it was that the British Government intervened and said that, in the interests of its own subjects and traders, and of its legitimate influence in the seas that wash the Indian coasts, this state of affairs must not continue. British flotillas appeared in these waters. British forces occupied the ports and towns on the coast that we see from this deck. The struggle was severe while it lasted but it was not long sustained. In 1820 the first general Treaty was signed between the British Government and the Chiefs; and of these or similar agreements there have been in all no fewer than eight. In 1839 the Maritime Truce was concluded, and was renewed from time to time until the year 1853, when it was succeeded by the Treaty of Perpetual Peace that has lasted ever since. Under that Treaty it was provided that there should be a complete cessation of hostilities at sea between the subjects of the signatory Chiefs, and a 'perfect maritime truce' – to use the words that were employed 'for evermore'; that in the event of aggressions on anyone by sea, the injured parties should not retaliate, but should refer the matter to the British Resident in the Persian Gulf; and that the British Government should watch over the peace of the Gulf and ensure at all times the observance of the Treaty...

Sometimes I think that the record of the past is in danger of being forgotten, and there are persons who ask – Why should Great Britain continue to exercise these powers? The history of your States and of your families, and the present condition of the Gulf, are the answer. ...We found strife and we have created order. It was our commerce as well as your security that was threatened and called for protection. At every port along these coasts the subjects of the King of England still reside and trade. The great Empire of India, which it is our duty to defend, lies almost at your gates. We saved you from extinction at the hands of your neighbours. We opened these seas to the ships of all nations, and enabled their flags to fly in peace. We have not seized or held your territory. We have not destroyed your independence, but preserved it. We are not now going to throw away this century of costly and triumphant enterprise; we shall not wipe out the most unselfish page in history. The peace of these waters must still be maintained; your independence will continue to be upheld; and the influence of the British Government must remain supreme.

...Chiefs, these are the relations that subsist between the British Government and yourselves. The Sovereign of the British Empire lives so far away that none of you has ever seen or will ever see his face; but his orders are carried out everywhere throughout his vast dominions by the officers of his Government, and it is as his representative in India, who is responsible to him for your welfare, that I am here today to exchange greetings with you, to renew old assurances, and to wish you prosperity in the future.'[219]

By today's standards, Lord Curzon's speech should of course be dismissed or branded as a case of colonialism at its most brazen and presumptuous, against the background of a British Empire that was riding the crest of its power, wealth and prestige, and as proof of England's imperialism, which had turned the Persian Gulf into a British lake. The speech was addressed to the Trucial Shaikhs, but *mutatis mutandis* the Shaikhs of Qatar, Bahrain, Kuwait, as well as the sultans of Oman and Zanzibar could have been included in the audience; and some aspects of it were not without validity even with respect to the "heavyweights" of the Gulf – Iran, the Ottoman Empire, and Saudi Arabia. They all benefited or suffered from this situation – depending on the eye of the beholder, and on which of the multifaceted effects of British presence is being emphasized. The speech also illustrates both the validity and fallacy of human expectations. In 1903 the Viceroy of India viewed with satisfaction the peace and prosperity spreading in the area thanks to Great Britain, and had little

---

[219] Lorimer, *Gazetteer*, 5: 2626-62 (Appendix P. Cruise of His Excellency Lord Curzon, Viceroy and Governor-General of India, in the Persian Gulf; the text of the address is on pp. 2638-39). "After Curzon's speech, an Arabic translation was read by Mr. Gaskin, Assistant Political Officer in Bahrain, and handsome gifts were distributed; each Shaikh attending in person received a sword from the Viceroy's hands, besides which a gold watch and chain and a sporting rifle were given to every Shaikh, and a rifle to every Shaikh's son. As the month of Ramadhan had now begun, no refreshments were served. The *Darbar* was then closed, and the Viceroy, the Naval Commander-in-Chief and the Shaikhs in succession took their departure from the "Argonaut", each receiving the guns due to his rank as he quitted the ship," p. 2639. See also Briton Cooper Busch, *Britain and the Persian Gulf, 1894-1914*, University of California Press 1967, pp. 259-62.

inkling of the extraordinary events that would make the Persian Gulf an ever more special and turbulent arena in the next hundred years until 2003 – and beyond.

The factor that raised the strategic and economic importance of the Persian Gulf beyond all expectations was the discovery of oil. In 1903 few suspected the vast wealth lying hidden underground and under the bottom of the sea, and the British lord would have been astounded had a magic mirror showed him the fabulously wealthy descendants of the impecunious Shaikhs at the turn of the next century and millennium,[220] or the substitution of the Pax Britannica by a Pax Americana, or again the turbulence that would agitate this second phase of peace imposed by the foremost world power.

The presence of oil was known in 1903, but only in the Persian province of Khuzistan, and exploration had not yet begun. The British firm D'Arcy had obtained a concession from the Persian government in 1901, and in 1908 the company's chief prospector George Reynolds struck oil at Masjid-e Suleiman. By the time World War I had broken out, production was starting, and the British Admiralty concluded a contract with the newly formed Anglo-Persian Oil Company to reserve the yield for its navy. Meanwhile the war itself transformed Ottoman Iraq into a battlefield between England and Turkey, while the rest of the Persian Gulf remained firmly under British control. The Allied victory in 1918 also meant the extinction of the multinational Ottoman and Habsburg empires and of the German colonial empire. The victors, primarily Great Britain and France, now occupied and controlled the formerly Ottoman-Arab Near East. The newly created League of Nations gave legal sanction to their authority, as mandate powers, to draw new borders, build new

---

[220] The Arab coastland of course had a long tradition of maritime trade, boat-building, pearling and fishing; this was especially true of Bahrain, and Dubai, as we have seen, was in 1903 becoming the foremost hub of entrepot trade in the eastern part of the Persian Gulf. The rulers themselves, however, participated little in mercantile activities, and the main beneficiaries were the merchants, many of them foreign, especially Indian. The modest conditions of the Shaikhs, their mansions and urban centers were still palpable in the 1950s, on the eve of the oil boom; this is amply documented by many testimonies, such as Sir Rupert Hay's *The Persian Gulf States*, Washington: The Middle East Institute, 1959.

nations, and fashion regimes of their preference in these new countries. Palestine, Trans-Jordan, Syria, and Iraq thus came into being as newly created states or mandate territories under British or French control. Saudi Arabia, however, not only escaped Allied occupation and its consequences but benefited from the Ottoman collapse to an extent that was to exceed even the greatest optimist's wildest dreams. On the one hand, Husain ibn Ali, the Hashimite *sharif* or ruler of the holy city of Mecca, now deprived of the earlier Ottoman and later British support, succumbed to the Saudi onslaught in 1925, and the Saudi emir added to his title that of King of the Hijaz. Luck had also smiled on the Saudis on the other, eastern fringe of Arabia. As we have already remarked, the Balkan War (1912-13) had caused enough trouble for the Ottoman Empire to impel it to withdraw its forces from Lahsa in 1913 (thus even before World War I brought British troops to Iraq), and the province immediately returned to the Saudi fold as al-Ahsa'. Had it not been for the Balkan War, the Turks could probably have retained Lahsa until the outbreak of the Great War, and British troops would have been landed not only in Iraq but also there to combat them. Bracketed by Kuwait to the north and the Trucial States to the south – all British protectorates – the Banu Khalid Arabs of al-Ahsa' might also have successfully clamored for a similar status. Bolstered by a treaty guaranteeing British protection, a sheikhdom of the Banu Khalid, possessing such ports as Ras Tannurah, Qatif, and Uqair, and established at the regional capital, Hufuf, would have come into being. The fertility of the oases of this province, especially famous for its dates, was proverbial; besides oasis agriculture and entrepot and caravan trade, fishing and pearling all added up to make this region a thriving one; its large Shiah minority gave it a further dimension of distinctiveness vis-à-vis the staunchly conservative Wahhabi sunnism of the Saudi state. Thus this hypothetical Sheikhdom of al-Ahsa, shielded by a treaty with Great Britain, might have survived like the other sheikhdoms along the Persian Gulf coast, until the 1930s when Western companies began prospecting for oil on its territory. World War II forced Britain to tighten her grip on – and protection of – the Persian Gulf area, a situation which lasted until 1971. By then, this Sheikhdom of al-Ahsa, or of the Banu Khalid, would have been the wealthiest country, per capita, on the planet, for under its soil is the world's largest concentration of oil.

This of course did not happen, and instead Saudi Arabia fell heir to this as yet unsuspected wealth. In 1932, still unaware of the fortunes in store under the soil of what later became Sharqi-yah (Eastern) Province, but basking in the prestige of having become the guardian of the Haramain – the holy cities of Mecca and Medina[221] – the Saudi emir Abd al-Aziz proclaimed himself king, and his country the Kingdom of Saudi Arabia.

Meanwhile in 1920 the League of Nations had designated Great Britain as the mandate power to administer Iraq, and the following year the British made the country a monarchy, offering the throne to Faisal, a son of the above-mentioned Hashimite Sharif of Mecca Husain. Faisal was crowned king of Iraq in August 1921, but the British mandate continued until 1930, when it was replaced by a treaty that provided for a special relationship between the two countries.

Although Iran escaped direct involvement in World War I, the heightened activity in the Persian Gulf could not but affect it in a number of ways, one being accelerated production of oil, with the construction of a refinery at Abadan by the Anglo-Persian Oil Company. The Company's principal agreement was with the Qajar government, but Shaikh Khaz`al of the Arab Ka`b tribe also received a share. He rose from the position of a local chieftain to an ever more autonomous warlord in Khuzistan; it was he who signed an agreement in 1910 allowing the British to build a pipeline from Masjid-e Sulaiman, on the eastern fringes of the province, to Abadan, where export facilities were being built. By the time World War I had ended, Khaz`al proclaimed Arabistan – an alternative name to Khuzistan – to be independent and sought British recognition. The last Qajar ruler, Ahmad Shah (1909-1925), was beset by a whole gamut of rebellions and separatist movements, and Iran came close to losing Khuzistan. Only in retrospect can we realize what a terrible loss it would have been. The attempt was thwarted in 1924 by a military campaign

---

[221] "Hadim ül-Haremeyn" or Guardian of the Two Holy Cities [of Mecca and Medina] had been one of the titles of the Ottoman sultan ; although the honor of the function passed to the Saudi monarch after Abd al-Aziz's conquest of the Hijaz in 1925, it was only King Fahd who officially adopted this title in 1986.

led by Reza Khan, who returned to Tehran in triumph with Khaz`al as his prisoner. This success in turn facilitated the deposition of the Qajar monarch and investiture of Reza Khan as Reza Shah, founder of the Pahlavi dynasty, in 1925. From then until the outbreak of World War II, the shah strove to strengthen his country politically and economically, efforts which included emancipation from excessive British influence and an enhancement of Persian national identity. To this end, in 1935 he ordered that the official name of his kingdom be changed from Persia to Iran, which in turn made the Anglo-Persian Oil Company change its name to Anglo-Iranian Oil Company. At the same time, however, extraction, refining, and exportation of oil continued to be under British control, and the distribution of the profits heavily favored Great Britain. Reza Shah's resentment of this made him lean toward Nazi Germany, but like the leaders of Iraq he bet on the losing side in World War II; Britain extended her control over southern Iran (just as Soviet Russia would soon do over the northern part of the country), and forced him to abdicate, enthroning his son Muhammad Reza in 1941.

Throughout World War II and even until the conflict between London and Tehran over Prime Minister Mosaddeq's nationalization of the Anglo-Iranian Oil Company in 1951, Iran was the main producer of oil in the Persian Gulf. Great Britain continued to be the dominant power there, and the Gulf thus still retained some of the characteristics of being "a British lake" even in these sunset years of the British Empire. The end was near, however, and it came with the general retreat of Britain from her colonies, beginning with India. We have seen that originally, the principal motivation for London's determination to control the Persian Gulf was its importance as a link between Great Britain and her most prized possession. Once India became independent in 1948, safeguarding this area became both less vital and unnecessarily onerous financially – unless protecting the new source of wealth, oil, justified the expense. The world had changed too much, however, for Britain to have the power to retain her monopoly. The 'Exclusive Agreements' of 1892 could not be repeated, and the British could only look on as their cousins the Americans penetrated the Persian Gulf in search of oil, influence, and security. The Iranian oil crisis of 1951-52 further accelerated this process. The embargo Britain succeeded in imposing upon Persian exports gave a boost to oil exploration and production on the Arab side, and to the realization that Arabia and the southern part of the Gulf itself might harbor the richest deposits in the world. Although the British received some share there, the main players henceforth were the Americans, and the stage was set to pass the guardianship of the Persian Gulf to the United States. Britain's withdrawal did not happen overnight, however, and until the process was consummated in 1971, the British presence continued to impose the Pax Britannica. It thus prevented what might have been an Iraqi invasion of Kuwait; it kept Iran from making attempts at annexing Bahrain and reclaiming the Tunb and Abu Musa islands; it played a protective role in the disputes over borders and territories claimed by Saudi Arabia at the expense of the Trucial sheikhdoms; it helped Abu Dhabi and Oman save the Buraimi – Al Ain oasis complex from Saudi annexation; and it played a decisive role in preventing the Masqat-Oman dichotomy from becoming permanent in the form of two separate states, a sultanate at Masqat and an imamate at Nizwa.

Meanwhile the above-mentioned dispute between the Persian government and the Anglo-Iranian Oil Company led to a bitter conflict whose grievous effects are still afflicting us today. Negotiations held in 1948 and 1949 produced an agreement, but the parliament rejected it and the government, headed by Muhammad Mosaddeq, nationalized the oil industry on 1 May 1951. Britain imposed an embargo on Iranian oil, and production and export were crippled. The young shah, accused of insufficiently supporting the national cause, was forced to leave the country, which thus came under the sole leadership of prime minister Mosaddeq. On the home front, among those who supported his program, was Tudeh, the Communist Party of Iran. Mosaddeq himself was not a communist but a patriot, a democrat and a friend of the West, especially of the United States. Initially, the American government sympathized with the Iranian position. The Persian statesman came to New York and Washington to plead Iran's case, and received support from President Truman. The presidential election of 1952 changed all that. True, President Eisenhower gave indications that he was leaning toward the course charted by his predecessor, but his sound instinct was thwarted by Secretary of State John Foster Dulles who gave the CIA permission to engineer a coup that in 1953 toppled

Mosaddeq and reinstalled the shah.[222] For the next twenty-six years Iran languished under the repressive regime of Muhammad Reza Shah.[223]

Although the crisis proved fatal to Dr. Mosaddeq's steward-ship, the process he had set in motion with respect to oil did not stop but in various forms continued and ultimately succeeded. On 29 October 1954 an agreement between the Persian govern-ment and an international consortium recognized the Iranian na-tionalization of its oil industry and stipulated an equal division of profits. For some time the consortium, in which British Petro-leum, the former Anglo-Iranian Oil Company, had a major share, retained considerable rights with respect to exploitation and marketing. Further agreements, however, increased Iranian con-trol, and since 1973 Iran has been in full charge of its oil indus-try.

The Shah may have had some merit, during the second phase of his reign, in defending Iran's economic interests. His increas-ingly repressive regime, however, alienated the majority of the citizens, and it also turned the enthusiastically pro-American

---

[222] An excellent account of this sad chapter of Iran's history can be found in Stephen Kinzer's *All the Shah's Men: an American Coup and the Roots of Middle East Terror*, Hoboken 2003.

[223] Secretary Dulles's motivation for allowing the CIA to engineer this coup bore certain similarities to that of Lord Auckland, Governor-General of India, for invading Afghanistan in 1839. Dost Mohammed, the Barakzai-Durrani Emir of Afghanistan, was an able and honest ruler determined to preserve his country's independence from Britain as well as from Russia. Auckland, however, found neutrality not good enough – prefiguring Dulles's statement that "neutrality is immoral" – and de-cided to replace Dost Mohammed with Shah Shuja, a Popalzai-Durrani emir ousted in dynastic struggle and living as an expatriate on a British pension in India. The result was the first Afghan War (1839-42), a dis-aster for the British and one of the causes of the Afghans' until then absent xenophobia and religious fanaticism, with consequences that are, as in the case of Iran, still with us. Both these Muslim countries were almost certainly saved from eventual Russian and Soviet domina-tion by Great Britain and the United States, whose merit was obscured by the flawed methods they used. This paradox acquires an especially absurd dimension in Iran, where Islam was shielded from the atheistic Bolshevik specter by the protective shadow cast by the... "Great Sa-tan".

Persians against the United States, which they blamed for the intervention and the subsequent unflinching support of the autocratic monarch. The coup engineered in 1953 ultimately contributed to the creation of a new problem. In 1978-79 popular pressure, this time backed by Iran's Shiite clergy, forced the shah to abdicate and leave the country. The movement's spiritual head, Ayatollah Khomeini, returned from exile in Paris on 1 February 1979 and assumed the leadership of a revolution whose outcome was the establishment of an Islamic Republic. Instead of seeing an enlightened patriot of the Mosaddeq mold replace the autocratic shah, the Persians thus saw their country delivered into the hands of an uncompromisingly religious figure and his group of Muslim clerics. Moreover, the revolution created a problem for the United States. While in 1953 the shah was briefly and promisingly replaced by a pro-American statesman and a democrat, in 1979 the man who came to power turned out to be an implacably anti-American theocrat.

The Islamic Republic of Iran was proclaimed on 1 April 1979. It has a president, an executive branch, a legislative branch, a supreme court, and a constitution (*qanun-e asasi*). The legislative body, *Majlis-e Shura-ye Islami*, is Iran's parliament, consisting of 290 members, who are elected for four year terms. There is a council of ministers presided over by the republic's president (at present Mahmud Ahmadi-Nejad, elected in June 2005). There are political parties.

In all these respects, Iran's political structure appears fairly similar to that of most democracies of the modern world. On closer look, however, we observe strikingly original, theocratic features, introduced by the Shiite religious establishment who created this republic.

First of all, the head of the state is not the president but a high-ranking Shiite cleric, whose function has the title *vali-e faqih*; it implies that the incumbent is an Islamic jurisprudent (*faqih*), who leads the faithful pending the return of the *mahdi*, a descendant of the Prophet Muhammad through his daughter Fatimah and son-in-law Ali. The *mahdi* or hidden imam, who at a certain point withdrew into occultation, is expected to make a messianic re-entry into the world and install a truly Islamic community. Shiite belief as to which descendant of Ali entered occultation is splintered among several groups, but those in Iran are the "Twelvers": In their case, the *mahdi* is the 12th imam, Muhammad al-Mahdi, also referred to as *al-Qa'im* and *al-Hujjah*, believed to have entered occultation in 874 of the common era.

The position and power of the *vali-ye faqih* emphasizes the theocratic nature of the Islamic Republic of Iran. This supreme leader is not elected by popular suffrage but selected for life by an assembly of religious experts. Iran has had two such leaders since the foundation of the republic: Ayatollah Khomeini, from the beginning till his death on 3 June 1989; and Ayatollah Ali Hoseini Khamenei, appointed the next day, 4 June, and still in office today.

The powers of the *vali-ye faqih* are formidable partly because he is not accountable to any elected body, nor is the assembly of experts that appoints him. The only checks and balances here are the tenets of Shiah doctrine and the *shariah* or Islamic law based on the Koran, hence the true nature of Iran as a theocracy. The result has been a restrictive regime of religious imposition on a nation that had nourished hopes for freedom when it emerged from the Shah's dictatorship.[224]

Iraq, as we have seen, was a kingdom created by Great Britain in the aftermath of World War I, and it remained under British influence for a number of years even after the abrogation of the mandate in 1930; this was formally expressed by a 'Treaty of Friendship' concluded for a duration of 25 years. Rising Arab nationalism sought to rid the country of the strictures imposed by foreign powers, but World War II and then the Cold War made this process complex and slow. This was further complicated by the discovery of oil also in Iraq; the deposits were in several places, but the richest fields are in the country's northeast around Kirkuk, and in the south near the Gulf and the Kuwaiti border.

---

[224] The dual government of present-day Iran, one religious, the other secular, is unique, but there was an interesting analogy in the Soviet Union with its version of dual government, one ideological and quasi-religious (the Marxist-Leninist scriptures, the prophetic-messianic role of Lenin, the church-like Communist party, the missionary zeal of spreading communism throughout the world), the other secular (the elected parliament, the president, the cabinet of ministers). In both cases, strict subordination of the secular to the ideological/religious was – and is – absolutely mandatory.

Pro-Axis leanings on the part of the Iraqi government during World War II forced the British to intervene with their Arab Legion of Jordan; fear of Soviet penetration led to increased American involvement during the Cold War. The Baghdad Pact formed in 1955 between Iraq, Turkey, and Pakistan, with the United States as the unofficial but vital partner, had the purpose of countering Soviet expansion. Iraqi nationalists, however, viewed this pact as yet another attempt by foreign powers to subordinate their country's interests to the imperialists' own ends. The coup – and revolution – which the army carried out in 1958 was an extreme expression of this resentment, and it was a bloody one. King Faisal II and the prime minister Nuri Said were killed, and a Republic was proclaimed. At first it followed a pattern common in such situations. Power was in the hands of army officers, whose leaders would in due course be displaced by other similarly short-lived strongmen. The new regime failed to demonstrate an ability to adequately cope with the country's problems and wisely exploit the tremendous economic potential offered by rising oil production, but it did achieve emancipation from foreign influence.

Abd al-Karim Qasim, the general who led the coup in 1958 and then became the Republic's first president, was in 1961 on the verge of ordering Iraqi troops to march into Kuwait. The scenario was both historic and prophetic. Until that year, Kuwait had had a formal treaty with Great Britain that made it the colonial power's protectorate, but the ruler, Abdallah III Al Sabah, terminated the treaty and declared independence. Qasim refused to recognize the sheikhdom's legitimacy, and on the grounds that Kuwait had been a dependency of Ottoman Iraq proclaimed his intention to reassert this tie. The precedent of Ottoman suzerainty over Kuwait had already been used by the second king of Iraq, Ghazi b. Faisal (1933-39). Like his father Faisal, Ghazi at first had paid little attention to his kingdom's little neighbor. On 23 December 1934, however, the government of Kuwait signed an agreement with a British company, leasing it the right to prospect for oil and extract it over a time span of 75 years. This awakened Iraq's interest, and in February 1939 Ghazi ordered Husain Fawzi, chief of staff of the Iraqi army, to occupy Kuwait. At the same time he ordered Ali Muhammad al-Shaikh Ali, *mutasarrif* or governor of the district of Basra, to do everything possible to facilitate the planned military campaign. The attack never took place, thanks to the realism of Naji Shawkat, the acting prime minister in the absence of Nuri Said, who had gone to London to attend a conference on the Palestinian problem. Naji Shawkat impressed upon the king the displeasure on the part of Britain, Iran, and Saudi Arabia which such an enterprise would cause. The king apparently never gave up the idea, but his death in an automobile accident on 4 April 1939 put an end to this stage of the project. The idea reemerged in veiled form when in February 1958 Nuri Said and King Husain of Jordan met to discuss a Federation of the Hashimite kingdoms of Iraq and Jordan. Both statesmen, the prime minister and the monarch, planned to invite Kuwait to join this new political formation. The project must have appeared to the Iraqis and Jordanians especially tempting because of the dramatic rise in Kuwait's oil production, but neither the Kuwaitis themselves nor their protectors the British shared this enthusiasm. At any rate, the new Federation itself was stillborn, for the project foundered in the above-mentioned coup carried out on 14 July 1958.

Iraq's designs on Kuwait did not die with the monarchy, and the new president, general Qasim, declared his determination to annex it on the same historical grounds as those advanced by his predecessor – that Kuwait had been part of Ottoman Iraq. On 25 June 1961 Qasim ordered Iraq's armed forces to prepare for military action that would lead to the occupation and annexation of Kuwait. The principality's ruler, Shaikh Abd Allah al-Salim Al Sabah, appealed to Great Britain for help, and the former suzerain acted forthwith, mobilizing an impressive array of its forces still present in the Middle East. By 6 July 1961, there were some 40,000 British troops in Kuwait, in addition to 6 warships with airplanes and paratroopers nearby. Kuwait also lodged a complaint with the United Nations, and despite Iraqi opposition the organization agreed on 2 July to discuss the problem although the principality was not yet a member. Meanwhile other Arab neighbors, in particular Saudi Arabia, voiced their concern and began to take action with a view to assisting Kuwait. A regiment of Saudi troops was sent to the Kuwaiti-Iraqi border and placed under British command, while others lent moral support. On 12 July the political committee of the Arab League met in an emergency session, and on the 13th the organization held the first of several sessions during which it welcomed Kuwait as a new member of the League. A significant component of the deliberations was a resolution to replace the British protective umbrella with one composed of military units of the Arab League. The last-mentioned alternative proved unnecessary, for faced with the British deterrent, Iraq desisted.

Qasim was overthrown in another army coup, and other officers followed until a new trend appeared: in 1968 the junta that seized and held power had a link with a political party, the Ba-ath. A politician, a civilian who had never experienced combat in war (though he liked to play the soldier by parading in military attire), eventually rose to the top: by 1979 Saddam Husain had become president, and was to steer the country's destinies until 2003. Had he been a wise statesman, or at least a realistic one, he might have led Iraq on a path of unprecedented rise in material well-being and cultural florescence. The country's potential was many-faceted, but oil wealth and a remarkably well educated, able, and quite secular urban class were its greatest assets. The Garden of Eden was in Iraq, we read (with some latitude of interpretation) in the Bible; a good government in Baghdad could have recreated this idyll by the turn of the new millennium.

Yet Saddam Husain ruined his country's chances by perverting the political process internally, and by reaching for forbidden fruit externally. His desire to become the unquestioned master of the Iraqis made him create a brutally repressive dictatorship; and his greed to acquire even more oil wealth made him invade Iran in 1980 and Kuwait in 1990.

The invasion of Iran affected primarily Khuzistan. In September 1980 Iraqi troops crossed the border and marched into this province, starting a war that would last until August 1988. An unavowed but no doubt principal motivation was greed driving the dictator of oil-rich Iraq to seize his neighbor's oil-rich province, while using the nationalist card on the grounds that "Arabistan" had a sizable Arabic-speaking population.[225] Another reason, paramount according to some observers, was Saddam's fear that Iran would stir up Iraq's Shiite majority against his eminently Sunni regime. The war, however, ground

---

[225] Le Strange, *The Lands*, pp. 232-47; Lorimer, *Gazetteer*, 7: 115-64, s.v. Arabistan; Schwarz, *Iran*, pp. 289 ff.; S. Soucek, "Arabistan or Khuzistan?", *Iranian Studies* 17 (1984), 195-213.

to an exhausting stalemate, and ended in 1988 with a return to the pre-war *status quo* but had cost Iraq an estimated $100 billion – besides the still more tragic loss of life.

Saddam Husain's accession to power coincided with the Soviet invasion of Afghanistan, an event that should have placed him on good terms with Washington. Moreover, the invasion of Khuzistan occurred soon after the outbreak of the diplomatic crisis between Iran and the United States, and the American administration was not averse to some degree of implicit siding with Iraq. He wasted this advantage by invading Kuwait. There was the usual ostensible justification – that Kuwait had been part of Ottoman Iraq – just as there of course was the real motivation, the principality's oil wealth. The resulting Gulf War is one of the most amply described recent events in both scholarly and general literature. Here we want to add a few somewhat unconventional comments. The Iraqi invasion on 2 August 1990 took the world by surprise, and was condemned by practically everybody, but not in the same manner. Most informed observers, aware of Iraq's historical fixation on Kuwait, remained skeptical of the apocalyptic interpretation and damning verdict passed by President George Bush, who compared Saddam Husain to Hitler planning to conquer or destroy first his neighbors and then the whole world, including the United States. A more nuanced condemnation came from Iraq's immediate neighbors – Saudi Arabia, Syria, Jordan, Turkey, and implicitly of course also Iran – who were angry and determined to resist Husain. And there was a man who too was angry and ready to return from Afghanistan, where he had successfully fought the Soviets, to his native Arabia in order to fight the Iraqis. These regional powers could have adequately thwarted Iraq's aggression, but this task was preempted by the United States. In fact, at least in the view of this author, the Turkish army alone would have defeated that of Saddam Husain. And if we visualize other possible combinations or alliances – Turkey with Iran, Turkey with Jordan and Saudi Arabia, we must conclude that the dictator's troops would not have had a chance.[226] What we do know is that the massive American

---

[226] It is also conceivable, indeed plausible, that regional resistance, if allowed to gain its own momentum, would have welcomed American help, whether directly or through the United Nations. That would have made a fundamental psychological difference; had Kuwait been liber-

operation and subsequent stationing of United States troops in Saudi Arabia, land of the Haramain, humiliated and enraged Muslims of Usamah ben Laden's mold. The path toward 9/11 was open.

The drama of the subsequent decade is well known. Suspecting Saddam Husain of developing weapons of mass destruction, successive American governments persuaded the United Nations to impose an embargo on Iraq in order to force its government to cease doing so. Iraq repeatedly denied any such activities, and inspection teams sent by the United Nations reported inconclusive but mostly negative findings. A stalemate ensued until the terrorist attacks of 11 September 2001. By then George W. Bush, the son of the president who had led the Gulf War of 1991, was president. Both he and his closest advisers, dominated by a new strand of political thinking advocating pre-emptive action and global exercise of American power, had been planning a "régime change" in Iraq, and the attack of 9/11 facilitated this project's execution. The first stage of the new "war on terror", liberating Afghanistan from Taliban despotism and depriving Usama ben Laden of a hospitable base, was a resounding, justified, and internationally acclaimed success.[227] Subsequently, however, the Bush administration persuaded the American people that the real man behind 9/11 had been Saddam Husain,[228] and it received

---

ated in this manner, the destructive resentment of non-Muslim intervention could have been avoided.

[227] At least in its initial stage. What should have been the essential purpose of the operation – eliminating the al-Qaidah in Afghanistan (and, little noticed, in Pakistan, the only Muslim country that is also a nuclear power), reducing its capability worldwide, capturing Usamah ben Laden, and reconstructing the war-torn country – has not been achieved, because the overwhelming part of the American effort swerved from those goals towards changing the regime in Iraq and capturing Saddam Husain.

[228] In fact, to Usamah ben Laden, Saddam Husain was a godless secularist who had to be eliminated, and Iraq was one of the few Arab countries – in contrast to Saudi Arabia for example – where al-Qaidah could not operate, so that in this sense President Bush acted as Usamah's unwitting proxy. One exception was the northeastern segment of the country, a part of the so-called "no fly zone" patrolled by British and American aircraft in order to protect its Kurdish population

unstinting support on the road toward the invasion of Iraq in March 2003.[229]

The invasion and subsequent attempted pacification has now reached a crucial stage epitomized by the parliamentary elections of December 15, 2005 and the formation of a new Iraqi government in May-June 2006.[230] The invasion, occupation, reconstruction, and political process are subject to conflicting interpretations and predictions. Throughout its long history, Mesopotamia has needed either a strong central authoritarian power (Babylonia, Assyria, Baghdad as the center of the Abbasid Islamic Empire, Baghdad under a strongman), or the presence of a Middle Eastern superpower (pre-Islamic Iran, Islamic Ottoman Empire), or of a global superpower (Great Britain in the first half of the 20th century, the United States in the 21st century), to avoid disintegrating into separate ethnic and religious segments. The professed goal of the United States, to create a unified and stable Iraq, may be realizable as long as the Iraqi government is supported by a sufficient American military presence.

For our purposes, the main interest lies in the fact that the war and the subsequent military presence of the United States cannot but further enhance the role of the Gulf, which holds the key to the logistics of the Allied operation, with the ever-present role of oil in the background. The air link, sure enough, is important. Foreign troops arrive and leave by air, the wounded and the dead are evacuated by air. But most of the matériel comes by sea, and bases in places like Bahrain and Kuwait are indispensable. The

---

from government troops; a subsidiary branch of al-Qaidah apparently acquired a foothold there.

[229] An excellent and impressively well-documented analysis of the war's background is William R. Polk's *Understanding Iraq: The Whole Sweep of Iraqi History, from Genghis Khan's Mongols to the Ottoman Turks to the British Mandate to the American Occupation*, New York: Harper Collins, 2005. The title is misleading: the book's main focus is on recent and current events.

[230]Although deprived of official approval by the United Nations, the invasion and occupation was carried out in the name of a coalition. Indeed, besides the 130 thousand Americans and 20 thousand Britons, there were troops sent by other countries; the largest contingent came from Spain with some 5000 troops. A noteworthy detail is the fact that no Muslim neighbor – not even Saudi Arabia, Kuwait, or Turkey – contributed a single soldier.

importance of the Persian Gulf, already immense by virtue of its
being the world's richest supplier of oil, cannot but have grown
with its strategic role in the Iraq war and America's newly assumed guardianship of the entire Middle East.

The case of Kuwait in 1961 and other examples cited above
illustrate both the effectiveness of the Pax Britannica prior to the
Empire's definitive withdrawal from the Persian Gulf by 1971,
and the "change of guard" after that date, with the United States
stepping in to spread a Pax Americana over the area. The process
has gone through several stages and dramatic confrontations
against a background much more complex than that facing Great
Britain in the 19th century. There have been, however, certain
basic features common to the British and American enterprises.
The most salient one is the reassertion of the Gulf itself as the
absolutely essential platform of operations and dominance.
Without its control by the British navy, and then by the American navy and air force, any enterprise on land would have been
out of the question. In the 19th century and up to World War II,
this was a fairly straightforward proposition. For Britain, the
goal had been relatively limited: safeguarding the Gulf as a conduit of trade and of communications between India and London;
beyond that, military and political involvement on land with the
riparian countries was kept at a minimum. Since then, three new
facts came to complicate the gradual takeover of the task by the
United States. One was oil; another was the Cold War; the third
was an unexpected combination of Arab nationalism with Islamic radicalism, both further inflamed by the Palestinian-Israeli
conflict. To this we might add the special role unusual political
leaders can play in affecting the course of history. All have affected or have been affected by the manner in which America
has endeavored to spread peace and democracy, and to protect
her interests in the Persian Gulf.

Through all the human storms that have buffeted the Persian
Gulf since the mantle of its custody was passed to America, one
prerequisite, as we have said, has been constant: naval mastery.
American dominance of the Gulf's waters is as unchallenged
today as was the British dominance before World War II. The
process started well before Britain's withdrawal, for in 1949
ships of the US Navy MEF (Middle East Force) were given a
base in the Bahrain port of Mina Sulman, and office accommo-

dation was leased at the British Naval Compound in nearby Ju-fair. A new lease was signed, this time with the government of Bahrain, on 31 December 1971, thus almost immediately after Britain's official withdrawal. Although cooperation between Bahrain and the United States went through several difficult phases, the two governments have drawn ever closer, and on 1 July 1995 an agreement was signed making Bahrain the head-quarters of the Fifth Fleet, whose ships are now officially "home ported" at Mina Sulman. While the United States navy has its main base in Bahrain, it also benefits from the hospitality of sev-eral other Persian Gulf ports as stations of logistical and tactical support; the foremost among these is Dubai. The main American air force base is at Udaid in Qatar. Situated some 25 kilometers to the southwest of the emirate's capital Doha, it is equipped to accommodate up to 120 aircraft and ten thousand troops, and is one of the five USAF Prepositioned War Reserve Material bases in the Gulf (three others are in Oman and one is in Bahrain).

In 1968 Great Britain announced her intention to terminate her treaties with the Trucial Coast principalities by the end of 1971. This plan gave the native leaders time to prepare for inde-pendence, and by 1971 they had formed a federation that became known as the United Arab Emirates.[231] Shaikh Zayid bin Sultan, emir of Abu Dhabi, was the driving force behind this bold and successful process, and he became the federation's first presi-dent. Besides the Trucial States proper, Qatar and Bahrain had at first also joined the federation, but soon afterwards left it, and the definitive membership now consists of Abu Dhabi, Dubai, Sharjah, Ajman, Umm Qaiwain, Ras al-Khaimah, and Fujairah. These are also the names of their capitals, which in turn are ports on the Persian Gulf coast with the exception of Fujairah, located on the coast of the Gulf of Oman. Abu Dhabi dwarfs all the oth-ers in size and wealth, blessed as it is with 80% of the proven oil reserves found in the federation. The deposits are both on land and offshore. Some of those on land are in areas claimed both by Abu Dhabi and Saudi Arabia.

---

[231] Rosemarie Said Zahlan, *The Origins of the United Arab Emirates: a political and social history of the Trucial States.* London: Macmillan, 1978; eadem, *The Making of the Gulf States: Kuwait, Bahrain, Qatar, the United Arab Emirates, and Oman.* 2nd ed. Ithaca Press 1998, hence-forth cited as Zahlan 1998.

Shaikh Zayid bin Sultan died in November 2004, and was succeeded in the double post of emir of Abu Dhabi and president of the Federation by his son Khalifah bin Zayid. The oil wealth of this emirate is prodigious, and the recent rise in oil prices – partly caused by the Iraq war – further compounds this bonanza (some of this wealth is used to help the less fortunate small emirates of Ajman and Umm Qaiwain). Neighboring Dubai, next in size and wealth, stands out as a dynamic international business center. In Dubai City, the *khawr* or inlet that had been its harbor and site of traditional boat building was eclipsed by Mina' (Port) Rashid, a new harbor built outside; this modern facility is flanked by what ranks among the world's largest drydocks. Moreover, some twenty kilometers to the southwest of Dubai City, at Mina' Jabal Ali, was built what some claim to be the world's largest man-made harbor. Another illustration of the principality's business dynamism is that the company Dubai Ports World (*Mawani Dubai al-Alamiyah*), which already operates 22 ports worldwide, is in the process of purchasing the operation of 29 more ports from the British company Peninsular & Oriental Steam Navigation Company for $6.8 billion. The deal was to bring the number of ports operated by the Dubai company to 51 in thirty countries, including five in the United States (New York, Philadelphia, Baltimore, Miami, and New Orleans); concerns of security voiced by many senators, congressmen as well as other public and media figures have forced the Bush administration to cancel the inclusion of American ports, however.

The emirates of Abu Dhabi and Dubai have lately not only grown exponentially but boast some of the most dazzling features of an almost futuristic civilization. In Dubai, a series of artificial islands has been built off the coast that replicate the continents and large islands on the planet (a business venture, where real estate is being sold at astronomical prices and under stringent conditions). In a similar vein, in the vicinity of the federation's capital Abu Dhabi, the *Jazirat al-Sadiyat*, "Island of Delights", has been introduced to the international community by Shaikh Muhammad bin Zayid Al Nahyan, heir presumeptive to the throne, as a place of luxurious comfort and relaxation. Meanwhile the world's tallest building, at least 700 meters high, is reportedly planned in Dubai. This city has also become a hub of international air travel and tourism, with Air Dubai gaining

respect for its excellence. These are of course only the most con-
spicuous achievements. The whole infrastructure has undergone
rapid development, from public transportation to education and
health care.

If we step back and glance at the whole southern coast of the
Persian Gulf, we see an almost uniform scenario on the political
front. Kuwait, Saudi Arabia, Bahrain, Qatar, and the Emirates
are ruled by monarchic families rather than by autocratic individuals. These polities may be partly a result of the still recently
tribal structure of their societies, in which the heir presumptive is
not necessarily the Shaikh's son but another able man of the
family. Family rule in the Gulf States also has other effects, the
most noticeable being the fact that not only the sovereign but
much of the government consists of members of the dynasty,
starting with the prime minister and affecting the other vital
posts such as foreign affairs and defense. Thus the Al Sabah of
Kuwait, the Al Saud of Saudi Arabia, the Al Khalifah of Bahrain, the Al Thani of Qatar, the Al Nahyan of Abu Dhabi and the
other families of the Emirates all fill the principal posts in their
governments.[232] Until recently, their rule rested on the right bal-
ance of shared interests with other tribal leaders and the urban,
mainly merchant elites. The influx of wealth through the oil
boom has now enabled the rulers to develop centralized bureauc-
racies with which to defend their own privileges, but also to raise
the standard of living and quality of life for all citizens. The outcome has been a special kind of authoritarian welfare state presided over by a benevolent monarch. The undeniable good will
and success of this relationship has been marred, however, by a
lack of corresponding progress on the political level. The resulting social tensions and an awakening citizenry have forced all
the rulers to begin introducing reforms that include some degree,
or at least promises, of parliamentarian democracy. The point
departure is usually the *shariah* or Islamic law, which recom-

---

[232] *Al* (with a long *a*) is an Arabic word with the connotation of family,
clan, which is then identified by its specific name: *Al* Saud of Saudi
Arabia, *Al* Sabah of Kuwait, etc. It is easily confused graphically, and
to a certain extent semantically, with the superficially similar gram-
matical article *al-* (a short *a* here), so that the forms *al*-Sabah, *al*-
Khalifah etc. are common; and even phonetically: in colloquial Gulf
Arabic, the *a* in *Al* is also pronounced short like the article *al-*.

mends a consultative assembly, or so at least the more sophisticated theorists interpret the Koranic verse *"Wa-shawirhum fi l-
amri!"* ([O Muhammad,] consult them on matters of government!).[233] The *majlis al-shura* or consultative assembly has thus
been the usual initial innovation, and it is only recently that
elected parliaments with legislative powers in the Western sense
have begun to appear in some of the Gulf States.

Gulf Cooperation Council (GCC)

The Cooperation Council for the Arab States of the Gulf (*Majlis
al-Taawun li-Duwal al-Khalij al-Arabiyah*), usually referred to
by its abbreviated name Gulf Cooperation Council (GCC; *Majlis
al-Taawun al-Khaliji*), consists of the Arab states of the Persian
Gulf except Iraq, thus of Kuwait, Saudi Arabia, Bahrain, Qatar,
the United Arab Emirates, and Oman.[234] The initial step towards
its creation was taken at a meeting of the foreign ministers of
these countries in February 1981 at Riyadh; official inauguration
took place on 25 May of that year, when the heads of the six
states met at Abu Dhabi and approved a charter which stipulates
that the purpose of the alliance is to effect coordination, integration and inter-connection among the Member States in order to
achieve unity. The charter defines cooperation in the broadest
sense: political, social, economic, commercial, scientific, techni-
cal, cultural. The Council consists of three bodies: a Supreme
Council, which consists of the rulers themselves and meets once
a year (its chairmanship rotates in alphabetical order, and each
member has one vote); a Ministerial Council, which consists of
the six foreign ministers or other delegated ministers, and it
meets four times a year; and the General Secretariat in Riyadh,
the headquarters of the GCC.

Rather than being a structurally rigid organization, the Council functions more as a platform for the exchange of ideas and
the creation of institutions shared by the member countries. One
example is the formation of the Gulf University based in Bahrain. Nevertheless, the alliance has not so far quite been able to
resolve some disputes – mainly territorial – plaguing the relations between several of its members. Some problems go back

---

[233] Koran 3:159.
[234] Zahlan 1998, pp. 157-58.

several decades or even centuries, while others have appeared recently or are in the process of formation as a result of the members states' different relations with other foreign countries.

Oil in the Persian Gulf area

Oil plays a paramount role in this area, and is likely to do so well into the second half of the 21st century. Its commercial value cannot but grow, given the rising demand by an ever more industrialized and thus oil-thirsty world. It may be of interest to glance at this wealth from a simple comparative angle. Among the top ten oil-rich countries around the globe, the first five slots are occupied by Persian Gulf states:

Oil: Proven reserves (billions of barrels, 2005 estimate)

1. Saudi Arabia	262.7
2. Iran	133.3
3. Iraq	112.5
4. United Arab Emirates	97.8
5. Kuwait	96.5
Total	**704.7**

Comparison with the next six oil producing countries

6. Venezuela	78.0
7. Russia	69.0
8. Libya	38.0
9. Nigeria	34.0
10. Kazakhstan	26.0
11. USA	22.5
Total	**267.5**

The five petroleum-rich Persian Gulf states also possess large deposits of the other principal source of energy, natural gas. Iran and Qatar are number 2 and 3, on the world scale, with respect to proven reserves of natural gas, Russia being no. 1. Here is what Simon Romero, "A Dispute Underscores the New Power of

Gas," *New York Times*, 3 January 2006, C1 p. 1, writes: "Russia has the largest natural gas reserves, with 1,700 trillion cubic feet of the fuel, or 27 percent of the world's total, according to BP, the British oil and gas giant. Just two other countries rival Russia in natural gas reserves, Iran, with 971 trillion cubic feet, and Qatar, with 910 trillion cubic feet." If this estimate is correct, Iran and Qatar combined possess 1,881 trillion cubic feet, or almost one third of the world's total.

Conclusion

A Review and Ponderings About the Future

The role of the Persian Gulf has been noteworthy in several respects: as an avenue of trade and communications; as a source of valuable commodities extracted from its waters, from its bed, and from its surrounding coastland; and as a strategic naval and military area. Its northernmost shores witnessed, five thousand years ago, the birth of the first literate civilization, the Sumerian. The prosperity of Sumerian city-states and then of the Akkadian and Babylonian empires that flourished in Mesopotamia stimulated seaborne trade and links with both nearby and distant partners such as Dilmun (Bahrain), Magan (Oman), and Meluhka (the lower course and estuary of the Indus River). The earliest ships carrying commercial goods may well have plied the waters of the Persian Gulf, and this traffic was further stimulated by the Gulf's natural penetration inland through the splendid waterways of the two great Mesopotamian rivers, the Euphrates and the Tigris.

For over two millennia the city kingdoms and empires of Mesopotamia were the consumers and producers in this seaborne trade, while cities such as Ur and Agade and other capitals of these earliest civilizations also functioned as seaports. The governments themselves, however, showed little penchant for maritime ventures, whether for trade or conquest. The few known exceptions confirm this rule: King Sargon's (2334-2279) naval expedition to Dilmun, and King Sennacherib's (704-661) partly seaborne campaign to reduce Elamite cities for example. This is one of the reasons why the rest of the Gulf remained for a long time without history,[235] and why its early ports, fishermen, and seafarers, are anonymous. We have remarked in the introduction that at the time of the Sumerians, Elamites and Babylonians, the Gulf, not yet Persian, was referred to in their texts by an assortment of names such as the Lower Sea; in other words, it remained veiled in the anonymity of an alien expanse which the official establishments of the earliest political formations on its shores seldom engaged.

The foundation of the first historical Iranian empire, the Achaemenid, set in motion profound transformations in the ancient world, some of which also affected the Gulf. It became Persian, and not just by name. For the first time a sizeable portion of its coasts – the entire northern side – belonged to one national state, in contrast to the reduced shoreline at the head of the Gulf occupied by the Achaemenids' Mesopotamian predecessors. Moreover, the projection of Persian power did not stop at Iran's coasts: the Achaemenid Empire encompassed the entire Middle East, and thus also the whole Gulf. It was with its Persian identity that the Gulf entered the consciousness and writings of Greek geographers and historians soon after the conquest of Babylon by Cyrus the Great in 539 BC. The earliest political formations in the gulf area, the Mesopotamian ones, were now satrapies of the Persian Empire.

The solid and lasting nature of the Iranian state was demonstrated by the resilience with which it rode out the storm of Alexander's invasion and the subsequent period of Hellenistic rule in the Orient. What is more, by the time the Sasanians equaled the imperial magnitude of the Achaemenids, the Persian Gulf was more firmly anchored in Iran's political structure than it had ever been at the time of their illustrious forebears. The Aramaean and Arab principalities such as Characene/Mesene at the head of the Gulf and Gerrha in the middle of its southern shore, which had been vassals or docile neighbors under the Sasanians' Hellenistic and Arsacid predecessors, were now transformed into satrapies or new provinces under Sasanian governors. Iran's powerful rival to the west, the Byzantine Empire, disputed the possession of Syria and Mesopotamia, but the Persian Gulf always remained beyond its reach.

---

[235] But rich in prehistoric material civilization, as ongoing archaeological research in several parts of the Gulf area has revealed.

Under the Sasanians, the Gulf acquired a physiognomy which in the parlance of modern geopolitics could be called a Persian lake. A process had started toward a transformation of its southern coastland that was not only political and military but also cultural.

This process, however, evolved only gradually, and met with an opposite trend that had been gathering momentum: the movement of Arab tribes from the interior and southern regions of the Arabian Peninsula toward Syria, Mesopotamia, Oman and the Persian Gulf. Not only had it reached the coast just as the Sasanians were consolidating their rule in Iran, but it gained enough strength to establish rudimentary political formations or join existing principalities such as Gerrha and Tylos, the former Dilmun. Arabic names began to prevail over the existing ones, and the coastal and insular regions that had included Gerrha and Tylos became known as Bahrain. The Arabs then took an astonishing step: the desert nomads mounted a seaborne invasion of the Persian coastland. The attack, which happened during the minority of Shapur II, impressed him strongly. He vowed that once he became king he would not only retaliate but conquer Bahrain for his kingdom. He did so in 325 AD, a date which marks the start of the Sasanian counteroffensive and the inception of the "Persianization" of the Gulf's southern coast from Bahrain to Oman.

Shapur's successors fell heir to this enterprise and even expanded their maritime reach into the Arabian Sea towards Yemen. At sea and in the ports, a mixed Perso-Arab community of sailors and traders developed, stimulated by the wealth of Sasanian Iran and Iraq, and crisscrossed the Persian Gulf with precious wares and valuable commodities, many of these brought to the Gulf ports by sea all the way from Taprobana (Sri Lanka) or by caravans crossing the Arabian desert from Yemen or Syria. For three centuries, citizens of the virtual totality of the Gulf's circumference recognized one sovereign, the King of Iran. The area came close to becoming permanently Persian. Three centuries after Shapur's conquests, the Sasanian Empire was the only real power in the Persian Gulf, and had a good prospect of turning the southern rim of the Gulf into an overseas Iran.

The birth of Arab Islam put an end to this prospect. The inspired desert nomads defeated Sasanian troops in Iraq and ejected or subdued Persian governors and garrisons in the southern coastlands of the Persian Gulf, after which they repeated, this time with more lasting results, the exploit of their pre-Islamic ancestors by mounting a seaborne expedition to the Persian coast. By mid-7th century, a division of the Gulf into a Persian and an Arab half had occurred that has lasted till our own day. At the same time, however, the first three centuries of the unified Islamic empire created a link and mutual awareness between the two groups, further stimulating the growth of a mixed Persian and Arab community of mariners and traders so characteristic of the Persian Gulf.

At the time of the Abbasid caliphate, the seafarers and merchants of Basra and Siraf included many Persians; the accounts of their voyages were written in Arabic, however – at least the extant ones – even though the best-known hero of literary paraphrases of these adventures, Sindbad, had a Persian name. This may be partly explained by the fact that Basra, the western terminal of these voyages which spanned half the globe all the way to China, was the main port of the Arab caliphate of the Abbasids. When in the later Middle Ages new emporia grew up in the Gulf, the principal ones were along the Persian coast, but these had a strong Arab presence: the *maliks* or kings of Kish and Hormuz had an Arabic title and, though somewhat nebulously, an Arab provenance. As a rule they recognized the suzerainty of the nearest regional power in the Iranian interior, usually at Shiraz, Kirman, or Lar, while at the same time they often controlled useful coastal points on the Arab side of the Gulf.

From the Islamic conquest to the end of the Middle Ages, Iran was a country without its own national state – a circumstance that might seem to explain the relative independence of these partly Arab principalities along its coast. The Arab presence continued, however, even after the Safavids had reestablished this state,[236] and in fact grew in strength under the last two

---

[236] Dynasties of Iranian stock such as the Buwayhids had from an early time ruled in various parts or even most of the country, but their rule did not lead to the creation of a lasting and well defined national state before the rise of the Safavids. Only then did this creation become real, due to complex factors and despite seeming contradictions. Thus the Safavids themselves, as well as the Qajars, were of Turkic stock; the Buwayhids, of Iranian stock, were Shia like the Safavids (albeit of a

dynasties, the Zands and the Qajars, until in the second half of the 19th century the increasingly assertive Qajar government took steps to reclaim full control of the Persian littoral. Until then, during the 18th and 19th centuries, the Arab coastal shaykhdoms had not only commercial but also naval characteristics. In contrast, barring a few brief exceptions, Iran – even in its days of glory as the Achaemenid and Sasanian empires – never had a navy.[237] Like the Akkadian and Babylonian empires of antiquity, the Persian state too refused to engage the sea and left maritime matters to private individuals and coastal vassal principalities, which were mostly Arab. These mariners continued to arrive from their homeland across the Gulf, where similar coastal formations had made their appearance. Bahrain, Oman, Kuwait were only the most prominent of this counterpart of Siraf, Hormuz and Bandar Abbas.

Alongside similarities and ethnolinguistic kinships, however, there were significant differences between the maritime shaykhdoms and kingdoms on the two coasts. The first and most striking one is that in pre-oil times, those on the Arab side seldom attained the importance of their counterparts across the Gulf. The main reason must have been the difference in the economic and demographic strength of the hinterland: that of Iran substantially surpassed that of Arabia. Many more merchants visited Siraf, Kish, Hormuz, Bandar Abbas, Lingah and Bushire or resided there than came to Bahrain, Qatif or Kuwait, because Iran had more business to offer than Arabia. To be sure, Bahrain, as Dilmun and then Tylos, had been the great emporium in antiquity;

---

different subgroup, that of the Zaydi Shia), but embracing this major schism generated the nation-state building process only with the latter, to a considerable degree because of two catalytic external factors: the presence of two powerful Sunni rivals to the west and east, the Ottoman and Uzbek empires. The "Turkicness" of the Safavid and Qajar families, builders and consolidators of this national state, also reminds us that in their case the Persian identity of their kingdom was based on the fact that the language, culture and bureaucratic apparatus were Persian, but that the issue had no emotional or propagandistic connotations. The nationalistic element added to this "Persianness" is a recent phenomenon that appeared in the 20th century with the rise of Iran's last dynasty, the Pahlavis.

[237] In contrast to the Mediterranean, where the Achaemenids, as we have already pointed out, had a strong naval presence.

but after the establishment of the Persian state, ports on the Persian coast began to rival Bahrain; in the Islamic Middle Ages, despite its renown as the source and market of pearls, Bahrain ceded its place to Hormuz. It is thus no coincidence that when we examine the history of trading centers in the Persian Gulf, it is chiefly those on the northern coast that we deal with. By the same token, once European powers penetrated the area, it was primarily on that coast where they sought to establish their factories – from 1515, when the Portuguese occupied Hormuz and built a fort there, until the nineteenth century, when the British Resident, the "uncrowned king of the Persian Gulf,"[238] resided at Bushire. Only in the 20th century did the European presence swing back to the Arab side. This trend was the result of complex factors: an ever more assertive Iran impatient of any foreign presence, an inversely malleable and splintered Arab world willing to accommodate that presence, a new commercial dynamism of such principalities as Dubai, and newly discovered oil. The move of the British Residency from Bushire to Bahrain in 1947 was a symbol of this evolution.

While Iran had no unified national state from the time of the Islamic conquest until the end of the Middle Ages, there was none on the Arab side either. And like Qajar Iran, Saudi Arabia, when it arose as the major regional power on the Arab side, refrained from engaging the sea but left that business to the coastal shaykhdoms, which it tried with varying degrees of success to control. With the exception of the Sultanate of Oman between the 17th and 19th centuries, no regional power engaged the Persian Gulf in a major commercial or naval way. Trade and seafaring remained the domain of the smaller coastal units and myriads of enterprising Arabs, Persians, Indians, Armenians and others. Of naval wars there were virtually none; but that was compensated for by the brisk trade of piracy, which at times became the main industry of some of these shaykhdoms.

The fact that the Persian state never became a naval power eager to expand its maritime trade and acquire overseas possessions thus was not unique, but rather the rule among most landward-focused kingdoms of the Orient and indeed nearly everywhere else in the world, Europe being the exception. This may

---

[238] George Nathaniel Curzon, *Persia and the Persian Question*, London 1892, p. 451.

seem to contradict our earlier statement that in Sasanian times the Gulf became a Persian lake. That dominance was land-based, however: the entire circumference of the Gulf was Sasanian territory, and until the rise of Islam, no major rival, territorial or maritime, was in sight to threaten this dominance. The Sasanians needed no navy to impose or maintain their rule beyond the initial or occasional logistical necessity (as for example in the conquest of Yemen). The Arabian littoral virtually invited occupation by a powerful Iran, and the King of Kings did not have to build or maintain an expensive war fleet – in contrast to the challenge facing his Achaemenid predecessor during the attempts to conquer Greece. Meanwhile Persian ships, mariners and merchants continued to sail all the way to India and Sri Lanka, expanding a tradition that went back to the Achaemenids, or again to round the Arabian peninsula on the way to the Red Sea and East Africa, though again without any pronounced participation of the state. This state of affairs would then continue throughout history, in stark contrast to the course of action pursued by the Europeans once they penetrated the Orient. A vivid illustration of this contrast is offered by the very concept of "lake" in the strategic sense when applied to the Persian Gulf. In Sasanian times, it was "Persian", as we have said, because Iran occupied the land surrounding it; in the 19th century, it was "British" because cruisers of the Anglo-Indian navy patrolled its waters. In fact, this concept can be broadened and pushed back to the very inception of European presence in the Gulf. Lusitanian dominance too was essentially naval, although the Portuguese also relied on such bases as Hormuz.

As for the dominance itself, we can divide it into two phases, with a long hiatus between them: Portuguese (1515-1622) and British (1820-1971). Moreover, the second phase might never have happened had it not been for the fleets of the Arab principality of Ras al-Khaimah, which besides the honorable occupations of maritime trade and fishing increasingly lapsed into piracy, occasionally succumbing to the temptation of preying also on ships of the East India Company. It took the British, as we have seen, three expeditions to curb this redoubtable nest of corsairs; of these only the third expedition in 1819-20 fully succeeded. From then until 1971, the British were the undisputed, though rather reluctant, maritime masters of the Persian Gulf.

Their naval dominance gave rise, however, to a chronic dispute between an ever more assertive Iran and Britain. The dispute started right after the suppression of Ras al-Khaimah, when a British squadron was sent to chastise its parent Qasimi base, Lingah, which at that point was one of the most active ports on the Persian coast. The shaykh of Lingah was a vassal of the shah, and Tehran lodged a protest with the British envoy for what it considered an unacceptable encroachment. The British withdrew and Lingah ceased to be a problem, but the center stage was soon occupied by Bahrain, with which the British concluded a treaty but which Persia claimed as its possession. As we have seen, Bahrain was an intermittent bone of contention, albeit on a low level, between Britain as the guarantor of its independence and Iran as its persistent claimant, until 1968. Nor was Bahrain the only disputed place. The aforementioned islands near the Strait of Hormuz – Abu Musa, Greater Tunb and Lesser Tunb – began to be claimed by Iran by the end of the 19th century, while the British, in reversal of earlier statements, declared them to be part of the shaykhdom of Sharjah, hence under British protection. Here, the Persians went one step farther than in the case of Bahrain, for in 1904 they landed a small force on Abu Musa and established a tax-collecting post there; they soon withdrew, however, in response to British pressure. None of these variants of Persian assertion of a right to what they considered their share of the Gulf succeeded, for one overarching reason: British naval power, and the inverse lack of Persian naval power.

The string of Arab shaykhdoms along the southern coast, now relatively secure and well-behaved thanks to the treaties concluded with Britain, were glad to eschew the lumbering attempts of a briefly revived Ottoman Empire and Saudi Arabia at extracting tokens of vassalage from them, although at times they had to humor them with seeming subordination while the British chose to tolerate the contradiction. Meanwhile, on the northern side, the last vestiges of Omani and Qasimi presence were being extinguished by an ever more determined Qajar Iran. The Persian Gulf then seemed to settle into a fairly peaceful and prosperous existence, secure under British guardianship and basically undisturbed by the Ottomans and the Saudis. It functioned as an avenue of trade practiced by a transnational community of merchants: Arabs, Persians, Indians, Armenians and other groups who operated from a vast network of centers and ports encompassed in an area between Basra, Bushire, Hudaidah (in the Red Sea), Masqat, Zanzibar, and Bombay.[239] This thriving cosmopolitanism could make us forget the above-mentioned consolidation of Qajar Iran as a henceforward unified kingdom, which had an inherent strength far greater than that of its Arab neighbors, and which had finally reclaimed full control of its long and promising shoreline and the adjacent islands except the trio near the Strait of Hormuz. By the turn of the 20th century, two major obstacles stood in Iran's way to becoming the major regional power, or, put in different terms, the dominant power in the Persian Gulf: the lack of a navy, and the presence of Great Britain. It would have been reasonable to expect that once the first obstacle was corrected and the second removed, Iran would be able to assume this role.

Such a situation presented itself in 1971, the year of Britain's definitive withdrawal. By then Iran had a strong army and a growing navy,[240] and with geostrategy helping, it should have

---

[239] James Onley, "Transnational merchants in the nineteenth-century Gulf: The case of the Safar family," in *Transnational Connections and the Arab Gulf*, ed. Madawi Al-Rasheed, London and New York: Routledge, 2005, pp. 59-89, and other articles in this interesting volume, esp. Nelida Fuccaro, "Mapping the transnational community: Persians and the space of the city in Bahrain, c. 1869-1937," and Roland Marchal, "Dubai: global city and transnational hub."

[240] J.B. Kelly, *Arabia, the Gulf, and the West*, New York 1980, p. 80: "The Persians made no serious attempt to annex Abu Musa or the Tunbs until the 1930s. It was a time when Reza Shah was seeking to make his country's weight felt in the Gulf by the creation of a Persian navy. The assertion of Persian sovereignty over Abu Musa and the Tunbs, so Reza Shah reasoned, would serve to promote this object and at the same time challenge Britain's naval supremacy in the Gulf." Reza Shah's dream came true only in his son Muhammad Reza's reign, when upon Great Britain's termination of its protection treaties with the Trucial Coast principalities in November 1971 Iran took possession of the three islands. Both the timing and the event are revealing: Despite unquestionable growth in strength, the Persian navy could not risk a confrontation with the British; once that danger was removed, it proceeded to carry out the operation forthwith, for the navy of Ras al-Khaimah and Sharjah, the two directly concerned sheikhdoms, was no match for that of Iran.

been able to become the definitive guardian of the Persian Gulf. It even seems that this was the role in which the United States, Iran's chief ally and the overall architect of the containment of the Soviet Union, wished to see it. The cold war was still raging, and the specter of the Gulf's oil falling into Russian hands made the choice obvious. Until the Islamic Revolution of 1979, this was the thrust of American policy. It was basically correct, and had the democratic regime striven for by Dr. Mosaddeq been allowed to take root, the United States could not have had a better ally, nor the Gulf a better guardian. The Shah's dictatorial regime, however, was a festering wound on the Persian body politic which ultimately vitiated this role and provoked a revolution whose consequences still wait to be resolved; what is certain, however, is that at present, Iran is not the ally America could have had, nor is it the guardian of the Persian Gulf that it could and should be.

As it is, the United States is playing this part, and is likely to keep doing so for the foreseeable future. Its position has been cemented by defense treaties with Oman, Qatar, Bahrain and Kuwait, and is anchored in military bases there, besides a less formal though nonetheless real presence in Saudi Arabia and the United Arab Emirates – to say nothing of Iraq. This convergence of circumstances, chiefly Tehran's self-inflicted isolation and America's self-chosen – or perhaps forced – guardianship,[241] has reduced the role Iran is playing in the Gulf on all relevant levels – economic, political, military, and naval. It is only a matter of time, however, before Iran, more attuned to the conditions and exigencies of the 21st century, assumes a position of leadership among the Persian Gulf states. None of the Arab nations can match its all-round preponderance, not even if they are visualized as a unified bloc. Taken separately, the contrast becomes even more striking. Instead of being racked by conflicts arising from different religious or other ideologies, or from claims and counterclaims to certain islands and chunks of the continental shelf that are rich with oil, however, this future Persian Gulf community should find it more advantageous to cooperate in a

---

[241] Or again by the force of circumstances. In 1820 British guardianship was triggered by the need to curb the pirates of Ras al-Khaimah; in 1991 American guardianship was triggered by the need to thwart Iraq's occupation of Kuwait.

manner that reflects the age-old symbiosis of the Arabs and Persians living there. One of the characteristic and somewhat peculiar features of the past centuries, as we have pointed out, was the structural difference between the kind of Arab presence on the coast of Iran and the Persian one on that of Arabia. The Arabs as a rule acted through the prism of tribal associations and tended to form coastal principalities also in Iran; the Persians migrated more on an individual and family basis, anchoring their presence on the Arabian coast in the form of merchant and craftsman groups. While the former trend, a political liability to a newly assertive Iran, had ceased by the end of the 19th century, the latter, individual and apolitical, has continued and may even have increased in vigor during the recent rise of several Arab emirates as centers of international commerce, banking, and communications. Places like Dubai and Bahrain, neither of them endowed with oil reserves comparable to those of their neighbors, are the trailblazers in this new development that takes advantage of assets offered by the Gulf other than oil. Especially Dubai illustrates the benefits of what we could call the Persian Gulf symbiosis, for its business-friendly policy has attracted a great number of Persians along with their capital and dynamism. As a 4 December 2005 article in the New York Times by Hassan M. Fattah says, "Thousands of Iranians, most of them wealthy, are making the leap [from Iran to Dubai], investing in real estate, starting businesses and opening second homes, turning this desert country into an Iranian hub free of the corruption, American penalties and political turbulence they face in Iran ..." The article goes on to say that the Islamic Azad University in Tehran has a new Dubai campus, one of the shaykhdom's advantages being its proximity to Iran, a mere 45-minute flight across the Gulf. We have mentioned elsewhere that the city has become one of the major hubs of air travel between the West and the Orient, with Air Dubai gaining a reputation for reliability and excellence. Dubai's success may thus be attributed to a dynamic business-friendly climate, stimulated by a sound and improving infrastructure supported by an enlightened and participatory government. Moreover, Dubai is only the most successful of the Gulf states in this respect. Bahrain is another such case, and the others, from Kuwait to Ras al-Khaimah and Oman, are endeavoring, each in its way, to develop their economies independently of oil or in preparation for its eventual depletion.[242] In virtually all these respects, the Persian Gulf plays a pervasive and catalytic role, enabling the riparian countries to function as entrepots of maritime trade, as centers of multinational business, and as choice locations for international conferences, sports events and tourism.

---

[242] How soon this dreaded time will come is a matter of debate, for even expert estimates often disagree. Much depends of course on which country is meant, and on the rate of production. No observer suggests, however, the survival of this resource beyond the 21st century.

Part II

ATLAS OF THE PERSIAN GULF

Section 1. Specific Segments of the Persian Gulf
(four maps)

Section 2. The Eight Riparian States of the Persian Gulf
(sixteen maps)

Section 1.

This section contains a general map, a map showing the area in the political context of the riparian and neighboring countries, a map of the uppermost part of the Persian Gulf, and a map of the Strait of Hormuz.

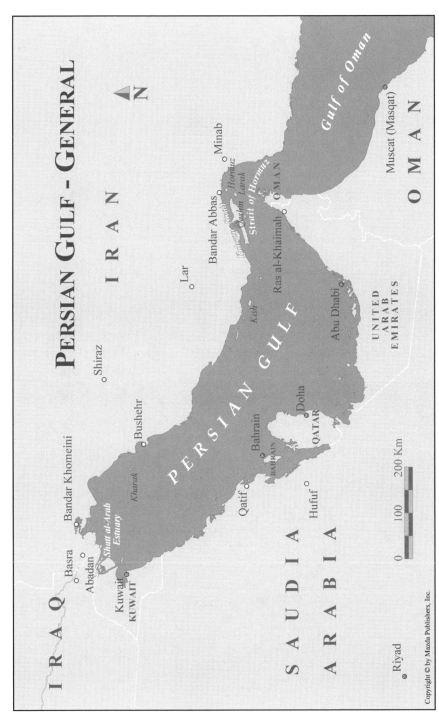

Map No.1: A general view of the Persian Gulf and the Gulf of Oman.

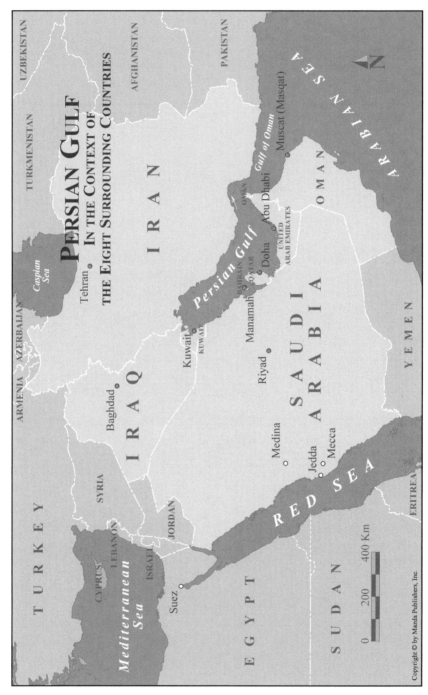

Map No. 2: The Persian Gulf in the Political Context of its Riparian Countries.

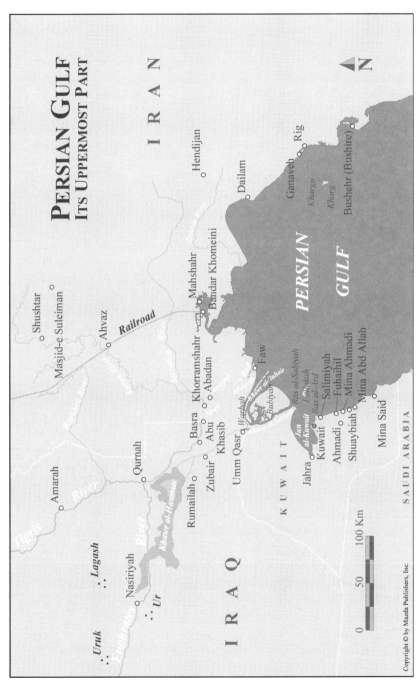

Map No. 3: The Uppermost Part of the Persian Gulf.

Map No. 4: The Strait of Hormuz and its Surroundings

This geographical formation is remarkable both for its natural features and for its historical as well as current importance. On the south, the strait is delimited by the Musandam Peninsula of the Sultanate of Oman, which is part of the Arabian Peninsula; on the north, it is bordered by Iran. The strait is named after the small island of Hormuz, situated some ten kilometers from the Persian coast and eighty kilometers due north from Cape Musandam.

Today this island, with a town of the same name, belies its glorious past when between the 14th and 17th centuries it was one of the greatest emporia of the Orient. However, in a broader sense the history of Hormuz neither began in the 14th century nor ended in the 17th. In antiquity and the Middle Ages until the year 1300 of the common era, the name Hormuz designated not this island but a port some forty kilometers due east by the estuary of the Minab River on the Persian mainland. The original Hormuz was already a busy international port when Marco Polo visited it in 1272 and 1293, but its renown as an emporium grew further after transfer to the insular location, to which it also brought its original name which gradually replaced Jarun, the island's earlier appellation. The insular kingdom which flourished there endured even after Albuquerque had conquered it, on behalf of King Manuel, in 1515 and proclaimed it as a dependency of Portugal. In 1622, Shah Abbas the Great, aided by ships of the East India Company, conquered Hormuz, which was then still under Portuguese suzerainty. Commercial activities moved back to the mainland to a location northwest of the island that the Europeans called Gombroon. The origin of this name is a matter of debate, but the relevance of the question is reduced by the fact that the site, renamed Bandar Abbas (or Bandar-e Abbasi, both of which could be translated as Port Abbas), became one of the principal ports of Iran.

Hormuz was a mostly barren island distinguished by salt mounds and extreme heat in the summer, and depended on water and victuals brought from the large neighboring island of Qishm. Wealthy citizens spent the hot season on the mainland in their villas and orchards around Minab, located on higher elevations in the Zagros piedmont.

The island of Kish, known in Arabic as Qais, farther west near the Persian coast, had in the 12th to early 14th centuries claimed primacy as the emporium of the Persian Gulf before it was eclipsed by Hormuz. The port of Lingah on the Persian coast, half-way between Kish and Qeshm, gained importance as a commercial port in the 17th to 19th centuries.

Across the Strait of Hormuz, if we proceed southward from the Omani border of the Musandam Peninsula, we see on the western, Persian Gulf coast six of the seven capitals of the United Arab Emirates: Ras al-Khaimah, Umm al-Qaiwain, Ajman, Sharjah, Dubai, and Abu Dhabi. The capital of the seventh emirate, Fujairah, is on the eastern, Gulf of Oman side of this configuration. Three of these centers – Ras al-Khaimah, Sharjah, and Dubai – have in recent centuries played noteworthy roles as ports for activities of varying kinds: maritime trade, boat-building, fishing, pearling, and piracy. Dubai especially was renowned as an important entrepot center, a role that has grown exponentially since the start of the oil boom; today, it is an ultra-modern, dynamic center of international business. Ras al-Khaimah gained in the late 18th and early 19th centuries a certain notoriety as a pirates' harbor, a role now replaced by its function as the capital of a modern emirate whose economy is based less on oil than on a diversity of assets ranging from fishing to tourism. Abu Dhabi has a shorter history than these other port cities, but that is compensated for by its function as the capital not only of this emirate but also of the whole federation, the United Arab Emirates. Its importance is further enhanced by the fact that this emirate overshadows the other six members of the federation with its enormous oil wealth.

Half-way between the cities of Dubai (and on the coast of this emirate) and Abu Dhabi is Mina Jabal Ali, one of the largest man-made harbors in the world. On the Gulf of Oman side we find the historical port of Khawr Fakkan, which has recently been developed as a modern harbor linked by highways with the city of Sharjah and other points on the Persian Gulf coast. Farther south on the coast of the Sultanate of Oman we see Suhar, a port with a long history but still in existence and active today, and Masqat or Muscat, the Sultanate's capital and also a renowned port with long history. On the other hand, the historical port of Julfar on the Persian Gulf coast a few kilometers to the north of Ras al-Khaimah is today only an archaeological site.

Finally we want to draw attention to two oasis complexes also shown on the map. They have had economic, strategic, or cultural importance and until recently were a bone of contention between two or more claimants. The oasis Al Ain is on the United Arab Emirates side of the border, that of Buraimi is on the Omani side; both are near the Saudi border, and Saudi Arabia had in the past claimed them as its possession. Arguments have now abated and Al Ain in particular is famous as the home of the University of the United Arab Emirates.

Also shown on the map are the islands Greater Tunb, Lesser Tunb, and Abu Musa. The question of their possession elicited little interest until toward the end of the 19th century the Iranian government began to consolidate its control of the semi-independent sheikhdoms along the Persian coast. The Qasimi sheikhs of Lingah had claimed ownership of the three islands, and when Qasimi rule was eliminated in 1887-88 by the government, Tehran considered itself the rightful possessor of the three islands despite counterclaims by the Emirate of Sharjah. The issue remained dormant, however, until Iran began to reinforce and expand its customs administration along the littoral and on adjacent islands. In 1904 Monsieur Dambrain, the Belgian director of Persian Customs, visited the three islands, pulled down the Sharjah flags, hoisted those of Iran, and installed two Customs guards. The British government intervened on behalf of its Trucial Coast clients, and Tehran acquiesced; between 1904 and 1971 Ras al-Khaimah thus exercized control of the Tunb islands, al-Sharjah of Abu Musa. As the date of British withdrawal, slated for 30 November 1971, approached, Iran revived its claims, and reached an agreement with Shaykh Khalid bin Muhammad of Sharjah on Abu Musa but not with Shaykh Saqr bin Muhammad of Ras al-Khaimah. Iranian troops occupied the islands, while the Emirate of Sharjah retained a limited right to Abu Musa's southern part. Nevertheless, the United Arab Emirates have not fully accepted the resolution and controversy flares up from time to time, partly fuelled by the discovery of oil in the vicinity of Abu Musa. It is also possible, and indeed realistic, to view the Persian possession of these three islands as part of the guardianship of the strategically and economically vital shipping lanes of the Strait of Hormuz, which only Iran has the adequate military potential to assume.

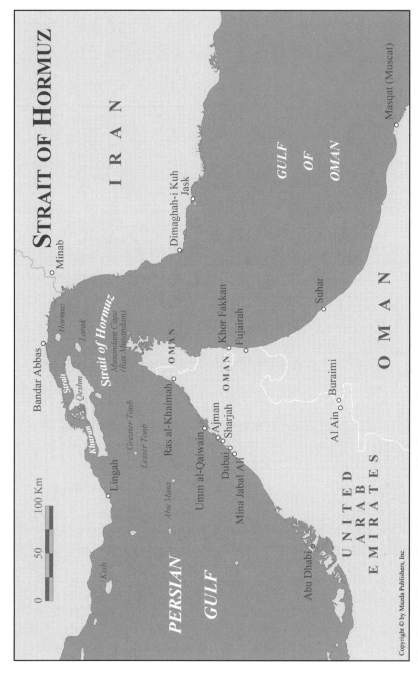

Map No. 4: The Strait of Hormuz and its Surroundings.

Section 2. The Eight Riparian States of the Persian Gulf

Introduction

Eight states border the Persian Gulf. Starting with Iran and proceeding counterclockwise, they are Iraq, Kuwait, Saudi Arabia, Bahrain, Qatar, United Arab Emirates (UAE), and Oman.

With its area of 1,648,000 sq km, Iran is the second-largest of the group after Saudi Arabia (1,960,582 sq km); its population of 68,278,826, however, dwarfs that of each of the other seven states, which have a combined population of 58,891,733. Iraq's 24,683,313 and Saudi Arabia's 24,293,844 are a distant second and third. Then come the UAE 3,440,000; Oman 2,807,125; Kuwait 2,183,161; Qatar 817,052; and Bahrain 667,238. The largest city is the capital of Iran, Tehran, with a population of 7,038,000 (UN, *Demographic Yearbook*, estimates for 2003).

Iran has the longest shoreline, along the northern side of the Gulf: approximately 900 kilometers, if we choose the estuary of the Arvand Rud/Shatt al-Arab on the northwest and the Strait of Hormuz on the southeast as the delimiters; the figure rises to some 1,440 kilometers if we include Iran's coastline along the Gulf of Oman.

Saudi Arabia and the United Arab Emirates occupy the greater part of the southern littoral, approximately 600 kilometers each. The large peninsula of Qatar, which juts out from the Arabian land mass into the Gulf, has a coastline of about 500 kilometers, while that of Kuwait is about 200 kilometers long. The Bahrain archipelago has some 161 kilometers of coasts, but even this small figure dwarfs the 58 kilometers of Iraq's shoreline.

Finally there is the special case of Oman, whose possession of the Musandam Peninsula on the southern side of the Strait of Hormuz qualifies it as a member of the Persian Gulf club and adds about 110 kilometers to the 1,972 kilometers of coastline the sultanate has along the Gulf of Oman and the Arabian Sea.

Besides the basic fact of having access to a gulf of vital economic and strategic importance, the eight countries also share a common religion and historical interaction. All these features go back to the early middle ages and some even to the remotest antiquity. Two, however, are of recent date and of paramount importance: oil and strategy.

Islam is the religion of the vast majority in the eight countries. This is a fundamentally unifying trait, but also a divisive one because of schisms that appeared in the very first century of this religion. All its three principal denominations are present in the eight states: Sunni or Orthodox Islam predominates in Saudi Arabia, Kuwait, Qatar, and the United Arab Emirates; Shia Islam is the official religion in Iran and claims the majority among the Arabs of Iraq and Bahrain, while forming an important minority in Saudi Arabia; and finally the Ibadi branch of Khariji Islam has tenaciously persisted in Oman.

Two of the three principal languages of the classical Islamic world, Arabic and Persian (the third being Turkish), are the official tongues of the Persian Gulf area. Like most languages, the actual spoken tongues display a broad range of dialects, especially in the case of Arabic; but there is only one officially correct, written and spoken, Arabic, which makes it a powerful unifying force for the cultural and political cohesion among the Arabs of the Gulf. Moreover, since Arabic is also the sacred language of Islam, educated Persian Muslims often possess an excellent knowledge of it, while their own language is as replete with Arabic loanwords as English is with Latin ones, a factor working towards a community of culture in the area. Both languages share the same – Arabic – alphabet.

In terms of the form of government, six of the eight states are hereditary monarchies, while two – Iran and Iraq – are republics. The reigning dynasties have roots that go back to the 18th or 19th centuries; the republics were established in 1958 (Iraq) and 1979 (Iran) through revolutions that killed the monarch in the case of Iraq, and forced him to flee abroad in the case of Iran.

1. IRAN
(The Islamic Republic of Iran, *Jumhuri-ye Islami-ye Iran*)

Iran is bordered by Iraq and Turkey on the west, by Azerbaijan and Turkmenistan on the north, by Afghanistan and Pakistan on the east, and by the Gulf of Oman and the Persian Gulf on the south. Its long coastline along the Persian Gulf and the Gulf of Oman extends from Iraq to Pakistan. The country's political, religious, and economic centers of gravity have in the last few centuries alternated between Qazvin, Isfahan, and Tehran, while the coastline, shielded from the hinterland by the long chain of the Zagros mountains, until recently had a special physiognomy in most respects – political, economic, religious, and ethnic.

Basic Statistical Data

Area: 1,648 square kilometers.

Population: 68 million, as of 2006.

Ethnolinguistic composition: Persian 51%, Azeri Turkic 24%, Kurdish 9%, and smaller groups.

Religion: Muslim 97% (89% Shia, 9% Sunni), Zoroastrian, Jewish, Christian, Bahai.

Capital: Tehran (7 million inhabitants; Greater Tehran, 14 million).

Administrative structure: 30 provinces (*ostan*-s), of which Khuzistan, Bushehr, Hormozgan, and Sistan/Baluchistan lie along the Persian Gulf and the Gulf of Oman.

Government type: dual, theocracy and democracy side by side, with theocracy as the ultimate arbiter.

Theocracy: *Vali-ye Faqih*, supreme religious jurisconsult who is the head of state; appointed for life by a closed group of Islamic jurisconsults.

Democracy: President, who also has the function of Prime Minister; elected by popular vote for a four-year term.

Political process: through political parties and political pressure groups.

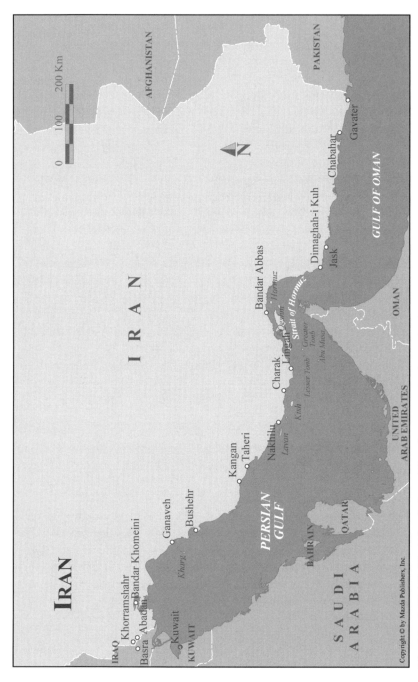

Map No. 5: IRAN (The Islamic Republic of Iran, *Jumhuri-ye Islami-ye Iran*).

2. IRAQ
(*al-Iraq, al-Jumhuriyah al-Iraqiyah*)

On the east Iraq borders on Iran; on the north on Turkey; on the northwest on Syria; on the west on Jordan; on the southwest on Saudi Arabia; and on the southeast on Kuwait. Its coastline on the Persian Gulf, between Iran and Kuwait, is exceedingly short – a mere 58 kilometers. This reduced length is substantially compensated for by the splendid waterways of the Shatt al-Arab and the two almost legendary rivers, the Euphrates and Tigris, which have always functioned as the country's double backbone and at the same time have been a link with the Persian Gulf and the Indian Ocean. In pre-modern times, before the birth of na-tion-states and ethnolinguistic and ethnoreligious identities, the two rivers also played a crucial role in the formulation of the concept of Iraq as a distinct country with its own cultural and economic bonds – a country that took shape in antiquity as Mesopotamia and has kept reasserting itself ever since. This identity received its current political and territorial form after World War I.

Basic Statistical Data

Area: 437,072 square kilometers.
Population: over 26 million.
Ethnolinguistic composition: Arabs (about 75%), Kurds (about 20%), Turkoman, Assyrian, and other, 5%.
Religion: Muslims 95% (two thirds Shia), the rest Christians, Sabaeans, Yazidis, Jews.
Government structure: Republic; there is a president and a prime minister. A new constitution was approved by a general ref-erendum in October 2005. The legislative branch is a uni-cameral *Majlis al-Watani* or National Assembly, consisting 275 seats.
Political parties: Yes.
Administrative structure: 18 *muhafazah*s or governorates; the governorate of Basra fronts the Persian Gulf.
Capital: Baghdad.

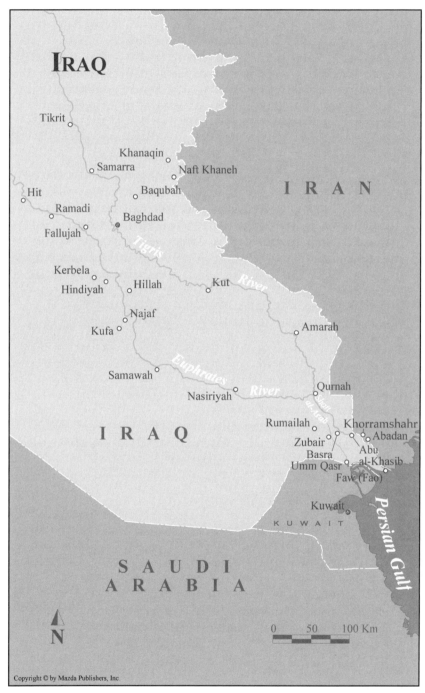

Map No. 6: Southern Half of Iraq from Tikrit to the Persian Gulf.

3. KUWAIT
(The State of Kuwait, *Dawlat Kuwait*)

With an area of 17,820 square kilometers, Kuwait is the second smallest of the group; its population of some 2,300,000 is the third smallest. Kuwait's distinctive, somewhat triangular territory lies at the northwestern end of the Persian Gulf; Iraq to the north and west, and Saudi Arabia to the south are its neighbors. In contrast to Iraq, Kuwait has a long and generous coastline; fairly straight from north to south, it is interrupted by the large Jun al-Kuwait or Bay of Kuwait, a splendid natural harbor; the city and port of Kuwait lie near Ras al-Ajuzah, a protrusion into this bay from the south. Kuwait also owns several islands to the east and northeast of this bay: Failakah, Bubiyan, and Warbah are the principal ones. Failakah is inhabited and contains important archaeological remains; Bubiyan and especially Warbah have considerable current political and strategic importance, for they overlook and almost block the approach from the Gulf to the short Iraqi shoreline, in particular to the Iraqi port of Umm Qasr, via the Khawr al-Zubair (also known as Khawr Abdallah), the widening estuary of the Zubair Channel.

Basic Statistical Data

Area: 17,820 square kilometers.
Population: 2,335,648; this figure includes 1,044,294 non-citizens.
Ethnolinguistic composition: 80% Arab, 9% South Asian, 4% Persian.
Religion: Muslim 85%; of these, 70% Sunni, 30% Shia.
Capital: Kuwait city.
Government structure: Hereditary monarchy of the Al Sabah family, of the "family rule" type.
The monarch's title is *amir* (emir), but *shaikh* is the usual title preceding the name itself.
Executive branch: chiefly the emir's relatives.
Legislative branch: A 50-seat Majlis al-Ummah or National Assembly is elected by popular vote for a 4-year term; no political parties exist, but specific groups do. In the 6 July 2003

elections, Islamists obtained 21 seats, government supporters 14 seats, independents 12 seats, and liberals 3 seats. Suffrage is limited to men starting at the age of 21.

Administrative structure: 5 governorates (*muhafazah*-s).

Map No. 7: Kuwait in the Context of its Immediate Surroundings

Iraq to the north and west, Saudi Arabia to the south, the Persian Gulf to the east. We can begin with the large island of Bubiyan and the small crescent-like Warbah island, both virtually uninhabited; they are separated from Iraq by the Khawr Abd Allah, also called Khawr al-Zubair, an inlet, wide at first but narrowing as it approaches the Zubair canal. The northern side of the Khawr Abd Allah also represents the entire Iraqi coastline.

From the inner end of the Khawr al-Zubair the land border between the two countries proceeds westward, passing through one of the most productive oil-bearing fields in the Persian Gulf, bracketed by Rumailah in Iraq and Rawdatain in Kuwait.

Bubiyan is separated from the Kuwait mainland by the narrow inlet Khawr al-Sabiyah. At its southern end (in fact, opening) we see the cape Ras al-Sabiyah, which marks the northern side of the wide entrance to the Jun al-Kuwait or Bay of Kuwait, the largest and best natural harbor in the Persian Gulf. The southern side of the entrance is marked by the cape Ras al-Ard. The city and port of Kuwait is some 10 km to the west-northwest of there near another cape, Ras al-Ajuzah. The bay then proceeds for some 28 km to its end near the oasis city of Jahra'.

Worthy of notice is the island of Failakah, not far from the entrance to the Bay of Kuwait. Despite its rather small size, it has great historical interest and has been inhabited since antiquity.

Several ports mark the Kuwait coastline from Ras al-Ard to the Saudi border. Four of these are terminals of pipelines bringing petroleum from the oil-rich fields in the hinterland: al-Ahmadi, Shuaibah, Mina' Abd Allah, and al-Zawr.

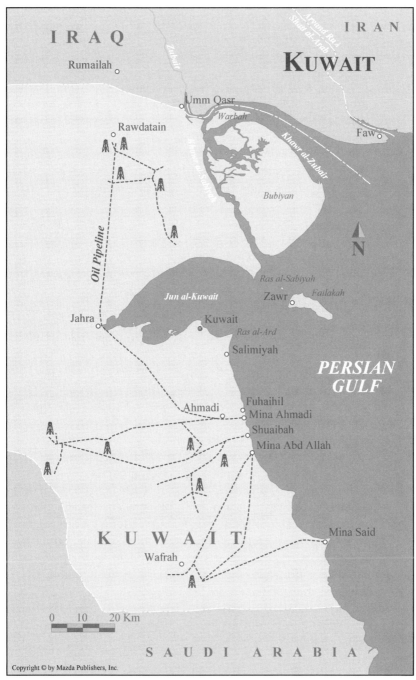

Map No. 7: Kuwait in the Context of its Immediate Surroundings.

4. SAUDI ARABIA
(The Kingdom of Saudi Arabia, *al-Mamlakah al-Arabiyah al-Suudiyah*)

Saudi Arabia has common borders with all the Persian Gulf countries except Iran, and, of course, the archipelago of Bahrain; it is also bordered on the north by Jordan and on the south by Yemen. The kingdom's long coastline along the Gulf, comparable to that of the United Arab Emirates, runs between Kuwait and Qatar; it is dwarfed in length, however, by the kingdom's Red Sea coast, which extends from Jordan to Yemen.

Basic Statistical Data

Area: 1, 960, 582 square kilometers.
Population: 27 million; over 5 million are non-nationals (2006 estimate).
Ethnolinguistic composition: overwhelmingly Arab.
Religion: Sunni Islam, mostly of the Hanbali rite, in its special form of Wahhabi Puritanism; important Shia minority in the Sharqiyah province.
Royal capital: Riyad, close to 5 million (2001 estimate).
Administrative capital: Jeddah, over 2 million.
The next two cities in size: Mecca, close to 1 million; Medina, over 600 thousand.
Government: Hereditary monarchy of the Al Saud family; the king is also prime minister. The cabinet of ministers is largely composed of members of the royal family.
Legislative branch: There is a *Majlis al-Shura* or Consultative Assembly, whose chairman and 120 members are appointed by the king. The *Qanun al-Asasi* or Constitution , introduced in 1993, is based on the *Shariah* or Islamic law. No political parties are permitted, but groups of candidates participated in the first nationwide election in April 2005 to municipal councils; conservatives were the winners.
Administrative units: 13 provinces (*mintaqah*-s); the Persian Gulf coast falls within the Sharqiyah province, whose capital is Dammam.

Map No. 8-1: The Persian Gulf Coast of Saudi Arabia

This map shows the Saudi coast from the border of Kuwait to that of Qatar. The principal ports and coastal features shown are Khafji, Saffaniyah, Jubail, Ras Tannurah, the island of Tarut, Qatif, Dammam, Dhahran, Khubar, Uqair, and Salwah. In the interior, we see Abqaiq, Mubarraz, Hufuf, and the capital of the kingdom Riyad. The bulk of the Saudi area shown on the map is the country's Sharqiyah or Eastern province; Hufuf was the provincial capital until 1952, when this function passed to Dammam.

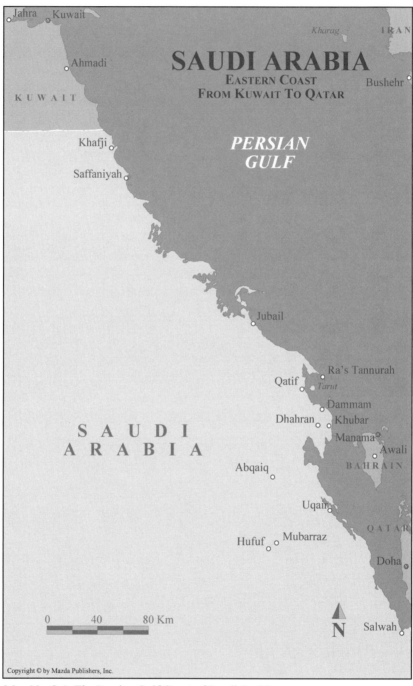

Map No. 8-1: The Persian Gulf Coast of Saudi Arabia.

Map No. 8-2. The Southern Part of the Sharqiyah Province

This is where the richest oil fields of the country are found about 80 km inland along a belt some 200 km long, just west of the oasis complex of Hufuf – Mubarraz (in addition to a number of other sites both to the north and south of there, as well as off-shore). The main processing installations extend from Jubail to Khubar. The cluster Dammam-Dhahran-Khubar epitomizes the transformation of Saudi Arabia as a result of the oil boom. Dammam, a small fishing village in the early decades of the 20th century, became the capital of the province, and the kingdom's largest port on the Persian Gulf; Dhahran, an uninhabited spot in the desert before 1935, was the site where the first oil strike occurred and is now an urban center hosting the headquarters of ARAMCO, a base of the Royal Saudi Air Force, and three international airports; Khubar, a modest fishing and pearling village in the 1920s, is now one of the principal residential and business centers of the area.

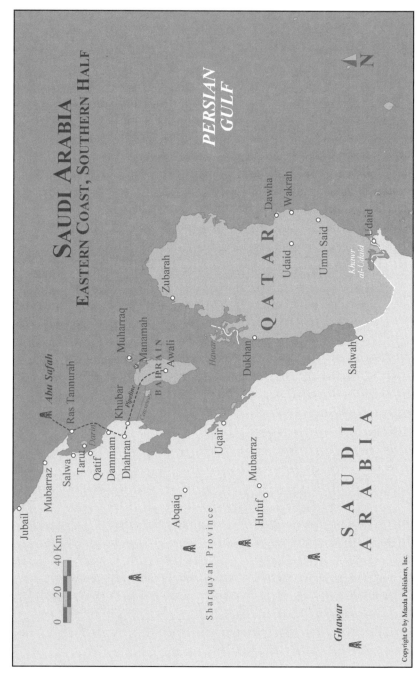

Map No. 8-2. The Southern Part of the Sharqiyah Province.

5. Bahrain
(Kingdom of Bahrain, *Mamlakat al-Bahrain*)

The Kingdom of Bahrain is an archipelago situated midway, longitudinally, down the Persian Gulf, but close to the Arabian coast, about halfway between northern Qatar to the east and the Dhahran-Dammam segment of Saudia Arabia's Sharqiyah province to the west. It is composed of 36 islands, of which the principal one, itself named Bahrain, towers over all the others in size. Muharraq, Umm al-Nasan, and Sitrah in their turn dwarf the rest. The kingdom also owns a secondary, smaller archipelago, that of the Hawar or Huwar Islands, situated some 30 kilometers southeast of Bahrain Island close to the southwestern coast of Qatar.

The main island, which in the past was also called Uwal or Awal, has the same physiognomy as the Sharqiyah province (roughly coterminous with the historical region of al-Ahsa) of Saudi Arabia. The prevailing desert climate would make it inhospitable if it were not for an important aquifer fed by water seeping in from the higher plateaus of the Arabian land mass. This aquifer, which also extdnds under the sea bed off Bahrain's northwestern coast, has been the source of springs and artesian wells that have enabled man to practice irrigated agriculture.

Basic Statistical Data.

Area: 665 square kilometers.

Population: 688 thousand (includes 235 thousand non-citizens).

Ethnolinguistic composition: Arab, 73%; Persian, 8%; Asian, 19%.

Religion: Shia Islam, 60%; Sunni Islam, 40%.

Government structure: Hereditary monarchy of the Al Khalifah family.

Executive branch: Cabinet of ministers appointed by the king.

Constitution: Adopted in December 2000 and approved by general referendum on 14 February 2001; it provides for a partially elected legislature, a constitutional monarchy, and an independent judiciary.

Parliament: bicameral, the *Shura* (Council) consists of 40 members appointed by the King; the House of Deputies also consists of 40 members, directly elected for four-year terms. Political parties are prohibited.

Administrative structure: 12 *mintaqah*-s (regions or municipalities).

Capital: Manamah.

Principal ports and coastal towns, starting with Manamah and proceeding clockwise: Mina' Salman, Askar, Jaww, Dur, Wasmiyah, Zallaq, Jasrah, Karbabad. Harbor installations, connected by pipelines with the refineries in the main island's interior, have been built on the island of Sitrah and extended for some four kilometers into the sea as wharves able to accommodate the largest oil-loading tankers.

Bahrain is the only site on the Arab coast of the Persian Gulf discussed in Kazaruni's description of Persian Gulf ports and islands. It may be instructive to glance at his account, written during the rule of Muhammad Shah Qajar (1834-48) (pp. 82-87).

> "The island of Bahrain lies [across the Gulf] opposite the ports of Tahiri and Aslu. ...On this island there is a fortress built five hundred years after the Ascension of Jesus, blessings on Him, according to an inscription on stone in the vestibule of this fortress[243]. The latter consists of four towers within eight towers withing sixteen towers, encompassed by three walls... and a ditch around the third wall. There is a fountain in the midst of the inner four towers with sweet tasty water. Now that this island has been seized by the Utub tribe, those four towers are no longer inhabited. In the past, Karim Khan Zand had granted the rule of this island to Shaykh Nasir Abu Shahri[244] and Shaykh Nasr, his son; these appointed their representative, who lived in this fortress and kept some of it in good repair. ...

---

[243] The author may, in fact, be referring to the fortress built by the Portuguese a short distance west of Manamah during their occupation of Bahrain between 1521 and 1602. There had been earlier fortifications on Bahrain, but by Kazaruni's time – first half of the 19th century – they would have been little more than archaeological ruins.

[244] Abu Shahri means "From Bushire".

The gardens and orchards of this island: Date palms are prevalent, the rest is fruit such as peaches, pomegrenades, grapes... Some Bahrain palm trees yield double harvests annually. Especially remarkable are oranges, citrons and lemons. The date palm orchards are allotted in the following manner: One third is earmarked as *vaqf* [pious endowment] for the benefit of ta`ziyahs [rituals of mourning] of the Fifth member of the Prophet's family and Lord of the Martyrs [Khamis-e Al-e Aba Sayyid ul-Shuhada = Husain], for defraying the costs of repairing bridges and mosques, and for travelers including the cost of shrouds for those who have died. ...Two thirds of the yield, not reserved as vaqf, are appropriated in their totality by the Banu Utub...

The other part of the revenue of the Banu Utbah comes from the 5500 baggarahs[245] engaged in pearling: each baggarah gladly pays the Banu Utbah the amount of 25 riyals farangsay; aside from that, [however], there are baggarahs working entirely for their own benefit.

They [the Banu Utbah] seize everything produced in Bahrain, and the helpless poor,...because of their inability and [lack of] strength [to leave], remain on the spot, passing their lives by tending orchards and cultivating fields throughout the four seasons and placing the entire harvests at the disposal of the Banu Utbah. What remains for those poor [peasants] is some rough cloth to cover their nakedness, and food barely sufficient to keep them alive and consisting of a starvation diet of inedible fish and dates.

Now despite the small size of Bahrain's population, no well-known Persian port is without two, three, four hundred houses inhabited by people from this island.

On this island, in the days of the rule of Shaykh Nasir Abu Mahiri[246] – sixty to seventy years ago – there were about 366 inhabited and prosperous villages. Here is a list of these villages, with the name and number of houses in each village:

On the [north-]east, there is a town (balad) called Manamah, the [capital] city of this island; the rest consists of villages pertaining to this city. ...In the midst of Manamah there is a bazaar with four hundred shops of all kinds. Every Friday artisans in many parts of Bahrain set out from their villages before sunrise, on their donkeys, and come to Manamah with

---

[245] A local type of ship.

[246] Shaykh Nasir of Bushire, of the above-mentioned Al Mazkur.

their wares and engage in commerce; one hour before sunset they depart on the return journey to their villages.

The city of Manamah has a strong fortress (hisar) and fortification wall (shahrband) with 28 towers and gates, one of which faces the harbor; there is a wharf (langargah) in this harbor. In the northern part of the city is a caravansary, all rooms are occupied by seafaring merchants (tujjar-e darya)... Manamah is more of a city than Abu Shahr [Bushire], its houses are tall buildings made of stone and plaster. There are some six thousand houses there, belonging to foreigners and locals, and 100 mosques ... Its caravansary consists of two storeys; and there are sixteen [other] caravansaries, all occupied and busy, with rooms whose doors face the sea. In its southern part is a fortress with four towers built by Sayyid Sultan, father of Sayyid Sa`id Khan of Oman in the days when he defeated the Banu Utbah ...[247]

Sahlah-e Sufla. It is a place whose soil is nothing but sand, with very good climate. The Banu Utbah own it, and have there a stable for horses. Four hundred of these are excellent mares, property of the Great Shaykh of the Utub; he keeps them there on account of the good climate.

Map No. 9-1: Bahrain and its Recent Acquisition, Hawar

This map shows Bahrain within the context of present-day political and economic relations. A causeway (Jisr al-Malik Fahd, lit. "The Bridge of King Fahd) built recently connects the main island with the Saudi coast just south of Khubar, and continues as a modern highway into the heart of Saudi Arabia's business and oil industry, encompassed by Khubar, Dhahran, Dammam and Qatif. A short distance to the north of this causeway and parallel to it lies a pipeline bringing oil to Bahrain's refinery at Rifa'. Some of this oil came from the Saudi offshore oilfield of Abu Safah, whose yield was being donated, as a gesture of cooperation and friendship, to Bahrain. This procedure had the purpose of helping Bahrain, whose oil reserves were nearing deple-

---

[247] The author is referring here to the brief conquest of Bahrain realized in 1800-1801 by the ruler of Oman, Sayyid Sultan (1792-1806). Two more attempts were made by his son and successor, Sayyid Sa'id, in 1816 and 1828, both equally ephemeral. See Lorimer, *Gazetteer*, 2: 841-54.

tion, to keep its refining and exporting facilities active. In 2004 a dispute between the two kingdoms regarding a special trade relationship treaty Bahrain had concluded with the United States caused a suspension of the agreement.

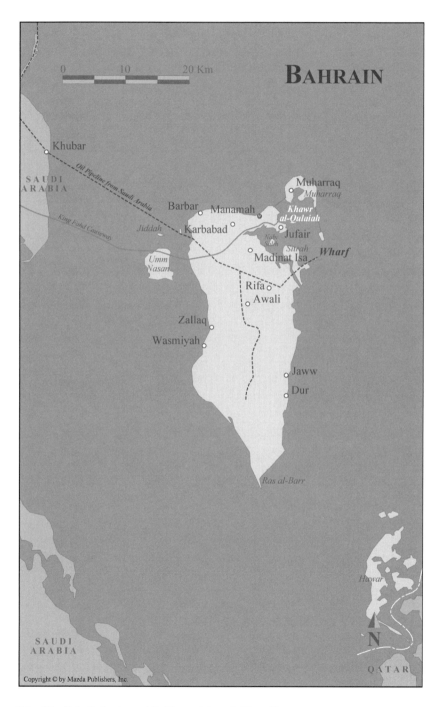

Map No. 9-1: Bahrain and its Recent Acquisition, Hawar.

Map No. 9-2: The Northeastern Part of the Main Island

This map shows the northern part as well as the second largest island of the archipelago, Muharraq, which is also the site of Bahrain International Airport. The Khawr al-Qulaiah to the south of Muharraq is a good natural harbor; part of it is Mina Sulman, now the principal US naval base in the Persian Gulf. Among other features worthy of notice, there are the ruins of a Portuguese fort, a vestige of intermittent Portuguese presence between 1521 and 1602, about 5 kilometers to the west of Manamah. Near the southern edge of the area shown on the map, we see Awali, the second important urban center on the main island; and the industrial sites of Rifa` al-Gharbi and Rifa` al-Sharqi, connected with the oil refinery further east near the island of Sitrah and its loading terminals.

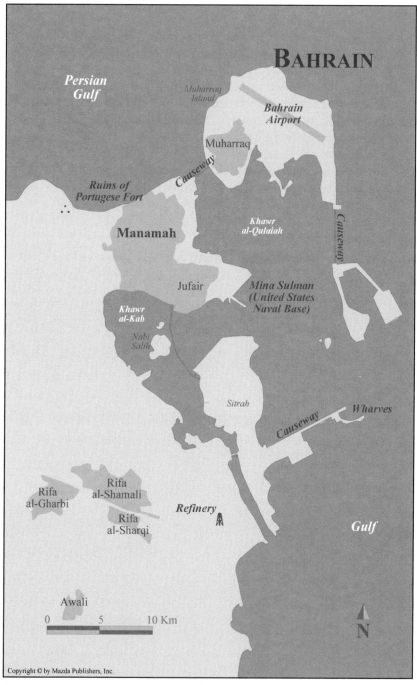

Map No. 9-2: The Northeastern Part of the Main Island.

6. QATAR
(The State of Qatar, *Dawlat Qatar*)

Qatar is a large, oblong peninsula that protrudes northward from the middle of the Gulf's southern coast, where its neighbors are Saudi Arabia and the United Arab Emirates.

Basic Statistical Data

Area: 11,437 square kilometers.

Population: 885 thousand (July 2006 estimate).

Ethnolinguistic composition: Arab 40%, Pakistani 18%, Indian 18%, Persian 10%, other 14%.

Religion: Muslims (Arabs, Pakistanis, Persians) 95%.

Capital: Doha (Dawhah).

Government structure: hereditary monarchy of the Al Thani family; the ruler has the title of *amir* (emir); in 2006, Hamad bin Khalifah Al Thani, since 1995; the cabinet of ministers is presided by Prime Minister Abd Allah bin Khalifah Al Thani, the emir's brother, since 1996; several other members of the family also have ministerial posts; the ministers are appointed by the monarch.

Constitution: drawn up by government, it was ratified by public referendum in 2003, was endorsed by the emir in 2004, and went into effect in 2005.

Legislative branch: a Majlis al-Shura or Advisory Council consists of 35 members, but is expected to be expanded to 45 members according to the Constitution; two thirds are to be elected by the public, one third to be appointed by the emir. There are no political parties

Administrative structure: 10 municipalities (*baladiyah*-s).

Map No. 10: The State of Qatar

We see the capital Doha (al-Dawhah in correct transliteration) on the peninsula's eastern coast. The rich oil fields extend along the central part of the western coast, approximately from Dukhan to Julahah; Qatar also owns several offshore oil fields in the vicinity of the islet of Halul some 80 kilometers to the east of the peninsula. The especially rich deposits of natural gas are mostly under the sea bed within Qatar's territorial waters and extended in a wide arc off the northeastern tip of the peninsula. Of historical interest is the city of Zubarah on the northwestern coast of the peninsula; in the 18th century it was the headquarters of the Al Khalifah, a clan of the Arab Utubi tribe, which had moved there from the Arabian interior. In 1783 their leader, Ahmad Al Khalifah, launched the conquest of Bahrain from Zubarah.

At the southeastern tip of the peninsula we see the deep inlet Khawr al-Udaid, whose southern shore is owned either by Saudi Arabia or by the United Arab Emirates, depending on whose maps are being consulted. Udaid, a small port town on the southern side of the narrow entrance to the Khawr Udaid, thus belongs to one or the other of these two states. We also see another Udaid, deeper in the peninsula's interior some 25 kilometers southwest of the capital Doha, which has in recent years been developed as a major US air force base.

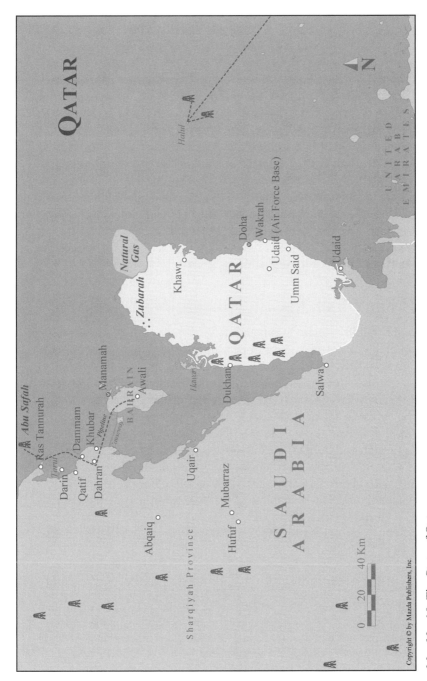

Map No. 10: The State of Qatar.

7. UNITED ARAB EMIRATES
(al-Imarat al-Arabiyah al-Muttahidah)[248]

The UAE is a federation of seven principalities (*imarat*) located along the lower southeastern shore of the Persian Gulf and, to a minor degree, along the Gulf of Oman. The principalities are, proceeding from west to east, Abu Dhabi, Dubai, Sharjah, Ajman, Umm al-Qaiwain, Ras al-Khaimah, and Fujairah. In each case, the name of the emirate is also that of its capital city. The federation is bordered by Saudi Arabia on the south and west, by Qatar on the northwest, and by Oman on the east. A glance at the map will reveal that except for Abu Dhabi and Umm al-Qaiwain, each emirate also possesses enclaves within the others' territories – a mosaic that defies verbal description and is best expressed and perceived cartographically.

Basic Statistical Data

Area: 82,880 square kilometers.
Population: 2,602,713 million (2006). The situation is compli-
    cated by the fact that a great portion, in fact the majority,
    consists of expatriates ranging from other Arabs to Western-
    ers to East Asians; the growth rate of the Imarati population
    is estimated at 1.54%.
Ethnolinguistic composition: 19% Emirati, all Arab; 23% other
    Arab and Iranian; 50% South Asian; 8% other expatriates.
Religion: Muslim (predominantly Sunni among the Arab popu-
    lation, but Shia among the considerable Iranian minority).
Capital: Abu Dhabi, capital of the federation and of the emirate
    of the same name.

---

[248] The official Arabic name of this union or federation is *imarat*, plural of *imarah*, principality, a word derived from amir, prince; this terminology has long since penetrated the English language as emir and
emirate, hence the preferred current name of this federation as Emirates. The titles of the individual rulers usually appear in Arabic as
shaykh, which again could be translated by its old English adaptation,
sheik. For the individual principalities, a frequently used term in English is the hybrid *shaykhdom*.

Government structure: a federation of seven emirates, all hereditary monarchies.

Ports and harbors: Fujairah, Khawr Fakkan, Mina' Jabal Ali, Mina' Rashid, Mina' Saqr, Mina' Zayid, Sharjah.

Maps 11-1 Through 12-3: Various Geographic Depictions of UAE

Map No. 11-1 shows the UAE within the context of the Persian Gulf group.

Map No. 11-2 shows the specific area of the Federation.

Map No. 11-3 is an attempt to make the extreme "gerrymandering" of its northern segment intelligible.

Maps No. 11-2 and 11-3 illustrate the disproportionately larger size of Abu Dhabi, the still considerable size of Dubai, and, conversely, the diminutive size of Ajman despite its ownership of two enclaves.

Map No. 11-2 is also an attempt to illustrate the location of the principal oil fields, both on land and offshore. Again, those of Abu Dhabi dwarf those of the other emirates. A point of interest is the fact that some of the most productive oil fields are in the same general area of the Persian Gulf where pearling used to be especially productive, on the so-called Great Pearl Bank.

Maps No. 12-(1,2,3) depict one of the not fully resolved territorial disputes troubling the relations among the Persian Gulf's Arab states. Map 12-1 represents the Abu Dhabi – and thus the UAE – version of the borders; Map 12-2, the Saudi version. To no one's surprise, all current publications issued in the UAE assert its version both textually and cartographically, while the opposite is true of Saudi publications. On the international scene, we encounter both versions, the choice probably dictated by which influence has prevailed in a given case. Thus the *Atlas of the Middle East* published by the National Geographic Society (Washington, D.C., 2003) shows the Saudi version (p. 46, United Arab Emirates); on the other hand, the *Atlas* published by the

Army of the Turkish Republic in 1993 shows on p. 33 the UAE version (although the publisher takes the precaution of stating, on the page facing the title page, that *"Devlet Hudutları kesin ve resmi mahiyet taşımamaktadır"* – "The international borders do not claim a definitive and official validity").

This dispute, which can be conveniently labeled as one over the Udaid area, is part of a larger one which has both economic and strategic implications and involves four states – Saudi Arabia, the UAE, Qatar, and Bahrain. One question is a region in the middle of the border between the two countries to the southeast of Abu Dhabi's Liwa oasis. It is on the Saudi side of the border, and the Saudis call it Shaibah, but the Emiratis prefer to call it Zarara, extending to it the name of a district on their side. This region harbors, according to recent discoveries and the latest estimates, 15 billion barrels of oil[249] or perhaps even more; as Zarara, it might be considered part of the Zarara region and thus a possession of the Emirates. The present border between the United Arab Emirates and Saudi Arabia was agreed upon in the "Jedda agreement" (*Ittifaqiyat Juddah*), signed in August 1974. Saudi Arabia renounced its claim to the Buraimi oasis[250] in return for the Emirates' renunciation of its claim to the Udaid area; as for the Zarara/Shaibah region, neither party seems to have cared at that point, and it is only with the discovery of oil there that it has become a bone of contention. Shaikh Hamdan bin Zayid Al Nihayan, minister of foreign affairs of the Emirates and chairman of the Permanent Commission on the question of the borders between the UAE and Saudi Arabia, recently stated that substantial   modifications are necessary. At present, both the Zarara/Shaibah area and the Udaid territory are held by Saudi Arabia, seemingly putting the United Arab Emirates in a position of weakness.

---

[249] By way of comparison, the proven oil reserves of the United States are 22 billion barrels.

[250] Buraimi in this sense has its broader historical connotation, which included also what is now known as the al-Ain oasis cluster, and the group was called by early Arab geographers Tu'am. Present-day Buraimi belongs to Oman, al-Ain to the United Arab Emirates; Saudi Arabia, since its formation in the 18th century until recently, had claimed the entire complex. Here too British protection of the Trucial Coast and Oman was the decisive factor.

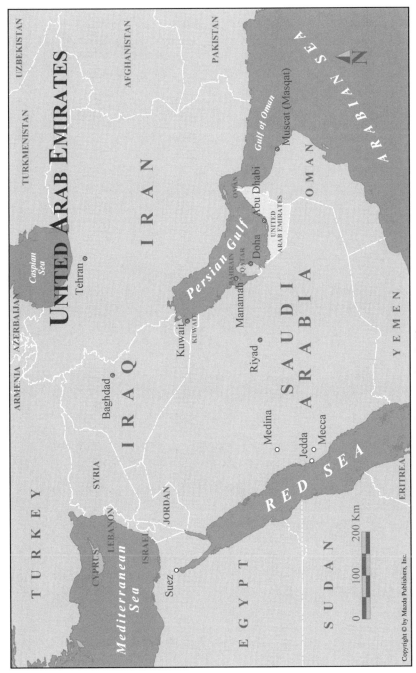

Map No. 11-1: The UAE within the Context of the Persian Gulf group.

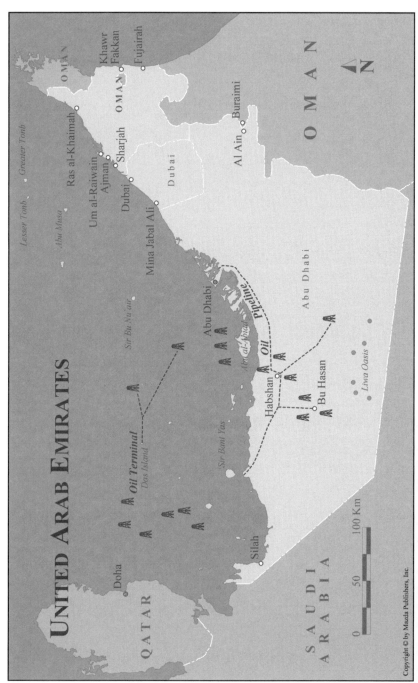

Map No. 11-2: The Specific Area of the Federation.

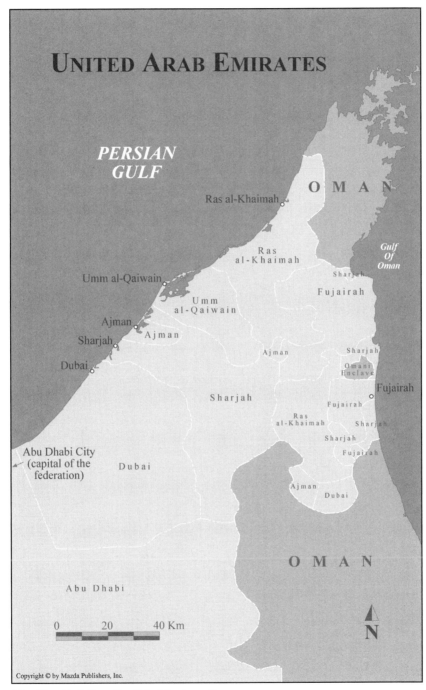

Map No. 11-3: Details of the Northern Segment.

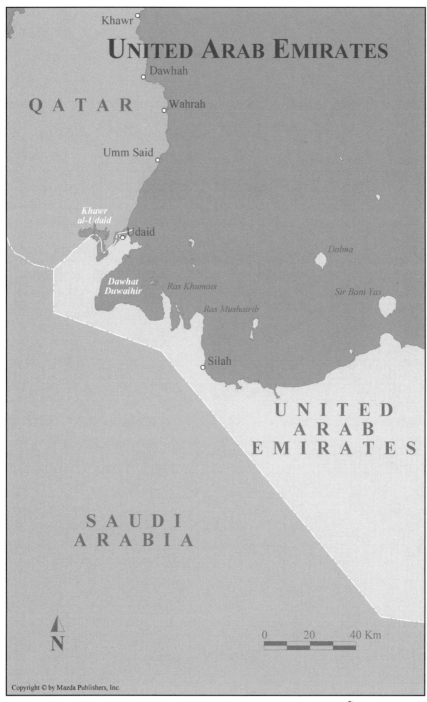

Map No. 12-1: The United Arab Emirates version of the federationŨs borders with Saudi Arabi and Qatar.

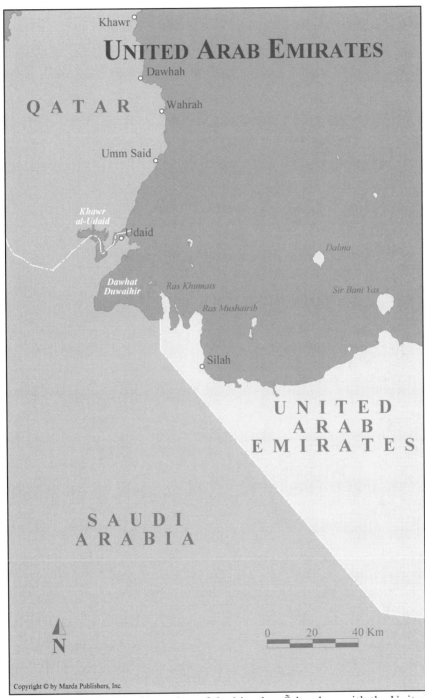

Map No. 12-2: The Saudi version of the kingdom̃s borders with the United Arab Emirates and Qatar.

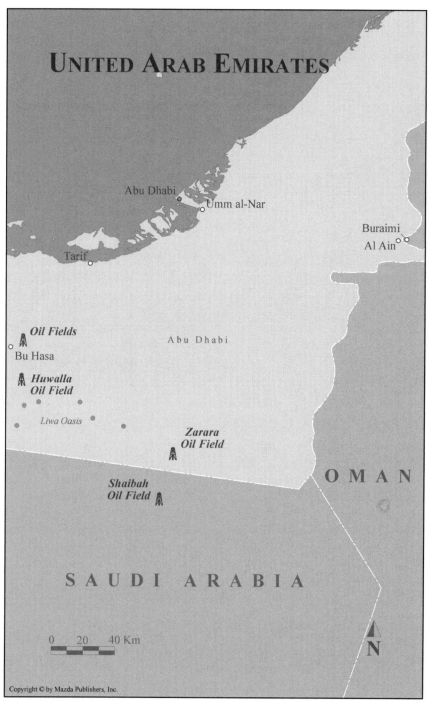

Map No. 12-3: The Zarara-Shaibah area (recently developed oil-rich region claimed both by the United Arab Emirates and Saudi Arabia).

8. OMAN
(Sultanate of Oman, *Soltanat Uman*)

With an area of 212,460 sq km, Oman takes the fourth place in the group under discussion, after Saudi Arabia, Iran, and Iraq, as does its population of 3,102,229 souls (July 2005 estimate; after Iran, Saudi Arabia, and Iraq). Situated in the easternmost segment of the Arabian Peninsula, it has common borders with the United Arab Emirates, Saudi Arabia, and the Republic of Yemen. Two additional special features of the Sultanate's territory are the small enclave of Nahwah within the United Arab Emirates, and a larger area that occupies the Musandam Peninsula and is separated from the rest of Oman by the same Federation.

Basic Statistical Data

Area: 212,460 square kilometers.
Population: 3,001,583, of whom 577,293 non-nationals.
Ethnolinguistic composition: Arab, but with both temporary and permanent minorities from Baluchistan, the Indian subcontinent, and East Africa; Oman's traditional ties with the last-named area have also produced a Swahili-speaking minority.
Religion: Islam, mostly of the Ibadi denomination.
Government: Hereditary rule of the Al Bu Said family; the ruler's title is sultan.
Executive branch: the sultan is also the prime minister, and the cabinet is appointed by him.
Legislative branch: a bicameral parliament (majlis); the upper chamber or Majlis al-Dawlah (State Assembly) consists of 58 members, who are appointed by the sultan; it has advisory powers only; the lower chamber or Majlis al-Shura (Consultative Assembly) consists of 83 members, who are elected by universal suffrage for 4-year terms; it is authorized to propose legislation but not to pass it. There are no political parties.
Capital: Muscat (Masqat).
Administrative divisions: 5 regions (*manatiq*, sg. *mintaqah*): Dakhiliyah, Batinah, Wusta, Sharqiyah, Zahirah; 3 governo-

rates (*muhafazat*, sg. muhafazah): Musandam, Masqat, Zufar.

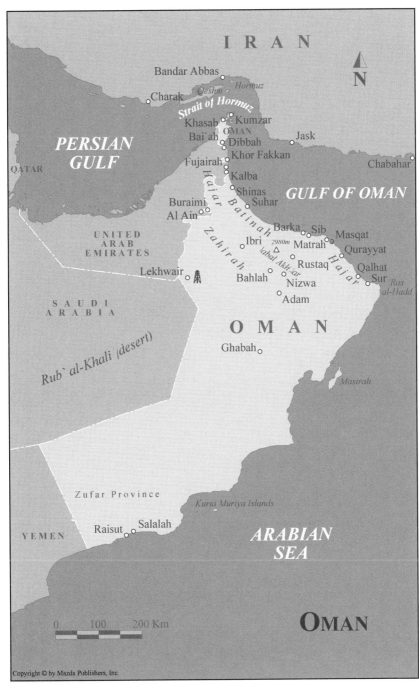

Map No. 13-1: The Sultanate of Oman

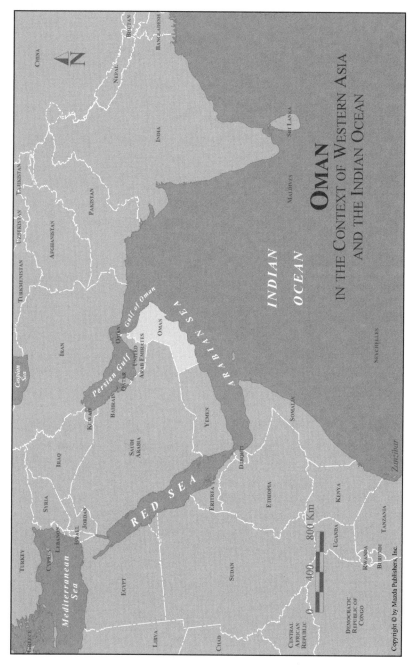

Map No. 13-2: Oman in the Context of Western Asia and Indian Ocean

Bibliography

Abd Allah, Muhammad Mursi. *Imarat al-Sahil wa-Uman wa l-Dawlah al-Su`udiyah al-Ula, 1793-1818*. al-Qahirah 1978.

al-Abid, Salih Muhammad. *Dawr al-Qawasim fi l-Khalij al-Arabi, 1747-1820*. Baghdad 1976.

Abu Hakimah, Ahmad Mustafa. *History of Eastern Arabia: the rise and development of Bahrain and Kuwait*. Beirut, 1965.

Adamiyat, Fereydoun. *Bahrein Islands: a legal and diplomatic study of the British – Iranian controversy*. New York: Praeger, 1955.

Afshar Sistani, Iraj. *Nam-e Khalij-e Fars*. Tehran, 2002.

Ainsworth, William Francis. *A personal narrative of the Euphrates expedition*. London, 1888. 2 vols.

_____, *The River Karun: an opening to British commerce*. London, 1890.

Aitchison, Charles Upherston. *A Collection of Treaties, Engagements and Sanads relating to India and neighbouring countries*. Calcutta, 1929-33. 5th edition.

Al Ahmad, Jalal. *Jazirah-e Kharg: durr-e yatim-e Khalij*. Tehran, 1960.

Albuquerque, Afonso de, 1500-1580. *The Commentaries of the great Afonso de Albuquerque, [1453-1515]*. London: Hakluyt Society, 1878. 4 vols. (the compiler of the Portuguese original *Comentarios do grande Afonso de Albuquerque*, Lisboa, 1576, was the author's son and namesake; the English translation, with an introduction and notes, is by Walter de Gray Birch).

Allen, Calvin H. "Indian merchant community of Masqat," *Bulletin of the School of Oriental and African Studies*, University of London, 44 (1981), 39-53.

_____, "The State of Masqat in the Gulf and East Africa, 1785-1829," *International Journal of Middle East Studies*, 14 (1982).

Allen, William Edward. *Problems of Turkish power in the sixteenth century*. London, 1963.

Anscombe, Frederick F. *The Ottoman Gulf: the creation of Kuwait, Saudi Arabia, and Qatar.* New York: Columbia University Press, 1997.

Arrian, 96-175. See Vincent, William. *Commerce and navigation...*

Asnad-e ravabit-e tarikhi-e Iran va Purtaghal: salha-ye 1500 ta 1758. Tarjamah va tanzim: Mahdi Aqa Muhammad Zanjani. Tehran: Markaz-e Asnad va Khadmat-e Pizhuhishi, 1382/2003.

Aubin, Jean. "Marchands de la Mer Rouge et du Golfe Persique au tournant des 15e et 16e siècles," in *Marchands et hommes d'affaires asiatiques dans l'Océan Indien et la Mer de Chine, 13e-20e siècles,* ed. Denys Lombard & Jean Aubin, Paris 1988.

_____, "Les Princes d'Ormuz du XIIIe au XVe siècles," *Journal Asiatique,* tome 241 (1953), pp. 77-138.

_____, "Le royaume d'Ormuz au début du XVIe siècle," *Mare Luso-Indicum* 2 (1973), pp. 77-179.

_____, "La ruine de Siraf et les routes du Golfe Persique," *Cahiers de la Civilisation Mediévale,* X-XII (1959).

_____, "Y a-t-il eu interruption du commerce par mer entre le Golfe Persique et l'Inde du XIe au XIVe siècle?", Lisboa: Centro de Estudos Históricos Ultramarinos, *Studia,* no. 11, January 1963, pp. 165-71.

Bacqué-Grammont, Jean-Louis. *Les Ottomans, les Safavides et leurs voisins: contribution à e'histoire des relations internationales dans l'orient islamique de 1514 à 1524.* Istanbul, 1987.

Bahrain Through the Ages. London, 1986-91. 2 vols. (Vol. 1: the archaeology; vol. 2: the history)

al-Bahrain al-thaqafiyah. al-Manamah: al-Majlis al-Watani lil-Thaqafah, 1994- (a periodical)

Bahrein, la civilisation des deux mers: de Dilmoun à Tylos: exposition présentée à l'Institut du Monde Arabe du 18 mai au 20 août 1999. Paris-Gand, 1999.

Baladhuri, Ahmad b. Yahya, d. 892. *Futuh al-buldan.* Ed. M.J. de Goeje. Leiden, 1866.

Barbosa, Duarte, d. 1521. *The Book of Duarte Barbosa: an account of the countries bordering on the Indian Ocean – completed about the year 1518. Translated and annotated by*

Mansel Longworth Dames. London: Hakluyt Society, 1918-21. 2 vols.

Bartold, Vasilii Vladimirovich. *An Historical Geography of Iran* (a translation from the Russian original, *Istoricheskiy obzor Irana*). Princeton University Press, 1984.

Beek, Martinus Adriaan. *Atlas of Mesopotamia; a survey of the history and civilisation of Mesopotamia from the Stone Age to the fall of Babylon*. London 1962. (Translated from the Dutch original, *Atlas van het Tweestroomland*)

Belgrave, James H.D. "The Portuguese in the Bahrain Islands 1521-1602," *Journal of the Royal Asiatic Society*, 1935, pp. 617-30.

_____, *Personal Column*. London, 1962.

_____, *The Pirate Coast*. London 1963 (based on the notes of Francis Erskine Loch, capitain of HMS Eden, one of the cruisers in the fleet that in December 1819 destroyed the pirate base of Ras al-Khaimah; there is now a Persian translation: *Sahel-e dozdan-e darya'i: safarnamah-e darya'i-e Lakh bih Khalij-e Fars... tarjamah-e Husain Zu l-Qadr*, Tehran, 1369/1990).

Bibby, Geoffrey. *Looking for Dilmun*. New York, 1969.

Blaeu, Joan, 1596-1673. *Atlas maior*. Amsterdam. There are a number of editions of this masterpiece of Dutch cartography. Also the following facsimile:

The third centenary edition of Johan Blaeu, *Le grand atlas: ou, Cosmographie blaviane*. Amsterdam, 1663/1967. 12 volumes.

Bosworth, Clifford Edmund. *The New Islamic Dynasties*. New York: Columbia University Press, 1996.

Bowen, R. "The Pearl fisheries of the Persian Gulf," *Middle East Journal*, 5 (1951), 161-80.

Bowman, J. "The Chrisitan monastery on the island of Kharg," *Australian Journal of Biblical Archaeology* 2/3 (1974-75), pp. 49-64.

Boxer, Charles. *The Portuguese Seaborne Empire, 1415-1825*. London, 1969.

_____. *Portuguese conquest and commerce in Southern Asia, 1500-1700*. London, 1985. (Variorum series)

Buckingham, James Silk, 1786-1855. *Travels in Assyria, India and Persia*. 2nd ed. London, 1830. 2 vols.

Busch, Britton Cooper. *Britain and the Persian Gulf, 1894-1914*. Berkeley and Los Angeles: University of Califormia Press, 1967.

Caetani, Leone. *Annali dell'Islam*. Milano, 1905-26. 10 vols. in 12.

The Cambridge Ancient History.

The Cambridge History of Iran.

Carls, Hans-Georg. *Alt-Hormuz: Ein historischer Hafen an der Strasse von Hormuz (Iran)*. München, 1982.

Castanheda, Fernão Lopes de, 1500-1559. *The first booke of the historie of the discouerie and conquest of the East Indias, enterprised by the Portingales,...Set foorth in the Portingale language, by Hernan Lopes de Castanheda. And now translated into English, by N.L. Gentleman*. Imprinted at London: By Thomas East, 1582. 164 leaves. English translation of *Historia do descobrimento e conquista de India pelos Portugueses*. (A new Portuguese ed. , 3rd , appeared at Coimbra, 1924-33).

Chardin, John. *The Travels of Sir John Chardin into Persia and the East Indies*. London, 1691.

Chesney, Francis Rawden, 1789-1872. Expedition for the survey of the Rivers Euphrates and Tigris. London, 1850. 2 vols.

Christensen, Arthur. *L'Iran sous les Sassanides*. 2nd ed., Copenhagen-Paris, 1944.

Cordesman, Anthony H. *Bahrain, Oman, Qatar, and the United Arab Emirates: challenges of security*. Boulder: Westview Press, 1997. See also other books and articles by this prominent specialist on the current situation in the Persian Gulf.

Curtin, Philip D. *The World and the West: the European challenge and the overseas response in the Age of Empire*. Cambridge University Press, 2000.

Curzon, George Nathaniel. *Persia and the Persian Question*. London 1892. 2 vols. (There is a Persian translation: *Iran va qaziyah-e Iran*. Tehran, 1349-50/1970-71. 2 vols.)

Daryaee, Touraj. "The Persian Gulf trade in Late Antiquity," *Journal of World History*, 14 (2003), 1-16.

Davies, Charles Edward. *The Blood-red Arab flag: an investigation into Qasimi piracy, 1797-1820*. Exeter 1997.

Idem. "Britain, trade and piracy: the British expeditions against Ras al-Khaima of 1809 and 1819-20," *Global interests in the Arab Gulf*, pp. 29-66.

Davies, David William. *Elizabethans errant: the strange fortunes of Sir Thomas Sherley and his three sons.* Ithaca: Cornell University Press, 1967.

Dejanirah Couto, Jean-Louis Bacqué-Grammont and Mahmoud Taleghani, editors, *Atlas historique du golfe Persique (XVIe-XVIIIe siècles)* = Historical Atlas of the Persian Gulf (sixteenth to eighteenth centuries). Turnhout: Brepols, 2006. (Text in French, English and Persian.)

Encyclopaedia Iranica. Ed. Ehsan Yarshater. London and Boston: Routledge & Kegan Paul, 1982-

The Encyclopaedia of Islam. 2nd edition, Leiden: Brill, 1960-2004. 12 vols.

English, Barbara. *John Company's last war.* London, 1971.

Faria e Sousa, Manuel de, 1590-1649. *The Portugues Asia on the History, Discovery and Conquest of India by the Portugues. Translated by Captain John Stevens.* London, 1695 (translation of the original, *Asia Portuguesa*, 1665-75, 3 vols.; a new Portuguese edition: Porto, 1945-47, 6 vols., with an introduction by M. Lopes de Almeida)

Farisi, Zaki Muhammad Ali. *National guide and atlas of the Kingdom of Saudi Arabia: maps, information, statistics.* Jeddah: Z.M.A. Farisi, 1989. (English version of the Arabic *al-Dalil al-Shamil lil-Mamlakah al-`Arabiyah al-Su`udiyah: khara'it-ma`lumat-ihsa'at*, Jiddah, 1989).

_____. *Farisi maps: Eastern region A to Z: Damam, Al Khubar, Qatif.* Jeddah: Farsi Maps, [1991].

Faroughy, Abbas. *Bahrein Islands, 750-1951.* New York, 1951.

_____. *Histoire du Royaume de Hormuz, depuis son origine jusqu'à son incorporation dans l'Empire persan des Séfévides en 1622.* Brussels, 1949.

Fiorani Piacentini, Valeria. *L'Emporio ed il Regno di Hormoz (VIII – fine XV sec. D.C.): vicende storiche, problemi ed aspetti di una civiltà costiera del Golfo Persico.* Milano, 1975. (Memorie dell'Istituto Lombardo – Accademia di Scienze e Lettere. Classe di Lettere – Scienze Morali e Storiche. Vol. xxxv – Fasc. 1)

_____. *Il Golfo nel XXI secolo: Le nuove logiche della conflittualità;* a cura di Valeria Fiorani Piacentini. Bologna: Società Editrice Il Mulino, 2002.

_____. "La Rinascita dell'economia di mercato in Iran: l'Emporio e il Regno di Hormoz dal 1300 al 1622," *Rivista Storica Itatliana,* 94 (1982), 490-507.

_____. "Siraf and Hormuz between East and West: Merchants and merchandise in the Gulf," *Global Interests in the Arab Gulf,* pp. 1-28.

Floor, Willem M. *Commercial conflict between Persia and the Netherlands, 1712-1718.* Durham: Centre for Middle Eastern and Islamic Studies, 1988.

_____. A description of the Persian Gulf and its inhabitants in 1756," *Persica* 8 (1979), pp. 163-85.

_____. *The First Dutch-Persian Conflict: The attack on Qeshm Island, 1645.* Costa Mesa: Mazda Publishers, 2004.

_____. "Pearl fishing in the Persian Gulf in 1757," *Persica* 10 (1982), pp. 209-22.

_____. *The Persian Gulf: A Political and Economic History of Five Port Cities, 1500-1730.* Washington, DC: Mage Publishers, 2006.

_____. "The Rise and fall of the Banu Ka'b, a borderer state in southern Khuzistan," Iran XLIV (2006), pp. 277-315.

Frye, Richard Nelson. *The Heritage of Persia.* Cleveland and New York, 1963.

Fryer, John, d. 1733. *A New Account of East India and Persia, in Eight Letters: being Nine years' Travels, begun 1672, finished 1681.* London, 1693. New ed. Hakluyt Society, 1909-15. 3 vols.

Fuccaro, Nalida. "Mapping the transnational community: Persians and the space of the city in Bahrain, c. 1869-1937," in *Transnational Connections,...* pp. 39-58.

Ghirshman, Roman. "L'Ile de Kharg dans le golfe Persique," Académie des Inscriptions et Belles Lettres [Bruxelles]. *Comptes Rendus,* 1958, pp. 261-71.

_____. "Ile de Kharg dans le golfe Persique," *Arts Asiatiques* 6 (1959), pp. 107-20.

_____. "L'île de Kharg (Ikaros) dans le golfe Persique," *Revue Archéologique,* 1959, pp. 70-77.

_____. *The Island of Kharg*. Tehran: Iranian Oil Operating Companies Publication, 1960.

Global Interests in the Arab Gulf, ed. Charles E. Davies, Exeter 1992.

Godinho, Vittorino Magalhães. *L'Économie de l'Empire Portugais aux XVe et XVIe siècles*. Paris, 1969.

Graham, Gerald Sanford. *The Politics of naval supremacy: studies in British maritime ascendancy*. Cambridge University Press, 1965.

Grummon, Stephen R. *The Rise and fall of the Arab Shaykhdom of Bushire, 1750-1850*. Baltimore: The Johns Hopkins University, PhD dissertation 1985 (University Microfilms 1985)

Gulvardi, Isa. *Jughrafiya-ye jazayir-e Irani-e Khalij-e Fars. Ustan-e Hurmuzgan. Shahristan-e Bu Musa (jazayir-e Bu Musa, Tunb-e Buzurg ve Tunb-e Kuchik)*. Tihran: Intisharat-e Sazman-e Jughrafiyayi-e Niruha-ye Musallah, 1381/2003.

Hakluyt, Richard, 1552-1616. *Principal Navigations*. London 1599. New ed. Glasgow: J. MacLehose, 1903-05. 12 vols.

Hamd Allah Mustawfi al-Qazwini, d. 1339. *Nuzhat al-qulub*. Ed. Muhammad Dabir Siyaqi, Tehran, 1336/1957-8; and el-Cazwini, *Kosmographie*, ed. Ferdinand Wüstenfeld, Göttingen, 1848-49.

_____, *The Geographical Part,...* ed. and tr. Guy Le Strange, Leiden-London 1915-19.

Handbuch des Persischen Golfs. 5th ed. Hamburg: Deutsches Hydrographisches Institut, 1976.

Hasan, Hadi. *A History of Persian Navigation*. London, 1928.
Persian translation: *Sarguzasht-e kashtirani-e Iraniyan: az dirbaz ta qarn-e shanzdahum-e miladi. Tarjumah-e Umid Iqtidari; tashih, tahshiyah, ta`liqat va payvastha, Ahmad Iqtidari*. Mashhad: Asitanah, 1371/1992.

Hawley, Donald. *The Trucial States*. London, 1970.

_____, *Oman and its Renaissance*. Rev. ed. London, 1984.

Hay, Sir Rupert. *The Persian Gulf states*. Washington, D.C.: The Middle East Institute, 1959.

Herodotus, 5th cent. BC. *History*. Book 4, chapter 44 (Darius and Scylax)

Hinds, Martin. "The First Arab conquests in Fars," *IRAN* 22 (1984), pp. 39-53.

An Historical Atlas of Islam. Atlas Historique de l'Islam. 2nd rev. ed. by Hugh Kennedy. Leiden: Brill, 2002.

Hourani, George Fazlo. *Arab Seafaring in the Indian Ocean in Ancient and Early Medieval Times.* 2nd edition ed. by John Carswell. Princeton University Press 1995.

Hoyland, Robert G. *Arabia and the Arabs, from the Bronze Age to the coming of Islam.* London and New York: Routledge, 2001.

Hudud al-`Alam: "The Regions of the World," a Persian Geography, 372 AH – 982 AD, translated and explained by Vladimir Minorsky, London 1970.

Hurewitz, Jacob Coleman. *The Middle East and North Africa in World Politics: a documentary record.* New Haven: Yale University Press, 1975-78. 3 vols. (vol. 1: European expansion, 1535-1914; vol. 2: British-French supremacy, 1914-1945; vol. 3: British-French withdrawal and Soviet-American rivalry, 1945-1975.) This is a new expanded edition of Hurewitz's *Diplomacy in the Near and Middle East*, Princeton University Press, 1956, 2 vols.)

Ibn Battuta, d. 1368. *Voyages d'Ibn Battuta; texte arabe accompagné d'une traduction, par C. Defrémery et B.R. Sanguinetti.* Paris 1854; new edition, 1969. 4 vols.; and *Travels of Ibn Battuta, A.D. 1325-1354, translated with revisions and notes from the Arabic text edited by D. Defrémery... by Hamilton Alexander Roskeen Gibb*, Hakluyt Society, Cambridge, 1958-2000, 5 vols.

Ibn Hawqal, fl. 943-977. *Kitab surat al-ard.* Leiden: Brill, 1967 (BGA, 2); and French translation by Gaston Wiet: *Configuration de la terre.* Paris: UNESCO, 1964-65. 2 vols.

Ibn Jubair, 1145-1217. *Rihlat Ibn Jubair... The Travels of Ibn Jubair*, translated by R.J.C. Broadhurst. London, 1952.

Ibn Majid, Ahmad, fl. 1489-98. *Kitab al-fawa'id fi usul al-bahr wa l-qawa`id...* Dimashq, 1971.

The English translation, accompanied by exhaustive annotation and commentary, of this classic Arab navigation manual has become a classic in its own right: Tibbets, Gerald, *Arab navigation in the Indian Ocean before the coming of the Portuguese: being a translation of the Kitab...,* London, Royal Asiatic Society, 1971. There is also a Persian translation, partly based on Tibbets' English translation: *Kitab al-*

fawa'id fi usul al-bahr wa l-qawa`id: A'inha-ye daryana-vardi-e kuhan dar Uqyanus-e Hind va Khalij-e Fars... tar-jumah az Arabi va tahshiyah, Ahmad Iqtidari; tarjumah az Ingilisi, Umid Iqtidari. Tehran, 1372/1993.

Ibn Ruzaiq, Humaid bin Muhammad. *al-Fath al-mubin fi sirat al-sadah Al Bu Sayidiyin.* Oman: Wizarat al-Turath, 1403/1983.

_____, English translation: *History of the Imams and Seyyids of Oman, translated by George Percy Badger.* London: Hakluyt Society, 1981. (Hakluyt series 1, no. 44)

Idrisi, ca. 1100-1166. *Nuzhat al-mushtaq fi ikhtiraq al-afaq. Opus geographicum, sive "Liber ad eorum delectationem qui terras peragrare student".* Naples: Istituto Universitario di Napoli, 1970-84.

India and the Indian Ocean, 1500-1800. Ed. Ashin Das Gupta and M.N. Pearson. Calcutta: Oxford University Press 1987.

Iqtidari, Ahmad. *Asar-e shahrha-ye bastani-ye savahil va jazayir-e Khalij-e Fars va Darya-ye `Uman.* Tehran, 1348/1969.

_____, *Az darya-ye Pars ta darya-ye Chin.* Tehran, 1364/1985.

_____, *Khalij-e Farsi.* Tehran, 1966.

IRAN: Journal of the British Institute of Persian Studies. London.

Iran in the Persian Gulf, 1820-1966. Anita L.P. Burdett and A. Seay, editors. Slough: Archive Editions... 6 vols.

Iraq and the Persian Gulf. London: British Admiralty, 1944.

Ives, Edward, d. 1786. *A Voyage from England to India in the year MDCCIV...* London, 1773.

Journal of Oman Studies. Muscat: Ministry of Information and Culture, 1975-

Kalus, Ludvík. *Inscriptions arabes des îles de Bahrain: contribution à l'histoire de Bahrain entre les XIe et XVIIe siècles...* Paris: Geuthner, 1990.

Kâtip Çelebi. *Cihannuma [Jihannuma].* Istanbul: Ibrahim Müteferrika, 1728.

Kazaruni Nadiri, Muhammad Ibrahim. *Tarikh-e banadir va jazayir-e Khalij-e Fars dar zaman-e Muhammad Shah Qajar;* ed. by Manuchihr Sutudah, Tehran, 1367/1988.

Kelly, John Barrett. *Arabia, the Gulf, and the West.* New York: Basic Books, 1980.

_____, *Britain and the Persian Gulf, 1795-1880*. Oxford: Clarendon Press, 1968.

_____, *Sultanate and Imamate in Oman*. Oxford: Oxford University Press for the Royal Institute of International Affairs, 1959.

Kervran, Monique. "Forteresses, entrepôts et commerce: une histoire à suivre depuis les rois sassanides jusqu'aux princes d'Ormuz," in *Itinéraires d'Orient: Hommages à Claude Cahen,* Bures-sur-Yvette, 1994, pp. 325-51 *(Res Orientales,* vol. 6)

Khwarazmi, Muhammad b. Musa, fl. 813-846. *Kitab surat al-ard*. Ed. Hans von Mžik, Leipzig, 1926.

Kinzer, Stephen. *All the Shah's men: an American coup and the roots of Middle East terror.* Hoboken, NJ: John Wiley, 2003.

Kroell, Anne. "Louis XIV, la Perse et Mascate," *Le Monde Iranien et l'Islam,* IV (1976-77), pp. 1-78.

Kumar, Ravinder. *India and the Persian Gulf region, 1858-1907; a study in British imperial policy.* New York: Asia Publishing House, 1965.

Kurşun, Zekeriya. *Necid ve Ahsa'da Osmanlı hakimiyeti.* Ankara: Türk Tarih Kurumu, 1998.

Landen, Robert Geran. *Oman since 1856: disruptive modernization in a traditional Arab society.* Princeton University Press 1967. 488 p.

_____, "Reconsideration of the history of Bahrain: a socioeconomic interpretation of events from 1783 to 1861," in *Bahrain Through the Ages*, vol. 2, pp. 393-408.

Lane, Frederick. "The Mediterranean Spice Trade: further evidence of its revival in the sixteenth century," *American Historical Review* 45 (1940).

Le Strange, Guy. *The Lands of the Eastern Caliphate.* Cambridge University Press 1905.

Lesure, Michel. "Un document ottoman sur l'Inde portugaise et les pays de la Mer Rouge," *Mare Luso-Indicum* 3 (1976), pp. 137-60.

Linschoten, Jan Huygen van, 1563-1611. *Itinerario, voyage ofte schipvaert, van Jan Huygen van Linschoten naer Ost ofte Portugaels Indien...* Amsterdam, M.D.XCVI. 3 vols. In 1.

_____, *The Voyage of John Huyghen van Linschoten to the East Indies*. From the old English translation of 1598 ...edited... by Arthur Coke Burnell... London: Hakluyt Society, 1885.

Livre des merveilles de l'Inde, texte arabe publié par P.A. van der Lith, trad. française par L.M. Devic. Leiden, 1883.

Lockhart, Laurence. *Nadir Shah: a critical study based mainly on contemporary sources.* London, 1938.

Longrigg, Stephen H. *Four centuries of Modern Iraq.* London, 1925.

Lorimer, John Gordon. *Gazetteer of the Persian Gulf.* Calcutta, 1908; and reprint, Gerrands Cross, 1986. 9 volumes (Part I: Historical, vols. 1-6; Part II: Geographical and Statistical, vols. 7-9).

Low, Charles Rathbone. *History of the Indian navy (1613-1863).* London 1877. 2 vols.

Luckenbill, Daniel David. *Ancient records of Assyria and Babylonia.* Chicago: University of Chicago Press, 1926-27. 2 vols.

Ma Huan. *Ying-yai Sheng-lan. 'The Overall survey of the Ocean's shores [1433]*; translated from the Chinese text...with introduction, notes and appendices by J.V.G. Mills. Cambridge University Press 1970.

Mandaville, Jon E. "The Ottoman province of al-Hasa in the sixteenth and seventeenth centuries," *Journal of the American Oriental Society* 90 (1970), pp. 486-513.

Marchand, Roland. "Dubai: global city and transnational hub," in *Transnational Connections,...* pp. 93-110.

Marr, Phoebe. *The Modern history of Iraq.* 2nd ed. Boulder: Westview Press, 2004.

Mas'udi, d. 956. *Muruj al-dhahab...* Beirut, 1965-66. 4 vols.; also French edition with Arabic text and French translation as Maçoudi, *Les Prairies d'Or,* texte et traduction par C. Barbier de Meynard et Pavet de Courteille. Paris, 1861-77. 9 volumes.

Maurizi, Vincenzo. *History of Seyd Said, Sultan of Muscat.* London 1819.

al-Mawsu'ah al-Arabiyah. Damascus. Vol. 8 (2003), entry "al-Khalij al-Arabi".

Mawsu'at al-Khalij al-Arabi. Prepared by Khalil Bahsun. Beirut, 1997. 2 vols.

Mehr, Farhang. *A colonial legacy: the dispute over the islands of Abu Musa, and the Greater and Lesser Tumbs.* Lanham: University Press of America, 1997.

Mojtahed-Zadeh, Pirouz. [Piruz Mujtahidzadah] *Security and territoriality in the Persian Gulf: a maritime political geography.* Richmond: Curzon Press, 1999. One of the foremost specialists on the subject of the modern Persian Gulf, this scholar has published a number of books and articles both in Persian and English. Two more examples:

_____. *Jazayir-e Tunb va Abu Musa.* Tehran 1375/1996

_____. *Jughrafiya-ye tarikhi-ye Khalij-e Fars.* 2nd ed., London, 1988.

Morgan, David. *Medieval Persia, 1040-1797.* London 1988.

Muqaddasi, 10th century. *Ahsan al-taqasim fi ma`rifat al-aqalim.* 3rd ed. Leiden: Brill, 1967 (*Bibliotheca Geographorum Arabicorum*, 3)

Muvahhid, Muhammad Ali. *Mubalaghah-e musta`ar: barrasi-ye madarik-e mawrid-e istinad-e shuyukh dar iddi`a bar jazayir-e Tunb-e Kuchak, Tunb-e Buzurg, Abu Musa.* Tehran, 1380/2001.

Nafisi, Sa`id. *Bahrain: Huquq-e 1700-salah-e Iran.* Tehran, 1330/1955.

Nasir-e Khusraw, 1004-1088. *Safarnamah.* Tehran, 1372/1993. English translation: *The Book of Travels (Safarnama),* translated by Wheeler M. Thackston, 1986.

Nicolini, Beatrice. *Il Sultanato di Zanzibar nel XIX secolo: traffici commerciali e relazioni internazionali.* Torino: L'Harmattan Italia, 2002.

Niebuhr, Carsten, 1733-1815. *Beschreibung von Arabien aus eigenen Beobachtungen...* Copenhagen, 1772.

_____, *Travels through Arabia, and other countries in the East, performed by Carsten Niebuhr, and illustrated with engravings and map.* Translated by Robert Heron, with notes. Edinburgh and London, 1792. 2 vols.

Nöldeke, Theodor. *Geschichte der Perser und Araber zur Zeit der Sassaniden nach der arabischen Chronik des Tabari.* Leiden, 1879.

Onley, James. "Transnational merchants in the nineteenth-century Gulf: The case of the Safar family," in *Transnational Connections in the Arab Gulf*, pp. 59-89.

Orhonlu, Cengiz. "Hint kaptanlığı ve Piri Reis," *Belleten* (Ankara), 34 (1970), pp. 235-54.

_____, "1559 Bahreyn Seferine âid bir raport," *Tarih Dergisi* (Istanbul), 17 (1967), pp. 1-18.

Outram, Sir James, 1803-1863. *Persian campaign in 1857.* London, 1860.

Özbaran, Salih. *The Ottoman Response to European Expansion.* Istanbul: Isis Press, 1994.

_____, *Yemen'den Basra'ya sınırdaki Osmanlı.* Istanbul: Kitap-yayınevi, 2004.

Parry, John Horace. *The establishment of the European hegemony, 1415-1715: trade and exploration in the age of the Renaissance.* 3rd ed. New York 1966.

Pellat, Charles. *Le Milieu basrien et la formation de Ǧahiz.* Paris, 1953.

Penrose, Boies. *The Sherleian odyssey, being the travels and adventures of three famous brothers during the reigns of Elizabeth, James I, and Charles I.* Taunton and London, 1938.

The Periplus Maris Erythraei; text with introduction, translation, and commentary by Lionel Casson. Princeton University Press, 1989.

Perry, John R. "The Banu Ka`b: an amphibious brigand state in Khuzistan," *Le Monde Iranien et l'Islam*, 1 (1971), pp. 131-52.

_____, *Karim Khan Zand: a history of Iran, 1747-1779.* Chicago University Press, 1979.

_____, "Mir Muhanna and the Dutch: Patterns of piracy in the Persian Gulf," *Studia Iranica* 2 (1973), pp. 79-95.

Persian Gulf States: a general survey. Alvin J. Cottrell, ed. Baltimore: The Johns Hopkins University Press, 1980.

Perspectives on the United Arab Emirates. London: Trident Press, 1997.

Peterson, John E. *Historical dictionary of Saudi Arabia.* Metuchen: Scarecrow Press, 1993.

Piri Reis, fl. 1526. *Kitab-i Bahriye.* Ankara: Türk Tarih Kurumu, 1935 (facsimile edition of one of the manuscripts); and a new edition in 4 volumes, with modern Turkish and English translations: Istanbul: The Historical Research Institute, 1988.

Polk, William Roe. *Understanding Iraq*. New York: Harper-Collins, 2005.

Potter, Lawrence G. , ed. *Iran, Iraq, and theLegacies of War*. Ed. by Lawrence G. Potter and Gary Sick. New York: Palgrave Macmillan, 2004.

_____, ed. *The Persian Gulf at the Millennium: Essays in Politics,Eeconomy, Security, and Religion*. Ed. Lawrence G. Potter and Gary Sick. New York: St. Martin's Press, 1997.

_____, *The Persian Gulf in Transition*. New York: Foreign Policy Association, 1998.

Potts, Daniel T. *The Arabian Gulf in Antiquity*. Oxford University Press, 1990. 2 vols.

_____, "From Qade to Mazun: Four notes on Oman, c. 700 BC to 700 AD," *Journal of Oman Studies*, vol. 8, part 1 (1985), pp. 81-95.

_____, "Khârg Island," article on line issued by CAIS (The Circle of Ancient Iranian Studies, SOAS [School of Oriental and African Studies, University of London]), 10 pages.

_____, "The Roman relationship with the Persicus sinus from the rise of Spasinou Charax (127 BC) to the reign of Shapur II (AD 309-379)," in Susan E. Alcock, ed., *The Early Roman Empire in the East*: Oxford: Oxbow Books, 1997, pp. 89-107.

Purchas, Samuel, 1577-1626. *Hakluytus posthumus, or, Purchas his Pilgrimes: Contayning a history of the world in sea voyages and lande travels by Englishmen and others*. London, 1625. The edition used here was issued in Glasgow, 1905-1907, 20 vols. (Hakluyt Society. *Extra series*, no. 14-30)

Qal`aji, Qadri. *al-Khalij al-Arabi*. Beirut, 1992.

Qasimi, Khalid bin Muhammad. *Bahrain: al-tarikh wa-al-hadir wa-al-mustaqbal*. Alexandria, 1999.

_____, *al-Khalij al-Arabi fi alam mutaghayyir: ru'yah tarikhiyah-siyasiyah*. al-Shariqah: Dar al-Thaqafah al-Arabiyah, 2000- (al-juz' 1: *al-Imarat..., al-Kuwait, al-Bahrain*)

Qasimi, Sultan bin Muhammad. *The Myth of Arab Piracy in the Gulf*. London: Croom Helm, 1986.

Qurani, Ali ibn Hasan. *Majlis al-Ta`awun al-Khaliji amama al-tahaddiyat*. Riyad, 1997.

Relations des voyages faits par les Arabes et les Persans dans l'Inde et la Chine dans le IXe siècle de l'ère chrétienne.

Texte arabe imprimé par les soins de feu Langlès, publié et accompagné d'une traduction française par M. Reinaud. Paris, 1845. 2 vols.

Rheda Backer, M. *Trade and Empire in Muscat and Zanzibar: Roots of British domination.* London and New York: Routledge, 1992.

Risso, Patricia. "Cross-Cultural perceptions of piracy: maritime violence in the Western Indian Ocean and Persian Gulf Region during a long eighteenth century," *Journal of World History*, 12 (2001), 293-319.

_____, *Merchants and Faith: Muslim commerce and culture in the Indian Ocean.* Boulder: Westview Press, 1995.

_____, *Oman and Muscat: an early modern history.* London, 1986.

_____, "Qasimi piracy and the General Treaty of Peace (1820)," *Arabian Studies*, 4 (1974), 47-57.

Roaf, Michael. *Cultural atlas of Mesopotamia and the Ancient Near East.* New York: Facts On File, 2004.

Ross, E. C. "Annals of Oman, from early times to the year 1728 A.D.," *Journal* of the Asiatic Society of Bengal, 43 (1874).

Roux, Georges. *Ancient Iraq.* New York: Penguin Group (USA), 1993. This is a translation of *La Mésopotamie: Essai d'histoire politique, économique et culturelle.* Paris, 1985.

Ruete, Emily. *Memoirs of an Arabian Princess from Zanzibar*, by Emily Ruete, born Salme, Princess of Oman and Zanzibar; with a new introduction by Patricia W. Romero. Princeton: Markus Wiener Publishers, 2000. This a reprint of a translation, London, 1888, from the German original *Memoiren einer arabischen Prinzessin.*

Ruete, Rudolph Said. *Said bin Sultan (1791-1856), ruler of Oman and Zanzibar: his place in the history of Arabia and East Africa.* London, 1929. The author was Emily Ruete's son.

Sadid al-Saltanah, Muhammad Ali, 1874-1943. *Bandar-e Abbas va Khalij-e Fars = I`lam al-nas fi ahwal Bandar Abbas...*Tashih va muqaddamah va faharis az Ahmad Iqtidari. 2nd ed. Tehran, 1363/1984. 780 p.

Saffet Bey. "Bahreyn'de bir vak`a," *TOEM* (Tarihi Osmani Encümeni *Mecmuası*), 3 (1328/1910).

Sahab, Abbas. *Atlas of geographical maps and historical documents on the Persian Gulf.* Tehran: Sahab Geographic and Drafting Institute, 1971.

Saldanha, Jerome Anthony. *The Persian Gulf précis.* Calcutta: Superinntendent of Government Printing, 1908; reprint Archive Editions, 1986.

Samarqandi, Abd al-Razzaq Kamal al-Din, 1413-1482. *Matla`-e sa`dain va majma` al-bahrain.* In R.H. Major, ed., *India in the Fifteenth Century,* London, 1857, part 1, pp. 5-7: Narrative of the voyage of Abd-er-Razzak Samarqandi in 1442.

Sauvaget, Jean. *Ahbar as-Sin wa-l-Hind: Relation de la Chine et de l'Inde, rédigée en 851.* Paris, 1948.

Savory, Roger M. "British and French Diplomacy in Persia, 1800-1810," *IRAN* 10 (1972) , pp. 31-44.

_____, *Iran under the Safavids.* Cambridge University Press, 1980.

Scammell, Geoffrey Vaughn. *The first imperial age: European overseas expansion, c. 1400-1715.* London, 1989.

Schwarz, Paul. *Iran im Mittelalter nach den arabischen Geografen.* Leipzig, 1929.

Seminar for Arabian Studies (London). *Proceedings of the Seminar for Arabian Studies.*

1- , 1971- Especially relevant are the following items:

*Fiorani Piacentini, Valeria, "Ardashir I Papakan and the wars against the Arabs: working hypothesis on the Sassanian hold of the Gulf," 18th Seminar, 1985, pp. 57-77.

_____, "Arab expeditions overseas in the seventh century AD – working hypotheses on the dissolution of the Sassanian State apparatus along the eastern seaboard of the Arabian peninsula," 32th Seminar, 2002, pp. 165-73.

_____, "The Mercantile Empire of the Tibis: economic predominance, political power, and military subordination," 34th Seminar, 2004, pp. 251-60.

*DeBlois, F., "Abu Tahir's Epistle to the Caliph al-Muqtadir: Studies on the History of Bahrayn and the Yemen," 20th Seminar, 1987: 27-35

*Al-Naboodah, H.M., "The Commercial activity of Bahrain and Oman in the early middle ages," 21st Seminar, 1992, pp. 81-96.

*Al-Tikriti, W.Y. "The South-east Arabian origin of the falaj system," 32th Seminar, 2002, pp. 117-38.

Severin, Timothy. *The Sindbad voyage*. New York, 1983.

Seydi Ali Reis, d. 1562. *Miratül-memalik*, ed. Mehmet Kiremit, Ankara, 1999. English translation by Armin Vambery: *Travels and adventures of the Turkish Admiral Sidi Ali Reis..*, London: Luzac, 1899; and a French translation by Jean-Louis Bacqué-Grammont: *Miroir des pays: une anabase ottomane à travers l'Inde et l'Asie centrale; récit traduit du turc ottoman, présenté et annoté...* Paris: Sindbad, 1999.

Shafiq, Ali. *Majlis al-Ta`awun al-Khaliji min manzur al-alaqat al-dawliyah*. Beirut, 1989.

al-Shamlan, Abd Allah Khalifah. *Bina' al-sufun al-khashabiyah fi dawlat al-Bahrain*. a-Manamah: Markaz al-Bahrain lil-Dirasat wa al-Buhuth, 1990.

Sherley, Evelyn Philip, 1812-1882. *The Sherley brothers: an historical memoir of the lives of Sir Thomas Sherley, Sir Anthony Sherley, and Sir Robert Sherley, knights*. Chiswick: Press of C. Whittingham, 1848.

Slot, B.J. *The Arabs of the Gulf, 1602-1784*. Leidschendam, 1993.

_____, *The Origins of Kuwait*. Kuwait: Centre for Research and Studies on Kuwait, 1998.

Sollberger, Edmond, and Kupper, Jean-Robert. *Inscriptions royales sumériennes et akkadiennes*. Paris, 1971.

Soucek, Svat. "Arabistan or Khuzistan?", *Iranian Studies*, 17 (1984), 195-213.

_____, "Piri Reis and Ottoman discovery of the Great Discoveries," *Studia Islamica*, 79 (1994), 121-42.

_____, *Piri Reis and Turkish mapmaking after Columbus*. London: Azimuth Press, 1996.

Steensgaard, Niels. *The Asian trade revolution of the seventeenth century: The East India Companies and the decline of the caravan trade*. Chicago: Chicago University Press, 1974.

Stocqueler, Joachim Hayward, 1800-1885. *Fifteen months' pilgrimage through untrodden tracts of Khuzistan and Persia*. London, 1832. 2 vols.

Strabo, 63 BC-24 AD. *The Geography of Strabo...* Ed. and trsl. By Horace Leonard Jones. London: Heinemann, 1954.

Subrahmanyam, Sanjay. *The Portuguese Empire in Asia, 1500-1700*. London, 1993.

Tabari, d. 923. *Tarikh al-rusul wa-l-muluk.*

The standard edition of the Arabic text is the following: *Annales quos scripsit Abu Djafar Mohammad ibn Djafari at-Tabari*, cum aliis edidit M.J. de Goeje. Leiden: Brill, 1879-1901. 15 vols.

A definitive English translation by a number of scholars is nearing completion:

The History of al-Tabari (Ta'rikh al-rusul wa'l-muluk). Albany: State University of New York Press. The following volumes are especially relevant:

The Ancient Kingdoms. Translated by Moshe Pearlmann. 1987 (= vol. 4)

The Sasanids, the Byzantines, the Lakhmids, and Yemen. Translated by C.E. Bosworth. 1999 (= vol. 5)

The Battle of al-Qadisiyyah and the Conquest of Syria and Palestine. Translated by Yohanan Friedmann. 1992 (= vol. 12)

The Revolt of the Zanj. Translated by Dawid Waines. 1992. (= vol. 36)

There is also a Persian translation: *Ta'rikh-e Tabari...* ; tarjumah-e Abu al-Qasim Payandah. Tehran, 1976. 16 vols.

Tadjbakhche, Gholem-Reza. *La Question des Iles Bahrein*. Paris, 1960.

Teixeira, Pedro, b. 1570. *The Travels of Pedro Teixeira: with his "Kings of Harmuz" and extracts from his "Kings of Persia"*. (Appendices: p. [153]-267, a) A short narrative of the origin of the kingdom of Harmuz and of its kings...; d) Relation of the chronicle of the kings of Ormuz [by Turan Shah ibn Qutb al-Din, d. 1378]. W.F. Sinclair, tr., London, 1902. This is a new translation of *The History of Persia...to which is added an abridgment of the lives of the kings of Ormuz by Touranxa...translated into Spanish by Antony Teixeira... and now render'd into English by Captain John Stervens*. London, 1708-11.

Thévenot, Jean de, 1633-1667. *The Travels of Monsieur de Thévenot into the Levant*. London, 1687. (French original: *Relation d'un voyage fait au Levant*)

Tibbetts, Geral R. see Ibn Majid

Tracy, James D., ed. *The Political Economy of Merchant Empires: State power and trade, 1350-1750.* Cambridge University Press, 1991.

_____, ed. *The Rise of Merchant Empires: Long-distanbe trade in the early modern world, 1350-1750.* Cambridge University Press, 1990.

Transnational Connections and the Arab Gulf, Edited by Madawi Al-Rasheed. London and New York: Routledge, 2005.

Tripp, Charles. *A History of Iraq.* Cambridge University Press, 2002.

Tudela, Benjamin. *The Itinerary of Benjamin of Tudela (1159-73).* Ed. M.N. Adler. London, 1907. 2 vols. In 1.

Tweedy, Maureen. *Bahrain and the Persian Gulf.* Ipswich, s.d.

Twinam, Joseph Wright. *The Gulf, cooperation, and the council: an American perspective; foreword by John C. West.* Washington, DC: Middle East Policy Council, 1992.

Uman wa-tarikhuha l-bahri. Masqat: Wizarat al-I'lam wa-l-Thaqafah, 1979.

Valdani, Asghar Ja`fari. *Huquq-e Iran-e bayn al-milal.* Tehran, 2002.

_____, *Tahavvulat-e marz'ha va naqsh-e zhi'upulitik-e an dar Khalij-e Fars.* Tehran, 1995.

_____, *Zhi'upulitik-e jadid-e Darya-ye Surkh va Khalij-e Fars.* Tehran, 1381/2002.

Varthema, Lodovico di, d. 1517. *The Itinerary lf Ludovico di Varthema of Bologna from 1502-1508,* as translated from the original Italian edition of 1510, by John Winton Jones... London: Hakluyt Society, 1863.

Vidal, F. S. *The oasis of al-Hasa.* New York, 1955.

Villiers, Alan John. *Monsoon Seas: the story of the Indian Ocean.* New York, 1952.

_____, "Some aspects of the Arab dhow trade," *Middle East Journal,* 2 (1948), 399-416.

Vincent, William, 1739-1815. *Commerce and navigation of the ancients in the Indian Ocean.* London, 1807-9. 2 vols.

Wellsted, J. R. *Travels to the City of the Caliphe, along the Shores of the Persian Gulf, and the Mediterranean.* London, 1840. 2 vols.

Whitehouse, David. "Sasanian maritime trade," *IRAN* 11 (1973), pp. 29-49.

_____, "Siraf: a medieval port on the Persian Gulf," by David Whitehouse and Andrew Williamson, *World Archaeology* 2 (1970).

Whiteway, R.S. *The Rise of Portguese power in India*. London, 1967.

Wilkinson, John Craven. *Arabia's frontiers: the story of Britain's boundary drawing in the desert*. London and New York: Tauris, 1991.

_____, *The Imamate tradition of Oman*. Cambridge University Press, 1987.

_____, "The Julanda of Oman," *Journal of Oman Studies* 1 (1975), pp. 97-108

_____, "The Origins of the Omani State," in Derek Hopwood, ed., *The Arabian Peninsula: Society and Politics*, London, 1972.

_____, *Water and tribal settlement in South-East Arabia*. Oxford: Clarendon Press, 1977.

Wilson, Arnold Talbot. *The Persian Gulf: an historical sketch from the earliest times to the beginning of the twentieth century*. Oxford: Clarendon Press, 1928.

Winder, Richard Bayly. *Saudi Arabia in the 19th century*. New York, 1965.

Wink, André. *Al-Hind, the Making of the Indo-Islamic World*. Leiden, 1990-
Vol. 1: Early Medieval India and the Expansion of Islam, 7th-11th centuries.
Vol. 2: The slave kings and the Islamic conquest, 11th-13th centuries.
Vol. 3: Indo-Islamic society, 14th-15th centuries.

Wüstenfeld, Ferdinand. "Jâcût's Reisen, aus seinem geographischen Wörterbuch beschrieben," *ZDMG* 28 (1964), pp. 397-493.

YaHusayni, Qasim. *Mir Muhanna-ye Bandar Rigi*. Tehran, 1374/1995.

Yapp, Malcolm. "British policy in the Persian Gulf," in *The Persian Gulf States*, pp.70-90.

Ya`qubi, d. 897. *Kitab al-Buldan*, ed. M.J. de Goeje, Leiden, 1892.

Yaqut, 1179-1229. *Mu`jam al-buldan*. Several editions; the best known is *Jacut's Geographisches Wörterbuch...*, edited by Ferdinand Wüstenfeld, Leipzig, 1866-73, 6 vols.

Yodfat, A. & Abir, M. *In the direction of the Persian Gulf: The Soviet Union and the Persian Gulf.* London: Frank Cass, 1977.

Zahlan, Rosemarie Said. *The making of the Modern Gulf States: Kuwait, Bahrain, Qatar, the United Arab Emirates, and Oman.* Rev. ed. Reading: Ithaca Press, 1998.

_____, *The origins of the United Arab Emirates: a political and social history of the Trucial States.* London and New York, 1978.

Zarrin-qalam, Ali. *Sarzamin-e Bahrain: az dawran-e bastan ta imruz.* Tehran, 1337/1958.

Index